Key Questions in Second Language Acquisition

This highly accessible introductory textbook carefully explores the main issues that have driven the field of second language acquisition research. Intended for students with little or no background in linguistics or psycholinguistics, it explains important linguistic concepts, and how and why they are relevant to second language acquisition. Topics are presented via a "key questions" structure that enables the reader to understand how these questions have motivated research in the field, and the problems to which researchers are seeking solutions. It provides a complete package for any introductory course on second language acquisition.

Bill VanPatten, formerly Professor of Spanish & Second Language Studies at Michigan State University, is now an independent scholar. He has had a long and distinguished academic career and has published widely in the fields of second language acquisition and second language teaching.

Megan Smith is an Assistant Professor at Mississippi State University. Her main research interests are in second language acquisition, particularly L2 syntax and psycholinguistics.

Alessandro G. Benati is Head of the English Department and Professor of English and Applied Linguistics at the American University of Sharjah. He is visiting and honorary professor at the University of York St. John and the University of Portsmouth.

Key Questions in Second Language Acquisition

An Introduction

Bill VanPatten

Chowchilla, CA, USA

Megan Smith

Mississippi State University

Alessandro G. Benati

American University of Sharjah, UAE

CAMBRIDGE
UNIVERSITY PRESS

CAMBRIDGE
UNIVERSITY PRESS

University Printing House, Cambridge CB2 8BS, United Kingdom

One Liberty Plaza, 20th Floor, New York, NY 10006, USA

477 Williamstown Road, Port Melbourne, VIC 3207, Australia

314–321, 3rd Floor, Plot 3, Splendor Forum, Jasola District Centre, New Delhi – 110025, India

79 Anson Road, #06-04/06, Singapore 079906

Cambridge University Press is part of the University of Cambridge.

It furthers the University's mission by disseminating knowledge in the pursuit of education, learning, and research at the highest international levels of excellence.

www.cambridge.org
Information on this title: www.cambridge.org/9781108486668
DOI: 10.1017/9781108761529

© Bill VanPatten, Megan Smith and Alessandro Benati 2020

First published 2020

Printed in the United Kingdom by TJ International Ltd. Padstow Cornwall

A catalogue record for this publication is available from the British Library.

ISBN 978-1-108-48666-8 Hardback
ISBN 978-1-108-70817-3 Paperback

To Murphy

      – BVP

To Hideki and Ayako

      – MS

To Bernadette, Grace, and Francesco and in
memory of AnnaMaria and Orazio Benati

      – AB

Contents

Foreword

Interest in second language acquisition (SLA) has been on a sharp rise for a few decades. Examining the acquisition and learning of non-native languages is important for multifarious reasons and, thus, of interest to students and scholars of linguistics, psychology, cognitive science, sociology, and many more disciplines. There is no shortage of introductory books on second language acquisition on the market, which is not surprising when one considers the many paradigms that contribute to the larger field. *Key Questions in Second Language Acquisition: An Introduction* is a unique and refreshing such book that stands out in this well-populated landscape. As an introduction to the field of second language studies in the broad sense, the book is as impressive as it is useful for a varied audience. The authors do a great job walking a novice student audience through decades of work in SLA, while providing a level of history of our discipline that offers insights and succinct review for even the more seasoned researcher. What stands out most from other texts available is the format. The tone and structure, aligning to key questions as the title suggests, make for a quite enjoyable and easy experience. I especially enjoy the "Consider this ..." excerpts, which facilitate this book being used at various levels of teaching on undergraduate and even graduate courses. The layout of the book is also logical in its flow as it incrementally builds knowledge that is needed for questions/topics covered downstream – another advantage for quick adoption of the book as a teaching tool.

Often with books of this type accuracy is sacrificed for the sake of perceived teaching needs: Details are changed knowingly or certain topics are foregone since they might be "too complex" for an introductory book. The authors have managed to find the perfect tone to engage, excite even, the reader while delivering a seriously large amount of information. Many difficult/dynamic questions are addressed without infantilizing the audience. And still, little to no prior knowledge is needed to get the full benefits of this book. In this respect, this book would be a very nice introduction even for the very seasoned linguist or psychologist who works on theory, language acquisition, or processing yet does not do so in the domain of sequential bi-/multilingualism. In a nutshell, this book is current, complete, well informed and well articulated. It is a must-have for everyone who studies or is interested in second language acquisition.

Jason Rothman
University of Reading
UiT, The Arctic University of Norway

Acknowledgments

Many thanks are in order for a book such as this one. First and foremost, we would like to thank the folks at Cambridge for their work in getting this book out, especially Helen Barton, who shepherded the proposal and the final manuscript through the review stages, and Charlie Howell, who managed the book during its production phase. Second, we would like to thank our family and friends for their support over the years. Such support cannot be understated because when the times get rough, they are the people you need to lean on. We also thank all the scholars who have influenced us over the years with their research and writings. A book such as this is always built on the work of many people. Finally, we thank our students who have inspired us to write an introductory book such as this one. We hope to have done the best job possible.

Abbreviations

ACC	accusative case
CEI	communicatively embedded input
CP	complementizer phrase
CPH	the Critical Period Hypothesis
ESL	English as a second language
FDH	the Fundamental Difference Hypothesis
FEM	feminine
FT/FA	Full Transfer/Full Access
L1	first language
L2	second language
MASC	masculine
MLAT	Modern Language Aptitude Test
NNS	non-native speaker
NOM	nominative case
NP	noun phrase
NS	native speaker
OPC	overt pronoun constraint
OVS	object-verb-subject (word order)
POS	poverty of the stimulus
PP	prepositional phrase
RC	relative clause
SLA	second language acquisition (as a research field)
SOV	subject-object-verb (word order)
SSH	the Shallow Structure Hypothesis
SVO	subject-verb-object (word order)
TP	tense phrase
UG	Universal Grammar
V2	verb second
VP	verb phrase
WM	working memory

Prologue

Second language acquisition (SLA) is a field of empirical and theoretical research that has been around since the early 1970s. For scholars interested in cognitive science (i.e., the interdisciplinary study of the mind and its processes), research on how a second language (L2) is acquired adds valuable data that can shed light on various hypotheses and offer novel insights into how the mind works. For teachers, basic facts about L2 acquisition can be informative for decision-making processes about methods, what to teach, what not to teach, and so on. (Note to the reader: In this book, we use SLA to represent a field of study and L2 acquisition to mean the actual acquisition of another language. Thus, when the reader sees SLA, that should be interpreted as a field of study interested in L2 acquisition.)

Regardless of the motivation for one's interest in research on L2 acquisition, it should be noted that the field of SLA is driven by underlying questions. Like any science or social science, SLA seeks answers to questions. The present volume is unique compared to other similar introductions to the field because it is organized around questions and not topics, theories, or research methodology. As the reader will see, Chapter 1 situates the origins of contemporary L2 research within the fundamental and original question of whether L2 acquisition is similar to or different from first language (L1) acquisition. As we see it, all questions currently driving the field stem from this fundamental question; that is, whether stated or not, lurking behind current research in L2 acquisition is the issue of similarities and differences between L1 and L2 acquisition. In most cases, this issue is implicit, as the researcher tends to have an underlying assumption about similarities and differences between the two contexts. So, for example, the researcher interested in motivation in L2 acquisition – a factor of little interest to researchers in L1 acquisition – may have already "determined" that something is different about L2 acquisition and this is why motivation is important to examine (see Chapter 8). As another example, researchers have wondered whether instruction on the formal elements of language (what people typically call "grammar") has an impact on how formal elements are actually acquired. In asking this question, the researcher is explicitly or implicitly making claims about how different L2 acquisition is from L1 acquisition (where there is no instruction).

It is impossible for a purposely short and introductory book to be exhaustive, so for the present endeavor we have selected a limited number of questions that we believe drive the bulk of L2 research (and theorizing) these days. We list them here with some brief introductory remarks – and the reader will note that most also form the chapter headings.

- Are L1 and L2 acquisition fundamentally the same or fundamentally different? We show how this question launched the field of SLA research in the early 1970s in Chapter 1. We do not address this question in this chapter but return to it in the Epilogue once the reader has reviewed research on the major questions that form the focus of this book.
- What does development look like? In Chapter 2, we describe various aspects of the ordered and staged development of formal features of language (e.g., sentence structure, inflections, and endings on verbs and nouns) while also touching on variation in such ordered development and any observed L1 influence on this development.
- What are the roles of input and output? One of the fundamental findings of the early research on L2 acquisition was the critical role that communicatively embedded input plays as the data for language acquisition. Chapter 3 reviews this idea while also addressing later hypotheses that communicatively embedded output (i.e., learner production) somehow affects acquisition.
- What is the initial state? Of concern to researchers since the early 1970s is whether or not L2 learners begin the task of acquisition by massively transferring their L1 into the "hypothesis space" for L2 acquisition. In Chapter 4, we explore research related to this question.
- Can L2 learners become nativelike? In Chapter 5 we address this question, looking at the outcome of L2 acquisition from a variety of perspectives. What will emerge from this discussion is that nativelikeness is not an all-or-nothing proposition, but that it likely depends on what aspects of language and language use we examine.
- Does instruction make a difference? Almost since the foundation of contemporary L2 research there has been debate about the extent to which instruction on the formal properties of language (i.e., what most people call "grammar") affects acquisition. We take up this question in Chapter 6.
- What are the roles of explicit and implicit learning? Increasingly, L2 researchers are converging on the importance and fundamental nature of implicit learning in L2 acquisition (i.e., learning without intent and without awareness of what you are learning). However, there is debate about the contribution of explicit learning and explicit processes in L2 acquisition. In a sense, the question raised here is related to the previous question about instruction. We take these issues up in Chapter 7.
- What are individual differences and how do they affect acquisition? Individual differences refer to non-linguistic things such as motivation, attitude, aptitude for learning, and working memory, among others. In Chapter 8, we focus on the most researched of the individual difference variables, namely, motivation, aptitude, and working memory. We purposely situate this chapter and the

question it addresses last in the book as much of how we interpret the research involves an understanding of how we answer other questions.

Because this is an introductory volume, we have purposely avoided a "scholarly style and tone." Instead, we have used a style that we hope is reader-friendly for the novice student of SLA. The three authors are experienced educators, having taught courses on SLA to teachers-in-training, novice researchers, graduate students, and other populations. We have concluded that introductory books that assume little background on the part of the reader are difficult to come by. So our target audience, again, is that novice student who is reading about the field of SLA for the first time. By extension, the reader could also be someone outside the field such as an administrator, parent, or anyone interested in the basics of L2 acquisition. We assume no background in any area related to SLA (e.g., linguistics, cognitive psychology) and do our best to explain as we go and simplify complex concepts where possible. In so doing, and in trying to keep this book as short as possible, we have necessarily been brief on some of the topics. Some topics that readers might find in a lengthier and more advanced work are not included in this volume. In addition, the reader will not find an exhaustive review of research with citation after citation that is found in tomes that are intended for more advanced readers and scholars (e.g., in the many "handbooks" on second language acquisition that are on the market these days). This book is different in intent and is not meant to compete with books used in advanced courses or advanced degree programs.

Along the same lines, we narrow our scope of discussion to what are traditionally called "syntax" and "morphology." Syntax refers to sentence structure while morphology refers to word structure (e.g., roots, inflections on words). We do this purposefully. One reason is to keep the book short. A second reason is that the crux of what we wish to talk about – differences between L1 and L2 acquisition – has largely been tied to these domains of inquiry. This does not mean that such things as the sound system (phonology), vocabulary (the mental lexicon), and other things aren't of interest to L2 acquisition more generally, and occasionally we make reference to them. But when it comes to comparing L1 and L2 acquisition, the locus of discussion has tended to be syntax and morphology. Because we have limited the scope of inquiry, we don't intend that readers will be experts in the field by the time they turn the last page. Instead, we hope to instill curiosity in readers so that continued engagement with more detailed volumes as well as primary sources is a result. For those readers who will not pursue more reading or work in the field of SLA, we hope we provide enough of the "basics" for whatever purpose that reader has in mind.

We also need to admit our biases up front. All scholars in SLA come to the task of synthesizing the field from a variety of perspectives. The three of us are trained linguists and thus we come to the task with a linguistic slant or bias. For example, we assume that the product of acquisition is an abstract, complex, and implicit system called "language" that defies easy explanation and looks nothing like text-book rules or descriptions language learners might find in a Google search. This perspective pushes us to always look at the research in terms of what it means to speak to the creation of this underlying "mental representation" of language. The particular approach that underlies this book is called "generative," which we will discuss in Chapter 1. In linguistics, the generative approach is the dominant framework informing theoretical and empirical advances. However, not all L2 researchers adopt a generative approach. Many have no theoretical approach to language at all. But we are firm believers that if we want to talk about language acquisition, we have to have a working theory of language. Readers who go on to pursue academic work in the field of SLA will encounter other approaches and can compare them to the one taken in this volume. Still, where appropriate, we point the reader to alternative ideas. And because none of us works in the field of social and cultural aspects of acquisition, the book leaves these perspectives to other experts. We do, however, touch on social aspects of acquisition in a special feature called "What about Social Factors?" in which we offer brief glimpses into how we might bridge the gap between linguistic approaches and social approaches. This may not be enough for the experts in social factors, but for an introductory book with a linguistic focus, we hope our intent is well taken.

We also point out that in addition to readings and follow-up questions at the end of each chapter, internal to each chapter are three features we hope will help the novice reader. One feature involves bolded words and phrases. Bolded words and phrases represent key constructs and ideas. Although these constructs and ideas are defined as we go, they are also included in a glossary at the end of the book. A second feature consists of call-outs, which are intended to draw the reader to a main idea in a particular section of the chapter. These are useful for reviewing after reading the chapter to recall key ideas. A third feature consists of boxes called "Consider this ..." The intent of these boxes is to invite readers to stop and think about something they have just read, to reflect before going on. We have found that such "stop and think" suggestions help readers consolidate ideas and also break up the reading process. If this book is used in a class, such boxes can also be used for classroom discussion.

We hope we have done our job for the novice reader. We hope we have done our job for the instructor who adopts this text for classroom use. Most importantly, we hope to instill in that novice reader a sense of wonder at the complexity of L2 acquisition both as a human endeavor and as a research enterprise. Although we have come a long way since the foundation of contemporary L2 acquisition research in the late 1960s, there are still things to be sorted out, research methodologies to be explored, and details that need examination. But at the heart of it all are the key questions that drive what we as researchers do, whether we acknowledge it or not. We hope these key questions remain with the reader long after finishing this book.

What Are the Origins of Second Language Acquisition as a Research Field?

In science, knowledge builds upon previous knowledge. New areas of inquiry and new disciplines have their origins in work that preceded them. Modern-day physics is built upon the physics of the nineteenth century, for example, which in turn was built upon Newton's ideas, which in turn had roots traceable to ancient Greece.

Although we may not be able to trace contemporary second language (L2) research to Plato or Aristotle, we can describe its origins in the twentieth century. And like other sciences, L2 acquisition also had its predecessors: linguistics and first language (L1) acquisition to be exact.

The Revolution in Linguistics and L1 Acquisition

The 1950s and the 1960s were an exciting time for both linguistics and language acquisition. Until that time, linguistics had been dominated by what was called **structural linguistics**. Structural linguistics looked at patterns of language; that is, it looked at observable aspects of sentences as they were actually used by people in order to make statements about the rules of language. For example, the structural linguist would look at the words *cat, cats, dog, dogs, plate*, and *plates* and determine that a regular singular noun is turned into a plural noun by adding an 's' sound. That 's' sound added to nouns would be called a "plural morpheme." (A **morpheme** is the smallest unit of language that carries meaning. Note that the 's' sound on a noun carries the meaning of "more than one": *dog* = one dog, *dogs* = more than one dog. We will examine morphemes in detail in Chapter 2.) Similarly, the structural linguist might look at sentences such as *John is tall, Is John tall?, Mary is studying*, and *Is Mary studying?* and conclude that a simple *yes/no* question with the verb *be* is formed by inverting the subject and the verb *be*. That linguist would also look at the following sentences, *Megan likes linguistics* and *Does Megan like linguistics?* and determine that a simple *yes/no* question with a full verb is formed by inserting an appropriate form of *do* before the subject and eliminating any inflection (ending) on the verb. Thus, the structural linguist would have two different "rules" or patterns for the formation of *yes/no* questions in English: one for *be* questions and one for *do* questions. At the same time, the structural linguist might look at what are called *wh*-questions: those questions containing interrogative words such as *why, who*, and *where*. They might look at sentences such as *John went to the store* and *Where did John go?* and determine yet a third rule for how questions are made in English.

At the same time, human (and animal) learning was dominated by the psychological theory of **behaviorism**. Under behaviorism, learning just about anything was seen as a result of an organism's response to a stimulus and the subsequent reaction to that response. Appropriate responses got some kind of reward. Inappropriate responses would get no reward or maybe even some kind of negative reaction. For example, a chicken runs to the gate of the coop (reaction) every time it hears the farmer approaching (stimulus). Why? Because in the past the chicken has repeatedly received food when the farmer comes to the coop. The chicken associates the footsteps of the farmer with impending food (reward). Another example is the daughter who answers the phone and hears her mother say, "I'm so glad you're home" (stimulus). The daughter tightens up inside (reaction) because she associates this phrase with all the times in the past her mother has called and used the same phrase before delivering bad news or complaining to her daughter about something. This kind of learning was termed **operant conditioning**.

> Under operant conditioning, language was seen as a behavior and not a mental construct. As such, it was learned like any other behavior: through the learning system of stimulus, response, and reward

B. F. Skinner applied behavioral psychology to language acquisition in his seminal book *Verbal Behavior* published in 1957. His claim was that children learn the structural patterns of the language around them the same way they learn anything else: through the learning system of stimulus, response, and reward. Skinner saw language primarily as a behavior and not as a mental construct. As such, he argued that language was learned like any other behavior. The prevailing notion of the time was that children imitated (response) what they heard (stimulus) and because of continued conversation by parents (one type of reward) or because parents said "how cute" and smiled (another type of reward) or because the child received something like a drink or food (yet another type of reward), children acquired language.

But something was brewing in the 1950s. For some, the basic ideas of structural linguistics and behaviorism as an explanation for language acquisition just didn't sit right. Two publications appeared at roughly the same time that gave voice to the concerns of those scholars. In 1958, Jean Berko Gleason published her famous study in which she tested young children's knowledge of word endings (inflections) for nouns, verbs, and adjectives in English. Without going into details here (see Exemplary Study), Berko found that children did not just imitate the speech around them. Instead, something internal to the child was extracting **rule-like knowledge** from the examples they were storing in their minds/brains. The conclusion from Berko's study was that children were much more "active" learners of language than could be claimed under something like behaviorism. Children weren't just imitating habits and then getting rewarded. They were actively (re-)creating language in their minds as they were exposed to language in their environment.

The following year, in 1959, Noam Chomsky published his famous critical review of Skinner's *Verbal Behavior*. In this seminal essay, Chomsky argued two basic points. The first was that unconscious linguistic knowledge was much more abstract and complex than a set of internalized habits, laying the groundwork for what would later be called the **generative revolution** in linguistics (more on that later). As we will see, Chomsky did not see language as something relatively simple to learn via stimulus and reinforcement, but as a very complex and intricate system that defied description by the psychologists of the time. For him language was not behavior; it was a mental construct. In other words, language was a system that existed inside the mind; something we could study through introspection. So we can introspect and determine that the word *himself* in *John knows himself well* refers to John and not to somebody else. But we can also think about the sentence *John told Bobby to buy the picture of himself* and determine that *himself* can only refer to Bobby and not to John. Then there's a third sentence, *John showed Bobby a picture of himself*, and we might say "Geez. *Himself* can refer to either Bobby or John." And finally, we might consider the sentence *Himself knows John pretty well* and say, "Well, that sentence is just not possible." We are not gathering sentences from people speaking. We are introspecting and thinking about language. And as we introspect, we begin to think about how language is constructed inside the mind.

Chomsky's second point was that learning anything could not be reduced to operant conditioning, no matter what neat experiments with rats, dogs, and chickens would suggest. He forcefully critiqued the very basic constructs of operant conditioning (e.g., stimulus, response, feedback) and showed how inadequate they were when one considered how quickly children acquire both language and concepts. He argued that children were not blank slates to be written on by their environments, but instead came to the learning task with something internal that guided their active processing of information to convert it into something usable at a given point in time. In a sense, Chomsky argued that children came prewired to learn certain things in certain ways. One of those things was language.

Exemplary Study

Berko, J. (1958). The child's learning of English morphology. *Word*, 14, 150–177.

Participants

- 12 native-speaking English adults
- 19 children learning English as an L1 between 4 and 5 years old (12 girls and 7 boys)
- 61 first-graders (5–7.5 years old, 35 girls and 26 boys)

Major Target Items

- noun plurals
- past tense on verbs
- third-person singular
- singular and plural possessive
- comparative and superlative of adjectives

Note: The items involved largely nonsense words for a total of 28 items.

Materials and Procedure

- picture cards with simple line drawings
- testing children individually, the experimenter held up a picture card and prompted the child to complete a thought. Example: [a picture with one bird-like animal] "This is a wug." [another picture with two of the bird-like animals] "Now there is another one. There are two of them. There are two _____." [the expectation was for the child to complete the sentence]

Results

- The 12 adults were unanimous in the way they supplied endings to nouns, verbs, and adjectives. Example: *wug → wugs* [wʌgz]; *gutch → gutches* [gʌʧɪz].
- There were no differences between boys and girls when matched for age.
- First-graders were better than pre-schoolers on some items, but of interest is where the two groups clearly deviated from adult-like patterns. These included plurals that needed to add /-ɪz/ as in *gutch → gutches*, past tense that required /-ɪd/ as in *mot → motted*, and third-person singular that required /-ɪz/ as in *nazz → nazzes*. What emerged was that children had adult-like rule-based knowledge for adding simple consonants and could do so on the nonsense words, but they tended not to be able to add an ending to nonsense words that required a syllable such as /-ɪz/ or /-ɪd/. So, they could easily pluralize *wug → wugs* [wʌgz] but could not easily pluralize *gutch → gutches* [gʌʧɪz].

Conclusion

- Children possess unconscious rules for noun, verb, and other inflections. They are not limited to imitating what they hear in the environment.

After the Berko Gleason and Chomsky publications, it seemed as though the dam had broken, and pushback against both structural linguistics and behaviorism began. Chomsky followed up his critique of Skinner's work with a number of publications that launched a new kind of linguistics called **generative linguistics**. The most cited of his early works was *Aspects of the Theory of Syntax*, which appeared in 1965. Generative linguistics sought to understand a number of things about language, including – but not limited to – exactly how languages were different and why they were different, what hidden properties there might be in languages that we don't see when we hear or read sentences, and

> Generative linguistics sought to understand a number of things about language, including but not limited to exactly how languages were different and why they were different, what hidden properties there might be in languages that we don't see when we hear or read sentences, and how language is organized in the mind/brain of the competent adult speaker.

how language is organized in the mind/brain of the competent adult speaker. The basic idea behind generative linguistics was that a person could generate an infinite number of sentences yet must have a finite set of "rules" to work with. How was this possible? And how was it that children acquired these "rules" without help?

Although generative linguistics has evolved over the years, it remains committed to understanding language as mental representation (competence) and not as a set of patterns observable in verbal behavior (some kind of performance). If we return to the examples of the *yes/no* questions from earlier, generative linguists would look to see not two different rules for *yes/no* questions depending on whether the verb was *be* or *do*, but instead to deeper properties that might actually reflect a "rule" that unified both types of question. The generative linguist might also include the *wh*-questions we saw earlier in this analysis to see if there is something common to all three types of question. Let's look at a classic example that Chomsky used with questions with *be*: *The man who is tall is sick* and its corresponding *yes/no* question *Is the man who is tall sick?* A simple rule or pattern for *yes/no* questions with *be* would be to move the first *be* to the front of the sentence, based on many examples one might hear, such as *John is sick/Is John sick?, Mary is studying/Is Mary studying?*, and *The baby's diaper is wet/Is the baby's diaper wet?* But moving the first *be* in *The man who is tall is sick* results in an incorrect question: **Is the man who tall is sick?* (An asterisk is used in linguistics to indicate a sentence that is not permitted in a language.) Chomsky reasoned that there must be something going on deeper and more abstract than "move the first *be* to make a *yes/no* question." What is more, he pointed out that no child ever makes an error such as **Is the man who tall is sick?* during language acquisition. And indeed the early research on child language acquisition showed that children's non-adult language was constrained; potential errors based on "imitation" and surface features of sentences just never happened. Chomsky surmised that something internal was guiding both the nature of language and the nature of language acquisition.

On the heels of Berko Gleason's work, data on L1 acquisition began popping up in the United States and Europe. Roger Brown's famous work on child language acquisition began to appear in the 1960s and culminated in his 1973 seminal book *A First Language.* In his work (and his colleagues' as well), Brown showed that language acquisition was stage-like and that particular parts of language were acquired in a particular order in English, regardless of children's social environment or status (as long as the children were not mentally impaired). As a preview to what we will see later, Brown showed, for example, that all English-speaking children first acquired *-ing* on the ends of verbs (e.g., *The car is slowing down*) before past-tense endings (e.g., *The car slowed down*) and both of these before present-tense third-person *-s* (e.g., *The car slows down*). No child acquires past tense before *-ing*, for example.

Also emerging in the 1960s and 1970s was work by Ursula Bellugi on developmental stages. What Bellugi showed was that in the acquisition of a particular structure, such as negation, one could find stages. That is, children do not magically begin producing negative sentences such as *John does not live here* but instead go through stages in which bits and pieces of the syntax of negation are added and refined until the child arrives at what looks like an adult-like representation. Again as a preview to what we will see in a later chapter, Bellugi showed that children start off with simple *no* + word or phrase to indicate negation (e.g., *no milk, no more soap*) followed by something that looked like a sentence because it had a subject and verb but *no* was still the negator (e.g., *I no want milk*). The staged development would continue until finally the child could produce helping verbs (*do, have*) and modals (e.g., *can, would, might*) with the correct negator *not* (e.g., *He doesn't like milk, I can't fix this*). Ordered development, whether the acquisition of a group of morphemes or the acquisition of a particular construction, showed up repeatedly in child language acquisition and in various different languages around the world.

At the same time, researchers began to look at the interactions between children and their caregivers in order to ascertain whether feedback (e.g., reinforcement, correction) and other aspects of behaviorism were at play. None could be found. In fact, repeated attempts to deliberately teach children language and to correct them did not work. Note: We're not talking about school-aged children who are corrected for the use of *ain't*, for example, by teachers and parents. We are talking about 2- and 3-year-olds corrected for *feets* and *Nobody don't like me*, as in the following example from David McNeill, published in the mid 1960s. A mother is attempting to overtly correct her child to see if the correction works.

CHILD: Nobody don't like me.
MOTHER: No, say "nobody likes me."
CHILD: Nobody don't like me.

(Eight repetitions of this exchange)

MOTHER: No, now listen carefully; say "nobody likes me."
CHILD: Oh! Nobody don't likes me.

McNeill's example was a deliberate attempt by one mother. Such attempts are rare. What the research did show was that parents and caregivers corrected children only for content or truth-value. Note in the following interchange how the parent does not correct for the form of the verb but for what the child is talking about.

CHILD: Look. Doggie lie down! (pointing to a cow in the field)
PARENT: No, honey. That's not a doggie. That's a cow.
CHILD: (still pointing) Cow! Cow lie down!
PARENT: Yes. Maybe he's tired.

By the time the mid 1970s had arrived, child language acquisition research – along with the generative revolution in linguistics – had pretty much sounded the death knell for behaviorism as an adequate explanation for child language acquisition. Children did not imitate their parents' language and get rewarded for it. Yes, they got rewarded for participating in conversations and for being truthful, but not for *how* they said anything. Children seemed to gradually work out the "rules" of language on their own without external influences.

What about Social Factors?

The picture painted here is that there is some sort of universalism in child language acquisition for speakers of the same language. A conclusion might be that social factors or context doesn't matter. Social factors and context matter a great deal for a variety of things in child language acquisition but not for the formal properties of language (e.g., syntax, rules of the sound system). Social context affects how children participate in conversations, the particular words they learn as opposed to others, and even how they might eventually see themselves as speakers of a particular language. For example, children in one social context may be raised so that swearing is okay, while others may be raised in an environment where swearing is considered ill mannered and to be avoided.

Of course, social context influences the particular dialect of a language that a child learns (e.g., English in South Boston, English in rural Georgia, English in Belfast, Black Vernacular English). Dialects are clearly tied to identity and children tend to identify with the community in which they are raised.

And, to be sure, social context and factors affect communicative modes that use language, such as writing and composition. Here the effect is not on the language itself (i.e., the formal properties) but on style, rhetoric, word choice, spelling, and even whether a person writes or doesn't.

But, again, social context does not seem to affect the acquisition of the underlying formal properties of language (i.e., how these things develop over time, as in the Berko Gleason and Brown studies). So, the child learning English in South Boston, the child learning English in rural Georgia, and the child learning English in Belfast, all acquire -*ing* before they acquire third-person -*s*, for example.

The Revolution in Second Language Acquisition

As in child language acquisition prior to the 1960s, L2 acquisition theory was dominated by behaviorism. L2 learners were viewed as acquirers of new habits, and these habits were learned using the same constructs as in L1 acquisition: stimulus, response, feedback, and their correlates. The situation was seen to be more complicated for the L2 learner because while learning new habits, the learner had to suppress old habits – the habits of the L1. Language-teaching circles in the military latched onto these ideas with the advent of the Army Method in the 1940s, which was translated into academic environments as the Audiolingual approach in the late 1950s and early 1960s. This approach to language acquisition in the classroom involved memorization of dialogues and various kinds of "drills" to practice vocabulary and sentence patterns. Suppression of L1 habits and the avoidance of errors were central to the Audiolingual approach. Errors were seen as either failure to learn or intrusive in the learning process. What is more, the L1 was considered to be the source of all errors. These ideas are best represented in the works of Robert Lado and his contemporaries.

Spurred by the rapidly changing landscape in child L1 acquisition and linguistics in the 1960s, several scholars interested in L2 acquisition began to question the application of behaviorism to non-native language acquisition. In this regard, two publications stand out as pioneering – and should be read by any student of L2 acquisition. The first was S. Pit Corder's famous essay, "The Significance of Learners' Errors" published in 1967. Corder argued that systematic errors in L2 acquisition were not symptomatic of faulty learning, but, as in child language acquisition, were windows into how the mind processed and stored language. Better yet, they were ways to understand how L2 learners (re-)created language in their heads. By careful study of "errors," we could come to know how L2 acquisition proceeds, determine some of the underlying processes, and look for commonalities across learners and languages. As Corder himself said,

> In 1967, the linguist S. Pit Corder argued that systematic errors in L2 acquisition were not symptomatic of faulty learning but, as in child language acquisition, were windows into how the mind processed and stored language.

A learner's errors provide evidence of the system of the language that he is using (i.e., has learned) at a particular point in the course (and it must be repeated that he is using some system, although it is not yet the right system) ... [Errors] provide to the researcher evidence of how language is learned or acquired, what strategies or procedures the learner is employing in the discovery of the language.

(Corder, 1967, p. 167)

Consider this ...

Corder discussed the significance of learners' "errors" and claimed that they would prob- ably provide evidence of a system. And if L2 acquisition turned out to be like L1 acquisi- tion in that the learner did not learn by imitation but by gradually building up an internal system over time, are "errors" actually errors? Think of this: An adult frog starts out as an egg, eggs hatch to release tadpoles with gills, tadpoles grow back legs, then the tadpoles' gills are replaced by lungs as they also grow front legs, and then the adult frog emerges. Is a tadpole an error because it isn't a frog yet? Is a tadpole with legs and gills an error because it doesn't have lungs?

The other publication that helped launch the field of contemporary research on L2 acquisition was Larry Selinker's 1972 essay, "Interlanguage." In an ambi- tious attempt to connect many ideas, Selinker argued a number of points. Here, we will consider only three. The first was that learners create what he called an **interlanguage**. This language was neither the L1 nor the L2 but was reflective of how the learner moved from one toward the goal of another. In this way, Selinker likened L2 acquisition to L1 acquisition but added in the one ingredient that the L1 learner did not have: an L1. That is, he added language transfer or influence as an essential ingredient in L2 acquisition. A second idea was that language was a complex and abstract mental representation in the vein of Chomsky's generative perspective. As such, L2 learners were as active in (re-)creating this representation as L1 learners were. A third major idea that Selinker offered was that L2 acquisition, for whatever reasons, was not uniformly successful. Whereas all children growing up in the same environment converge on the same linguis- tic system (mental representation), L2 learners do not. They are routinely non- nativelike in a variety of domains. Selinker termed this aspect of L2 acquisition **fossilization**.

Inspired by Roger Brown's empirical work in L1 acquisition, research on ordered development in the L2 context began to appear in the 1970s. Although we will visit this line of research in some detail in Chapter 2, a number of pioneers launched this line of empirical L2 research. (Prior to this time period, there was speculation about acquisition vis-à-vis behaviorism but no actual empirical research.) These pioneers included Heidi Dulay and Marina Burt, who in a series of studies in the early to mid 1970s demonstrated that child L2 acquisition of morphemes was ordered over time independently of the L1. For adult L2 learners, Stephen Krashen and his colleagues conducted similar research on the acquisition of morphemes in the mid to late 1970s. Again, ordered development was found and it looked similar to what children did.

About the same time and into the early 1980s, work inspired by Ursula Bellugi began to appear as L2 scholars looked at the acquisition of particular structures, namely negation, as in *John doesn't live here*, and *wh*-questions such as *Where does John live?* and *What time are you coming?* This work was published by scholars such as Henning Wode, John Schumann, Roar Ravem, and a number of others. Quickly, the research on ordered development spread from English as an L2 to other languages, notably Spanish, German, and French, with both classroom and non-classroom language learners.

In short, research on L2 acquisition was virtually non-existent prior to the 1970s. But because of the pioneering work in L1 acquisition and the field of linguistics – and also because of the seminal essays by Corder and Selinker – research on L2 acquisition seemed to explode, and by the 1980s, L2 research was a fruitful domain of inquiry. It was a young field but was quickly taking off. And it was challenging previously held notions about how second languages are acquired.

The Driving Question

The driving question that got the field of L2 acquisition going was whether it was similar to or different from L1 acquisition in terms of underlying processes.

Although the flurry of research that cropped up in the 1970s and continued afterward was inspired by the work in L1 acquisition, very quickly the field began to coalesce around a singular question: Is L2 acquisition like L1 acquisition? To the average person on the street this may seem like a dumb question. Of course L2 acquisition is not like L1 acquisition! Adults are adults and children are children. Their brains are different, their motivations are different, their environments are different ... and the list continues. Nonetheless, both Corder and Selinker suggested that at least in some respects – perhaps at their core – L1 and L2 acquisition shared similarities and probably involved identical *underlying* processes in spite of the differences we see on the outside. The key term here is "underlying," with the suggestion that no matter what the motivations, environments, or other non-language-related factors, something deep in the mind of humans was at the core of both L1 and L2 acquisition. Here is a quote from Corder on this matter:

It still remains to be shown that the process of learning an L2 is of a fundamentally different nature from the process of primary acquisition. If we postulate the same mechanism, then we may also postulate that the procedures or strategies adopted by the learner of the L2 are fundamentally the same.

(Corder, 1967, p. 164)

As the empirical research emerged in the 1970s and 1980s, at first it seemed as though L1 and L2 acquisition were more similar than they were different. As we will see later on ordered development (Chapter 2), there was considerable overlap between ordered development in English L1 and English L2, for example. But enough differences seemed to surface that the pendulum swung in the opposite direction and some claimed that L1 and L2 acquisition were different. One of the most influential hypotheses to emerge came from Robert Bley-Vroman in the late 1980s and was called the Fundamental Difference Hypothesis. We will review Bley-Vroman's hypothesis in detail in Chapter 5. For now, we will suggest that answering the question of L1 and L2 acquisition similarities and differences hinges on how we define terms like "process," "procedure," "strategies," and so on. What is more, it also hinges on what kind of data we look at – a point we will touch on below – and what we mean by both "similar" and "different."

We will not answer the question of whether L2 acquisition is the same as L1 acquisition here. It is our aim to lay out the issues in each chapter of this book and then revisit this question in the Epilogue. For now, we will simply say that, for whatever reason, many scholars simply decided that L2 acquisition was different from L1 acquisition and the early driving question of the empirical research seemed to have faded by the 1990s. Indeed, many people accepted Bley-Vroman's hypothesis that the two acquisition situations were fundamentally different. However, it is our contention that the question has never really gone away and remains central to the research and theorizing in L2 acquisition. It lurks beneath the major questions that scholars have been addressing over the years – the questions that are the core of this book. For this reason, you will see us return to this driving question from time to time and, again, address it in a summary form in the Epilogue to this book. It is also our contention that Bley-Vroman's hypothesis was flawed in a number of ways and not sustainable given the vast amount of research conducted since the 1980s. Does this mean that L1 and L2 acquisition are fundamentally the same? Once more, we will refrain from addressing that question until the end of this book.

Some Observations on Data Types

A recurring difference in comparing L1 and L2 acquisition is the type of data gathered. Because pre-school children tend not to be literate, the kinds of data gathered are oral or comprehension based. Oral data may be spontaneous; that is, the researcher may simply put a recording device in a room and record the child during play, eating, and other everyday activities. Oral data may also be elicited using puppets or pictures. If you review the Berko experiment in the Exemplary Study in this chapter, you will see the use of elicited oral data with children. Another kind of oral data used with children are those collected when the researcher says something like "Bill, ask the lady in the picture where she wants to go" or "Ask the doll what time it is."

Researchers might also collect comprehension data in L1 acquisition. For example, researchers have tested children on active sentences (*The cow kicked the horse*) and passive sentences (*The horse was kicked by the cow*). The child would be given stuffed-animal toys and asked to act out a sentence spoken by the researcher. If the child understood the sentences, he or she would demonstrate this by manipulating the stuffed animals accordingly. The real target of such research was the comprehension of passives. If children interpreted passives like actives, they would mistakenly show the horse kicking the cow for *The horse was kicked by the cow* (which pre-school children regularly do – it seems that passive sentences are a "late-acquired structure" in English L1).

Clearly, researchers are limited in the kind of data they can obtain from preschool and pre-literate children. However, the same is not true for, say, adolescents and adults acquiring an L2. Nonetheless, in the early days of L2 research, researchers tended to use the same kind of methods used in child language acquisition research. For example, the research conducted by Heidi Dulay and Marina Burt mentioned earlier used a picture narration task, as did some of the research by Stephen Krashen and his colleagues, also mentioned above. In these studies, participants saw an array of pictures that told a story. The researcher would ask participants a question or several questions about each picture to elicit language production focused on meaning (i.e., talking about the story). Other researchers used semi-spontaneous oral production data in which they interviewed L2 learners about topics related to their lives, hopes, dreams, experiences, and so on. Still others used comprehension data, and some combined both oral and comprehension data.

Since the early days of L2 research, however, researchers have generally moved away from oral production data – especially spontaneous and semi-spontaneous oral data. Just about every type of data has been used. Here is a partial list.

- spontaneous writing (e.g., email samples, chat room samples)
- elicited writing (e.g., sentence combining, picture description, video summary, compositions assigned in classes)
- grammaticality judgments (indicating whether a sentence is possible or impossible in a language)
- truth-value tasks (indicating whether a sentence "fits" with what preceded it)
- sentence interpretation tasks, aural and written (e.g., matching what is heard/read to a picture, answering questions about who did what to whom)

- self-paced reading (comparing reading times on different kinds of sentences, e.g., grammatical versus ungrammatical, logical versus illogical)
- eye-tracking (e.g., tracking unconscious pupil movement during sentence reading using similar stimuli to self-paced reading)
- paper-and-pencil tests (e.g., cloze tests in which every fifth, seventh, or tenth word has been deleted from a reading and the participant fills them in, classroom tests, results from standardized language tests such as the TOEFL)
- grades in language courses.

Again, this list is partial. You might guess that the kind of data collected depends on what the researcher is looking at, and you will be partially correct. However, over the short life span of L2 research, we have seen almost an explosion of techniques to gather data – and we have also seen that questions researched in the past could be researched again with a new data-gathering technique to see if the same results obtain. We have also seen that sometimes techniques are misapplied or that conclusions are reached prematurely because the data collected are limited in what they can actually address.

These and other issues regarding the type of data collected and the conclusions based on those data will surface periodically in this book. As we will see, the issue always comes back to whether or not a particular technique measures underlying mental representation. For now, if you are unfamiliar with empirical L2 research, it is important for you to simply keep in mind that two researchers with two distinct data-collection techniques could come to different conclusions regarding the same question they are investigating. This makes the field a bit complicated and there have been a number of volumes already published on data-collection techniques in L2 research.

Consider this ...

Given the differences in types of data used in L1 and L2 acquisition, do you think they have an impact on how we view first "versus" second language acquisition and whether they are similar or different? In what way?

Conclusion

As of the writing of this book, L2 acquisition as a research field is only 50 years old. If we take Corder's 1967 essay as the starting point for all contemporary theory and research on L2 acquisition, then compared to other empirical fields, including the sciences and many social sciences, L2 research is a relative new-comer. After all, physics, chemistry, and math have been around for centuries if not millennia. Nonetheless, a lot has happened in five decades in terms of research findings, theory development, debates, and general growth of the field. When Corder published his seminal essay, a person could count on one hand the number of journals devoted to L2 theory and research. Now, the journals number well beyond a dozen (e.g., *Studies in Second Language Acquisition, Language Learning, Second Language Research, Linguistic Approaches to Bilingualism, Bilingualism: Language and Cognition, Applied Psycholinguistics, The International Review of Applied Linguistics, Instructed Second Language Acquisition, The Modern Language Journal*). In addition, major publishing houses in Europe, North America, and else-where have series and sub-series devoted to L2 research (e.g., Routledge/Taylor Francis, John Benjamins, Multilingual Matters, Blackwell, Cambridge, Oxford, Bloomsbury, Georgetown University Press). There are dozens of conferences in which L2 research forms the core of the conference or is regularly featured in the conference (e.g., The Second Language Research Forum, The American Association of Applied Linguistics, The British Association of Applied Linguistics, EuroSLA, Generative Approaches to Second Language Acquisition, The Boston University Conference on Language Development).

All of this leads us to the simple claim that L2 acquisition is a vibrant and busy field of inquiry. Although its roots are in linguistics and child language acquisition, the field of L2 research has evolved to include cognitive and social perspectives. Sometimes these perspectives are at odds. Sometimes they are not. And sometimes it seems they are at odds but a closer look suggests that perhaps they are not.

Recap

In the present chapter, we have touched upon these major ideas and issues.

- In the 1950s and 1960s, we saw the beginnings of a revolution in linguistics and in language acquisition that would challenge prevailing beliefs.
- Language is not a set of rules or patterns but something much more abstract and generative in nature.
- L1 acquisition does not involve the internalization of "habits" mimicked from the environment. Instead, a linguistic system evolves in the child's mind/brain over time. That evolution involves staged and ordered development.
- The revolution in L2 research began in the 1970s and demonstrated that as with children, a second language is not learned through repetition and imitation. Instead, the learner's linguistic system evolves over time.

- The initial driving question – and one that lurks beneath the surface of current research – is to what extent L1 and L2 acquisition are the same thing or involve the same processes.
- How we measure acquisition (i.e., the type of data we examine) influences how we talk about acquisition and the conclusions we draw from it.

REFERENCES AND READINGS

- Bellugi, U. (1967). *The acquisition of negation. Unpublished doctoral dissertation,* Cambridge, MA: Harvard University Press.
- Berko, J. (1958). The child's learning of English morphology. *Word,* 14, 150–177.
- Brown, R. (1973). *A first language: The early stages.* Cambridge, MA: Harvard University Press.
- Chomsky, N. (1957). *Syntactic structures.* The Hague: Mouton.
- Chomsky, N. (1959). A review of B. F. Skinner's *Verbal Behavior. Language,* 35, 26–58.
- Corder, S. Pit. (1967). The significance of learners' errors. *International Review of Applied Linguistics,* 5, 161–170.
- Dulay, H. & Burt, M. (1974). Natural sequences in child second language acquisition. *Language Learning,* 24, 37–53.
- Krashen, S. D., Houck, N., Giunchi, P., Birnbaum, R., Butler, J., & Srei, J. (1977). Difficulty order for grammatical morphemes for adult second language performers using free speech. *TESOL Quarterly,* 11, 338–341.
- Pinker, S. (2007). *The language instinct: How the mind creates language.* New York: Harper Perennial.
- Rowland, C. (2014). *Understanding child language acquisition.* London: Routledge.
- Selinker, L. (1972). Interlanguage. *International Review of Applied Linguistics,* 10, 209–230.
- Skinner, B. F. (1957). *Verbal Behavior.* New York: Appleton-Century-Crofts.

FOLLOWING UP

1. Read S. Pit Corder's 1967 essay on the significance of learners' errors (see References and Readings). List and describe five major points he makes in this essay.

2. It is common belief that children learn an L1 effortlessly and easily. We now know the following to be true:
   - Acquisition begins in the womb as the later-stage fetus starts to process sounds from the environment.
   - Children first babble, then enter a one-word stage.
   - At some point, children begin to put two words together, eventually getting to something that looks like a sentence by the age of 3 years.
   - An adult-like grammar is in place by the age of 4.5 years but there are gaps in some areas.
   - Some of these gaps aren't filled in until the child is much older, well into primary school and sometimes middle-school age.

It would seem that if children do nothing but spend their waking hours learning language, they spend thousands of hours doing so: over 13,000 hours by the age of 4.5. How does this scenario fit with the "effortlessly and easily" description of acquisition? What do you think people mean by "effortlessly and easily"?

3. When children acquire the past tense in English, they tend to follow this sequence:
   - In the first stage, verbs are not marked for past tense. Children use "bare" verbs such as *eat* and *talk* when referencing past tense.
   - In the next stage, children exhibit control over high-frequency irregulars (e.g., *ate, went*) but not regular past tense.
   - In the subsequent stage, regular past-tense markings emerge (e.g., *talked, looked*) but there is also an unlearning of the irregulars so that they are treated as regulars (e.g., *eated* or *ated, wented* or *goed*).
   - In a final stage, the irregulars reassert themselves (e.g., *ate, went*) and past-tense marking looks adult-like. It takes the child until about the age of 5 to get to this stage, and there may still be a few gaps for infrequent verbs.

Can these stages be accounted for by imitation and reward? Why or why not?

4. Structural linguists were concerned with observable patterns of language. As such, they were concerned with possible sentences in a language and tried to describe those. Generative linguists have been concerned with both what is possible and what is not possible in a language. For example, the contraction *wanna* is possible in this sentence, *Who do you wanna call about this?* but it is not possible in this sentence, **Who do you wanna call Jim about this?* (instead you have to say *Who do you wanta/want to call Jim about this?*). Likewise, the contraction *I've* is possible in *I've done it* but not possible in **Should I've done it?* To look at what is possible and impossible, generative linguists rely on intuitions about language or sometimes they ask speakers "Which sounds better to you? X or Y?" Structural linguists relied on what people said. Which do you think is a better way to determine "what's in people's heads" (i.e., their underlying competence)?

5. Conduct an online search for recent Second Language Research Forum (SLRF) meetings and/or for recent EuroSLA meetings. Examine the titles for papers on L2 acquisition. What strikes you about the titles?

2   What Does Development Look Like?

In nature, there is ordered development. Any person who has taken a science class has probably seen how chicken eggs are fertilized and what the development of a chick embryo looks like over the 21 days it takes for the chick to emerge from the shell. If not, you might want to Google "development of chick embryo." What is clear is that the development of the embryo is ordered or staged, such that something must happen before other things can happen. This is all pre-programmed into the genetics of the egg, of course. The same is true for the development of an oak tree from an acorn and the development of a snowflake from molecules of water.

So too in L2 acquisition there is ordered development. That is, there are ways in which an L2 system grows in the mind of the learner that are universal across all learners of the same language. Such ordered development does not mean that there is no variation among individuals, but such variation does not alter the stages themselves. And of course, in Chapter 8 we will touch on individual variation that affects rate of development and how far learners get. To examine ordered development, we will review four major research areas in L2 research:

- morpheme orders
- developmental sequences
- U-shaped development
- markedness relationships.

At the appropriate points, we will also discuss the role of L1 influence in the developmental process of L2 acquisition.

Morpheme Orders

You may recall from Chapter 1 that morpheme order research began in response to research in child L1 acquisition. Roger Brown studied how children acquire particular morphemes over time in English. To review, a **morpheme** is the smallest unit of language that carries meaning. So, a word like *dog* is a morpheme and carries the meaning of a canine-like animal. The *-s* marker that is attached to the end of a noun is a morpheme and means "more than one." So, *dogs* consists of two morphemes: the morpheme *dog* and the morpheme *-s*. The plural *-s* marker is what is called an **inflectional morpheme**, meaning that it gets attached to a noun to add to its meaning (i.e., *dog* has one meaning and *dogs* has the same meaning with the added meaning of more than one). Likewise, the verb *watch* is a morpheme and means using the eyes to focus on something. We can add the inflectional morpheme *-ed* to the verb and add the meaning of "happened in the past": *watch + -ed = watched*.

As we touched on in Chapter 1, Roger Brown investigated how children acquired various morphemes over time. These morphemes included inflectional morphemes for nouns (plural marker, possessive marker, as in *the boy's hat*), for verbs (past-tense marker, third-person marker for present-tense *-s* as in *eats*, progressive marker *-ing* as in *eating*), in addition to articles (*the, a/an*), copular ("linking") verbs (*be,* and contracted *be*, as in *the boy's hungry*), *be* as auxiliary (as in the *boy is coming* and *the boy's coming*), irregular past-tense verbs (such as *ate, went*), among a few others. What Brown found was that linguistically unimpaired children, regardless of social status or home life, acquired the morphemes in a universal order over time. The order looks like this (with a few things left out for simplicity here):

> progressive *-ing* (e.g., *eating*)
> ↓
> plural *-s*
> ↓
> irregular past (e.g., *went, ate*)
> ↓
> possessive *-s*
> ↓
> full copula *be* (e.g., *Snail is slow*).
> ↓
> articles (e.g., *a/an, the*)
> ↓
> regular past (e.g., *watched, cooked*)
> ↓
> third-person *-s* (e.g., *eats, cooks*)
> ↓
> full auxiliary *be* (e.g., *The snail is crawling*)
> ↓
> contracted copula *be* (e.g., (*The snail's slow*)
> ↓
> contracted auxiliary *be* (e.g., *The snail's crawling*)

By acquired, Brown meant that in the samples he took, the children were accurately using a morpheme 90 percent of the time in spontaneous speech over several contiguous time periods. Of course, there are individual differences in how long children take to acquire each morpheme and how long they take overall, but the point here is that regardless of differences in rate, all children acquired the morphemes in the same order over time. Brown's work was subsequently corroborated by others.

In the 1970s, L2 researchers began to look at children and adults acquiring English as an L2 in and out of classrooms. Some of these researchers were Heidi Dulay and Marina Burt and Stephen Krashen and his colleagues, among many, many others. In fact, by the early 1990s, dozens of studies looking at morpheme orders and their universality had been reported. Taken together, these studies found that, with some slight variations, there was a universal order of morpheme development for all L2 learners of English. This prompted Stephen Krashen to claim there was a "natural" order of English morpheme acquisition for all learners of English regardless of context, L1, age, and so on. His order looked like this, with groups of morphemes acquired before other groups of morphemes:

> -*ing*, noun plural, copula *be*
> ↓
> auxiliaries, articles
> ↓
> irregular past
> ↓
> regular past, third-person singular present tense (-*s* as in *talks*), possessive on nouns (-*s* as in *John's*)

Other researchers, notably Roger Andersen and Bill VanPatten, took another look at the morpheme studies and questioned whether it was appropriate to group noun-related morphemes with articles with verb-related morphemes (and so on) all in the same study. After all, why should we care about the relative order of, say, plural -*s* and past tense? Andersen and VanPatten independently looked at, for example, just verb-related morphemes and found a universal and inalterable order in all studies. What is more, this order matched that found for first-language learners. That order looked like this:

> progressive -*ing* (*eating*)
> ↓
> regular past (e.g., *watched, cooked*)
> ↓
> irregular past (e.g., *went, ate*)
> ↓
> third-person -*s* (e.g., *eats, cooks*)

In short, when morphemes were tracked by the category to which

> When morphemes are grouped by category (e.g., verb-related morphemes), it appears that there is a universal, invariant developmental order for all learners regardless of context, L1, and other external factors.

they belong, it looks like indeed there is a universal or "natural" order for L2 acquisition and that this order closely resembles the order for child L1 acquisition.

However, a universal morpheme order only obtained with spontaneous or semi-spontaneous speech. That is, the data establishing morpheme orders for L2 learners was the same kind of data used for establishing orders for child L1 learners: speech samples in which the participants are actively engaged in communicating information. The morpheme orders could be altered, especially for adults, if non-spontaneous, non-communicative data were used, such as fill-in-the-blank tests, untimed writing samples where participants' attention was directed to "how well they wrote," and other activities where the adult's attention could be directed to what Stephen Krashen has called **monitored output**. Monitored output can occur in those situations in which a learner has formally studied grammar and under certain conditions (e.g., there is time) can apply consciously learned rules and formal features to edit speech or writing. Most researchers now accept that monitored output is not reflective of what is actually in a learner's implicit mental representation of language, a point that will be further developed in this book. For this reason, the kind of data researchers use to talk about language acquisition becomes paramount to understanding L2 acquisition.

Consider this ...

Why would researchers want to restrict data to that collected via spontaneous or semi-spontaneous speech? Why not use monitored output? One reason, of course, is to have a more direct comparison to child L1 acquisition and child/adult L2 acquisition. If the data sets aren't similar, then differences found between the two kinds of acquisition could be traceable to research methods and not to actual differences. Another reason is that researchers are more interested in what's in the unconscious or implicit system in the learner and not what that learner knows consciously. This is an important issue and one that we will visit again later in this book when we talk about the effects of instruction (Chapter 6).

The vast majority of research on morpheme orders has been conducted with English. The reason for this is that once it was established that English morpheme orders were unaffected by instruction, context, gender, the L1, and other variables (see other chapters in this book), researchers concluded that there must be orders in other languages as well. That is, we could posit the idea in the abstract of morpheme orders because of the compelling evidence from English; we did not actually need to see these other orders. Nonetheless, in spite of the general acceptance that there is some kind of universality to morpheme orders, some researchers have suggested that the orders were affected by the L1. In 2009, Zoe Pei-su Luk and Yashuro Shirai published an article in which they reviewed morpheme order development by learners with Japanese as an L1. What they found was that for the noun-related morphemes, Japanese did seem to affect what the English L2 learners were doing compared to learners who, for example, had Spanish as a native language. They did not report the same for verb-related morphemes, which to date seem to form a universal order regardless of L1. A study published in 2016 by Akira Murakami and Theodora Alexopoulou also suggested L1 influence on morpheme order development. However, their conclusions must be taken with a grain of salt because of the numerous methodological differences in their study. For example, they looked at only six morphemes, did not group them by function (as did Andersen and VanPatten, for example), used written data collected from exams (which of course is subject to Krashen's monitored output), and also did not follow the standard procedure of looking at morpheme development over time. In short, it is difficult to take their research as any serious challenge to universality of morpheme development.

At this point in time, it seems that sets of morphemes are acquired in a particular order regardless of the factors already mentioned. It may be, however, that noun-related morphemes (plural marker -s, possessive -s) are somehow affected by first-language influence (at least in the case of Japanese as L1). What is more, learners do not zip through morpheme orders and acquire them quickly; the process is slow. In some cases for some learners, late-acquired morphemes hardly appear in their communicative speech.

Not a lot of work has been done on morpheme orders in other languages. However, research in various languages has looked at non-native patterns of development for small sets of morphemes in Spanish, Swedish, German, and other languages. For example, in Spanish as an L2, it has been documented that learners acquire 3rd-person singular before they acquire other verb forms and that singular verb forms are acquired before plural verb forms. For the reader unfamiliar with Spanish, the language has unique person–number markings on verbs in almost all tenses and moods. In the present tense, for example, the morphemes are these:

> 1st singular: -o (or the variant -oy). Examples: *como* 'I eat'; *voy* 'I go'
> 2nd singular: -s. Examples: *comes* 'you eat'; *vas* 'you go'
> 3rd singular: nothing/"bare" verb. Examples: *come* 'he/she eats'; *va* 'he/she goes'
> 1st plural: -mos. Examples: *comemos* 'we eat'; *vamos* 'we go'
> 2nd plural: -is or -n depending on dialect. Examples: *comeis/comen* 'you all eat'; *vais/van* 'you all go'
> 3rd plural: -n. Examples: *comen* 'they eat'; *van* 'they go'

Thus, learners of Spanish exhibit a morpheme order for person–number endings resembling this:

nothing/bare verb (e.g., *come*)
↓
-o, -s (e.g., *como, comes*)
↓
-n, -mos, -is (e.g., *comen, comemos, comeis*).

Developmental Sequences

In the previous section, we reviewed the ordered development of different parts of language (e.g., noun-related morphemes, verb-related morphemes, articles, copular verbs). **Developmental sequences** refers to the acquisition of a particular item or structure. How does a learner get control over past-tense endings? How does a learner get control over making *yes/no* questions (e.g., *Does Bill write about acquisition? Do you like to read about acquisition?*)? How does a learner get control over negation (e.g., *Bill doesn't write about physics. You won't read about acquisition.*)? As we saw in Chapter 1, research on developmental sequences was inspired by the research of Ursula Bellugi and others in acquisition. Edward Klima and Ursula Bellugi published a paper in 1966 in which they established three stages of development that all child L1 learners traverse during the acquisition of negation in English.

> Stage 1. The negator 'no' (sometimes 'not') is placed in front of or behind a sentence or phrase. Examples: *Not have coffee, No singing song, No I see truck, Not Fraser read it.*
> Stage 2. The negator moves internal to the sentence. Unanalyzed chunks of language such as *can't* and *don't* are used and may mean the same thing as *no* not. Examples: *There no squirrels, You can't dance* (meaning 'You aren't dancing').
> Stage 3. Auxiliaries and modals are acquired and used correctly with *not*, in both contracted and uncontracted forms. But children may still omit auxiliary or copular *be*. Examples: *I don't have a book, Paul can't have one, I not crying.*

In the late 1960s and early to mid 1970s, researchers such as Roar Ravem, Henning Wode, and John Schumann (among others) began to look at negation in L2 development. What emerged after a number of years was that the acquisition of negation was stage-like just as it was in L1 acquisition. What is more, the stages (1) were strikingly similar to those for L1 acquisition and (2) were similar across learners of different L1s.

> Stage 1. The negator 'no' is placed in front of a sentence or phrase. Examples: *No book, No is happy, No you pay it.*

Stage 2. The negator moves internal to the sentence. Unanalyzed *don't* appears as a variant of *no* (i.e., the learner has not yet acquired *do* as an auxiliary) Examples: *He no can shoot good, They not working, I don't have a car, I don't can play good, He don't like job.*

Stage 3. Modals appear and are used correctly with *not*, but largely in contracted form. Examples: *I can't play, It wasn't so big.*

Stage 4. *Do* appears as an auxiliary and is used correctly with *not* in a variety of persons and tenses. Examples: *She didn't believe me, He didn't say it, He doesn't know anything.*

Three points about developmental sequences are important to mention here. The first is that learners do not seem able to skip stages. That is, a learner does not go from Stage 1 to Stage 3 of negation without spending some time in Stage 2. To be sure, learners may go through a stage very quickly and if we are not there to document it, we might not see it. A second point about developmental sequences is that they cannot be reordered. Stage 3 cannot become Stage 2 and vice versa. Finally, although the stages are universal, learners show individual rates of passing through each one, just like children in L1 acquisition are shown to have individual rates of progressing through their development. Thus, one learner may make it through the stages of acquisition in two years while another might take four years. Others may never make it to the final stage after a decade.

Developmental sequences have been well documented for other structures in English, such as *wh*-questions (*what, when, where, why, how*) and relative clauses (e.g., *The man who came ..., The man who I saw ...*). Developmental sequences have been established in other languages for various structures as well, such as word order in German and copular verb acquisition in Spanish. In short, staged development for a particular structure is a well-researched phenomenon. As in the case of morpheme orders, learners take time to go through these stages – years, in fact. Some learners do not make it to the last stages, as noted earlier for negation.

> The L1 does not seem to affect the universality of staged development. But the L1 may affect how long a learner stays in a particular stage of development of a given structure.

Once again, something like staged development seems impervious to L1 influence. Whether you are a Chinese speaker, a Spanish speaker, or a Turkish speaker, you will show evidence of these stages. You won't skip stages and you won't reorder the stages. However, your L1 may influence how quickly you pass through them or how long you spend in a stage. For example, Spanish is a language with pre-verbal negation, as in *Juan no estudia mucho* 'John doesn't study much.' French is a language with post-verbal negation, as in *Jean n'étudie pas beaucoup* 'John doesn't study much.' (*Pas* is the negator in French; the *ne/n'* is redundant and is often eliminated in spoken French, e.g., *Jean étudie pas beaucoup.*) Both French speakers and Spanish speakers will show evidence of Stages 1 and 2 of negation, but the Spanish speakers may linger longer in these stages presumably because of the similarity to Spanish. In other words, L1 influence may be "trig-gered" in developmental sequences when a stage in acquisition resembles some-thing in the L1. This idea was advanced by Roger Andersen back in the 1980s and, while not widely researched, has received support in the empirical research on developmental sequences.

To be sure, there is some variation among learners but not in terms of the stages themselves. For example, two different learners do not create two different devel-opmental sequences for negation. The four stages for negation outlined above are universal. But the two learners may show some individual differences in a given stage. For example, one learner might use *no* more as a negator than *not* in Stages 1 and 2 whereas another learner might use them equally or may not use *not* at all. What is more, stages aren't neatly divided such that Stage 1 suddenly disappears and Stage 2 suddenly appears. There is overlap among stages so that if you collect data at just the right time, you might get a learner showing evidence of Stages 2 and 3 at the same time, for example. This makes the learner's internal system look variable at a given point in time. And as in the case of morpheme orders, research on developmental sequences is based largely on spontaneous or semi-spontaneous speech used to communicate ideas.

Consider this ...

Developmental sequences are said to be universal. This suggests that everyone learning English negation begins with the *no* + word/phrase stage. What does this suggest about the starting point for L2 acquisition? Do learners begin with universal tendencies or pre-dispositions? Is there L1 transfer from the outset? Can you think of some other possibility? In short, what do you think about this: The L1 may be the "starting point" for L2 acquisi-tion, but as soon as the data start coming in to the learner, transfer may be "suppressed" until a time when a stage of acquisition looks something like a structure in the L1. We will review these and related ideas in Chapter 4.

U-Shaped Development

Another phenomenon documented in the acquisition of particular structures over time is what is called **U-shaped development**. The name derives from the shape of a graph line if you plotted out what the development looks like over time. An ideal situation is depicted in Figure 2.1.

What Figure 2.1 represents is that at Time 1, the first time the researcher observed the participant, the participant seemed to do rather well on the structure, with an accuracy of about 95 percent. Then at Time 2, the participant seems to have got

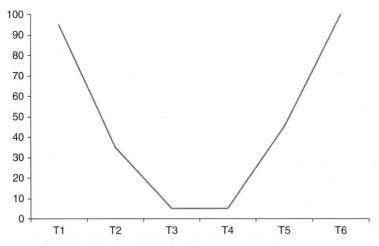

Figure 2.1 Classic U-shaped development

worse in performing with the structure (35 percent accuracy), finally bottoming out at Time 3 and Time 4 (5 percent accuracy). Then at Time 5 we see a marked increase in accuracy (45 percent), with the participant performing with almost perfect accuracy in the end (Time 6). When we step back and look at the graph line, it resembles a "U." Hence the name of the phenomenon.

On what kinds of structures do we see a developmental trend like that in Figure 2.1? The classic case is with the acquisition of irregular past tense – and this seems to be true for L1 and L2 learners. At first, the learner performs rather well with a handful of highly frequent irregulars, such as *was, came, went*, and *ate*. Less frequent irregulars like *drove, swam*, and *bought* haven't even been picked up by the learner yet. Subsequently, the learner begins to develop regular past tense, which is formed by adding some form of the /t/ sound to the ends of verbs (e.g., *watched* ends in a [t] sound, *warmed* ends in a [d] sound, and *wanted* ends in a [ɪd] sound). As regulars begin to creep into the learner's system, the irregulars get "regularized." So the learner stops saying *went* and might say *goed* or even *wented*. Accuracy in production of these irregulars may drop to zero. After a period of time, the irregulars begin to creep back in, especially the highly frequent ones, until the learner is once again saying *went, ate*, and *came* with 100 percent accuracy. When the accuracy of these irregular verb forms in the past is plotted over time on a graph, it looks like the one in the graph.

Another typical U-shaped pattern emerges with plural marking on nouns. Learners may start off correctly with various irregular plurals such as *feet* and *sheep*. Later, as they acquire regular plurals such as *dogs, watches*, and *books*, they tend to regularize the irregulars, producing variations such as *foots* and *feets*, *sheeps*, and others. Eventually, these drop out and the irregular forms the learner started with emerge once again.

U-shaped development has been more studied in L1 acquisition than in L2 acquisition, yet there are a few studies that have documented U-shaped patterns. Again, once the pattern showed up in early L2 research and was found not to be influenced by L1 (except see below with markedness), scholars took such behavior to be a given. Related to U-shaped behavior is a term called **backsliding**. Backsliding refers to learners seemingly going back to an earlier stage of learning a structure and thus performing in a "worse" or less accurate way. So if a learner is clearly at Stage 3 of negation and then Stage 2-type structures begin to dominate, we might say that the learner is backsliding. Backsliding does not appear to be a predominant feature of L2 acquisition but it has been documented for some learners.

Markedness Relationships

Languages have what linguists called **unmarked and marked structures** or **lesser-marked** and **more marked** structures. Markedness refers, in a general sense, to how typical and frequent one version of a structure is compared to other versions. Markedness often entails what is called an implicational hierarchy. In an implicational hierarchy, if a language has Z it also has A, but if it has A it does not necessarily mean it has Z. One of the classic examples of markedness and an implicational hierarchy is found in relative clauses.

Relative clauses are those dependent clauses that modify a noun. So, for example, in *The man who came to dinner ...*, *who came to dinner* is a relative clause that modifies *the man*. There are different types of relative clauses depending on the grammatical role they fulfill. Here are all of the relative clauses in English.

> Subject. The relative clause modifies the subject of a sentence. In *the man who came to dinner was Fred*, the relative clause *who came to dinner* modifies *the man*, which is the subject of the main clause *The man was Fred*.
> Object. The relative clause is the object of a verb. In *I know the man who you invited to dinner, the man* is the direct object of the verb *invited*.
> Indirect object. The relative clause is the indirect object of a verb. In *I know the man who you served dinner to, the man* is the indirect object of the phrase *served dinner to*.
> Oblique. The relative clause is the object of a preposition. In *I know the man who you talked about, the man* is the object of the preposition *about*.
> Genitive. The relative clause is the possessor of something. In *I know the man whose dinner you burned, the man* is the possessor of *the dinner*.
> Object of comparison. The relative clause is the object of a comparison involving *than*. In *I know the man who you are a better cook than, the man* is the object of the comparison *better cook than*.

In English, and other languages that have similar relative clauses – not all do – subject relative clauses are by far the more frequent. They are considered unmarked or the least marked of the relative clauses. Object of comparison clauses, on the other hand, are infrequent and are said to be marked or more marked and less typical. What is more, these relative clauses exist in an implicational hierarchy. Each relative clause lower on the list implies the clauses above it but not below it. So if a language has oblique relative clauses, it also has subject, object, and indirect object relative clauses. But we can't make any predictions about clauses below oblique; the language may or may not have them. Looking at the two extremes, if a language has object of comparison clauses, then it has all of the clauses above it. If a language has subject relative clauses, we cannot infer anything about other clauses. We'd have to see if the language has any of those.

Markedness plays a complex role in L2 acquisition. First, as in L1 acquisition, unmarked or lesser-marked structures tend to be acquired before marked or more marked structures. In the case of relative clauses, we would expect learners to comprehend and produce subject relative clauses (way) before they could comprehend and produce object of comparison clauses. We might also expect learners to make fewer non-nativelike versions of subject relative clauses before they would do the same with something like object of comparison clauses. What does this mean?

Some languages have what are called resumptive pronouns within relative clauses. Resumptive pronouns duplicate the grammatical function of the relative clause itself. For example, for an object relative clause, the resumptive pronoun *him* is inserted into the clause: *I know the man who you invited him to dinner.* In this case, the object pronoun *him* duplicates the function of *the man*, which is the original object of the verb *invited* (i.e., *I know the man. You invited him to dinner.*). For object of comparisons, the sentence with a resumptive pronoun would be *I know the man who you are a better cook than him* (i.e., *I know the man. You are a better cook than him.*). Languages like Arabic require the use of such pronouns in relative clauses. Languages like Spanish and English do not; in fact, they aren't allowed in these languages. Yet both Spanish and Arabic learners are known to produce resumptive pronouns when first working with relative clauses or accept them on what are called "grammaticality judgment tests" (tests in which you give a learner sentences, some grammatical and some ungrammatical, and ask the learner to indicate whether a sentence sounds "good" or "bad"). However, resumptive pronouns should "disappear" earlier from learner language with the unmarked or lesser-marked relative clauses than before the marked or more marked relative clauses. And if learners are not making non-native sentences with resumptive pronouns in oblique relative clauses, they are probably not making them in sentences above these clauses on the implicational hierarchy we reviewed earlier.

Markedness also plays a role in L1 influence. There was considerable research conducted in the 1970s and 1980s in which it was shown that marked structures are less likely to be "transferred" into L2 learning than unmarked structures. **Transfer** is a somewhat ill-defined term in L2 acquisition but can refer to any situation in which there appears to be L1 influence on L2 acquisition or performance. For example, if you hear someone speaking English and detect a "foreign accent," you are likely noticing some kind of L1 transfer of that person's L1 sound system into the L2 sound system. How transfer actually happens is not entirely clear, which in part is why the concept is a bit ill-defined. Nonetheless, the idea of transfer (or **L1 influence**) is widely accepted as a phenomenon in L2 research circles.

> Markedness plays a role in constraining language transfer. Learners seem less likely to transfer marked structures from their L1 into the L2 learning process than they are to transfer unmarked ones.

Returning to the issue of markedness and transfer, here's one example of how markedness constrains transfer (meaning how it keeps transfer from doing whatever it wants to do). The example comes from phonology (the study of sound systems). Languages may have what is called a voiced/voiceless contrast for consonants. Voicing occurs when the vocal cords vibrate. The cords do not vibrate when a consonant is not voiced. You can try this yourself by placing your fingers gently on your throat and making the /s/ sound several times and then making the /z/ sound several times. You should feel a vibration when pronouncing /z/ but not /s/. Other voiced/voiceless pairs of consonants include /d/ and /t/, /b/ and /p/, and /g/ and /k/. In terms of markedness, there is an implicational hierarchy for voiced/voiceless contrasts of consonants. The unmarked position is word initial, as in *dot* vs. *tot*. The more marked position is in word-final or syllable-final position, as in *Tod* vs. *tot*. Some languages have voicing contrasts in all positions, such as English. Others do not. What has been observed in L2 research is that learners are less inclined to transfer the voiced/voiceless contrast in final position into the L2, whereas they may readily transfer the contrast in initial position. In addition, learners whose L1 has the voiced/voiceless contrast in all word and syllable positions seem to have no difficulty acquiring these contrasts in their L2. Learners whose L1 does not, tend to have a harder time acquiring marked voicing contrasts. Thus, markedness constrains or affects the role of L1 influence.

Summary So Far

In this chapter we have reviewed several key findings about how L2s grow in the mind of the typical, unimpaired learner. We will summarize them here.

- *Language development is ordered.* It is ordered in that various forms and structures are acquired over time in orders that seem universal to all learners of a given language. We saw this in three ways.

- o Morpheme orders. Morphemes, the smallest units of meaning, are acquired in a particular order over time. So, for example, in English, -ing on verbs is always acquired before 3rd-person -s, and past-tense marking is acquired somewhere in between.
- o Developmental sequences. In the acquisition of a given structure, learners will show evidence of staged development. We demonstrated this with the acquisition of negation in English, describing the four stages established by researchers.
- o U-shaped behavior. In the acquisition of a given structure, learners sometimes show evidence of starting out well with something (normally with a few target samples of the structure or form), then their accuracy "plummets." Over time, they regain accuracy on the form or structure.
- *Language development is constrained.* We saw how the construct of markedness affects how language is acquired. In general, we noted the following:
  - o Learners acquire unmarked structures before marked or more marked structures.
  - o Learners are more likely to exhibit non-nativelike performance with more marked structures than unmarked structures.
  - o Learners are less inclined to transfer marked structures from the L1 to the L2.
- There is some individual variation in ordered development, but it does not affect the overall universal patterns of ordered development we see in learners.

The general idea is that language acquisition is not completely idiosyncratic such that each and every learner does something completely different from other learners. There is something universal about language acquisition. That is, when it comes to the formal features of language (i.e., the purely grammatical aspects of language), learners seem to be guided and constrained by "something." That something is, most likely, not external to the learner; it is internal to the learner. In other words, something inside the learner's mind, some kind of mechanism or device (possibly mechanisms or devices) is pushing learners along one path as opposed to another. Something internal to the learner is causing -ing to be acquired before past tense in English. Something internal to the learner is causing Stage 2 of negation before Stages 3 and 4. To go back to our example of resumptive pronouns for a minute, it's clear that resumptive pronouns in relative clauses are due to something other than the languages in question. English doesn't have them, so learners couldn't have been taught them or couldn't have heard them. Arabic-speaking learners of English might transfer resumptive pronouns into English, but Spanish-speaking won't do this because Spanish doesn't have resumptive pronouns either. That both groups of learners produce or accept relative clauses with resumptive pronouns suggests that something independent of the L1 and independent of the language they are exposed to drives language acquisition. Something internal to the learner is causing the appearance of resumptive pronouns in relative clauses or for subject relative clauses to appear before oblique relative clauses. We will return to the issue of constraints in the next section.

In addition to the above, it is worth underscoring two related aspects of acquisition. The first is that, as the morpheme studies and developmental sequence studies show, acquisition is piecemeal. Many people think, for example, that a person first acquires the present tense, then the past tense, then the future tense, and so on. In fact, this is codified in a lot of language-teaching materials – especially for modern languages such as Spanish, French, Russian, and Arabic. However, as we saw, this is not the case. At a given point in time, a learner may be "sketching in" pieces of language related to the present tense while also "sketching in" pieces of language related to the past tense. The second point worth underscoring is that acquisition is much slower than most people assume or admit. As pointed out above, it can take years to pass through the developmental sequences described earlier. And because of individual differences in rate of acquisition, for some learners it can take many years. In short, when we look at such things as morpheme orders, developmental sequences, U-shaped behavior, and so on, we are not talking about learning a language in a month or two months. In spite of the advertisements of some commercial "teach yourself" materials, it is not possible to learn Spanish in just 30 days. At least not in terms of putting together an underlying system.

A final observation about development is the role of L1 influence or transfer. It is widely assumed among teachers and lay people that the L1 is the source of all learning problems for the L2 acquirer. These ideas date way back and were codified in behaviorist theory, which we reviewed in Chapter 1. Although there is no doubt that the L1 does influence L2 acquisition in some way, it is also clear that in many respects L1 influence is constrained. In some cases, we see evidence of language transfer and in some cases we do not. In some cases it affects one piece of the puzzle but not another piece of the puzzle.

Consider this …

Prior to the 1970s there was no empirical evidence to speak of on how L2 learners' linguistic systems grew over time. The revelation of ordered development, constrained L1 transfer, and other facts about L2 acquisition struck a blow to behaviorism and the idea that learning language was learning habits (see Chapter 1). What you must consider at this point is that the research discussed in this chapter has been collected on classroom learners, non-classroom learners, and learners who are in mixed environments (i.e., they may be in a classroom learning for some part of the day but then they leave the classroom and are in a community in which the L2 is the dominant or only language). It seems, then, that context is not a major factor affecting how language acquisition unfolds over time. This is not to say it has no impact, but context does not seem to play a major or determining role in ordered development. This has consequences or implications for how people conceptualize language instruction. What do you think these consequences and implications might be?

Exemplary Study

Ellis, R. (1989). Are classroom and naturalistic acquisition the same? *Studies in Second Language Acquisition*, 11, 305–328.

Participants

- 39 beginning students of German as an L2
- L1 = English, Spanish, Arabic, French, Mauritian Creole
- location: London
- the students were taught by different instructors using different techniques and approaches
- some students were fulfilling requirements, while others intended to pursue more study of German after this initial course

Major Target Item

- German word order
- previous research on immigrant non-classroom learners in Germany revealed the following developmental order:
    1. subject-verb-object: *die kinder spielen mim ball* 'the children are playing with the ball'
    2. adverb preposing: *da kinder spielen* 'there the children play' (the adverb 'there' is placed at the beginning of the sentence before everything else in this example)
    3. verb separation: *alle kinder muss die pause machen* 'all the children must the pause make' (modals and helping verbs, *muss*, are separated from main verbs, *machen*)
    4. inversion: *dann hat sie wieder die knocht gebringt* 'then has she again the bone brought' (this begins to look like actual German word order in which the inflected verb, *hat*, appears in the second position of the sentence no matter what is in first position – in this case an adverb; thus the subject appears after the verb, and the main verb, in this case a past participle, appears at the end of the sentence)

5. subordinate clause verb end: *er sagte dass er nach hause kommt* 'he said that he to home came' (this is standard German word order; note that unlike simple or main clauses, the inflected verb comes at the end of the subordinate clause)

Materials and Procedure

- participants were put into pairs with cut-up pictures, not knowing what the other person was looking at; together they had to talk without showing the picture in order to work out what was in the pictures and what story the pictures told
- at the end, one of the participants was required to tell the story (i.e., produce something like a short monologue)
- each pair of participants performed three picture tasks at two intervals: the first interval was after 11 weeks and the second interval was after 22 weeks
- all pair work was recorded and subsequently transcribed
- an analysis of the self-corrections made revealed minimal self-corrections, suggesting the learners were engaged with the task communicatively and not to produce correct sentences in German (when they did correct, it was not for word order or sentence structure)

Results

- Only 17 learners produced enough sentences involving the different components involved in German word order.
- An analysis of production revealed an implicational order that looked like the naturalistic order described above.
- Thus classroom learners of German first produced adverb preposing followed by verb separation followed by inversion.

Conclusion

- Both classroom and non-classroom learners seem to follow similar developmental paths and are constrained by both the nature of language and learner-internal mechanisms (see below).

Knowing More Than What You Are Exposed To

Another interesting but often overlooked feature of L2 acquisition is that, just like L1 learners, people come to know more about the L2 than what they are exposed to. What is more, they come to know things about language that are impossible to know given the language they are exposed to. Let's look at a few examples to see what this means.

In English, we can contract such things as *want to* to *wanna, going to* to *gonna*, and *I have* to *I've*, as in the following examples.

(1) Who do you want to invite to the party? → Who do you wanna invite to the party?

(2) I'm going to try a new look. → I'm gonna try a new look.

(3) I have decided that doesn't work. → I've decided that doesn't work.

At the same time, the following contracted sentences are impossible in English. (Remember that an asterisk means a sentence is not possible.)

(4) Who do you want to tell Alex the news? → *Who do you wanna tell Alex the news?

(5) I'm going to the store now. → *I'm gonna the store now.

(6) Should I have said that? → *Should I've said that?

Every English speaker knows that (4)–(6) are bad sentences because the contractions "sound odd." But nowhere are they taught this. What is more, these are not even mistakes that children would ever make when learning English as an L1.

Now let's look at an example from Spanish. Spanish allows null subjects. Null subjects are "hidden" subjects, meaning a sentence is perfectly grammatical without a subject or subject pronoun in it. Here are some examples.

(7) *Escribo un libro/Yo escribo un libro.* 'I'm writing a book.'

(8) *¿Qué quería? /¿Qué quería él?* 'What did he want?'

What is more, null subjects are required in certain instances, such as time expressions, weather expressions, "existential" statements, and when a subject is unknown.

(9) *Llueve.* 'It's raining' (*Ello llueve* is ungrammatical in almost all dialects.)

(10) *Es la una.* 'It's one o'clock.' (*Ello es la una* is ungrammatical in almost all dialects.)

(11) *Hay café en la cocina.* 'There's coffee in the kitchen.' (*Allí hay café en la cocina* is ungrammatical in all dialects.)

(12) *¡Me robaron!* 'They robbed me!' (But I don't know who the 'they' are; this is more like 'I was robbed.' Here *Ellos me robaron* would be incorrect.)

Every speaker of Spanish knows when null subjects are possible and when they are required. Of particular interest is (12), that people come to know that overt-subject pronouns in Spanish must have antecedents. That is, *ellos* in (12) is only possible if the speaker knows exactly who the robbers are (e.g., John and Paul, the boys down the street, two men the speaker met at a bar). Again, children do not show evidence of making mistakes with sentences in which null subjects are required.

In short, people come to know not just what is possible in a given language but also what is impossible. No one tells them what is impossible and, as indicated, people just don't make mistakes with such impossible structures during L1 acquisition.

The same is true in L2 acquisition: Learners come to know more than what they are exposed to or taught. This is well known in the research. L2 learners of English come to know when contractions are possible, and they know this not because they are taught. And like children learning English as an L1, L2 learners don't make such mistakes. The same is true for the examples in Spanish. It is documented that L2 learners come to know when null subjects are required (i.e., when "overt" subject pronouns are not allowed) just like L1 learners do. Again, no one teaches an L2 learner of Spanish how null and overt subjects work, and certainly no one teaches them that overt pronouns must have an antecedent.

This particular situation in acquisition has been termed the **poverty of the stimulus**. This term means that the stimulus (language) learners are exposed to does not contain any obvious data in it about the impossibility of a particular structure. What is important to keep in mind is that learners are only exposed to possible sentences and structures. Somehow, something inside their minds must "infer" what is impossible. And just because something hasn't been encountered in the language the learner has been exposed to doesn't mean it's impossible. Perhaps the learner just hasn't encountered it yet and it is possible.

> Learners obtain knowledge about grammaticality and ungrammaticality or possibility and impossibility that goes beyond just the grammatical and possible structures they hear or see in the language that surrounds them.

In addition to impossibility, learners may come to know that certain things are possible even when they haven't encountered them previously. A classic example is ambiguity, as in *John said he broke his leg yesterday*. This sentence can be understood in two ways: John made the announcement yesterday (Yesterday John said he broke his leg) or that the leg breaking occurred yesterday (Yesterday John broke his leg). Hidden behind this ambiguity are two distinct syntactic structures for the sentence, and these two distinct structures permit two different interpretations of the sentence. The question is, how do people know this? They aren't taught this and there is nothing in the language they encounter that would tell them there are two interpretations. They just know.

In short, a significant part of L2 development, then, is projecting beyond the data learners are exposed to (we will see another example in the section below on constraints). They obtain knowledge about grammaticality/ungrammaticality or possibility/impossibility that goes beyond just the grammatical and possible structures they hear or see in the language that surrounds them. No one teaches them. They just seem to know.

Consider this ...

What we look at in L2 acquisition and what we see as "patterns" in what learners do may depend on the kind of data we get. For example, research on acquisition orders and developmental sequences requires spontaneous or semi-spontaneous oral data. The research is interested in what learners *do*. Research on the poverty of the stimulus, however, cannot rely on oral data – at least not on oral data alone. This research is interested in what learners unconsciously *know*. That is, to find out what learners believe are impossible sentences in a language, their underlying knowledge has to be probed. This is because what learners produce would, presumably, be what is possible at a given point in time in their developing systems; learners don't produce what is impossible in their linguistic systems. Why can't the researcher simply infer that if the learner doesn't produce something while speaking, that thing must be impossible in the learner's system?

Constraints on Acquisition

Once again allowing for certain (limited) individual variation, we saw earlier that two adjectives that describe acquisition are *ordered* and *constrained*. It should be clear what we mean by ordered. What do we mean by constrained and constrained by what?

The term constrained means that a process or action is compelled or forced along a particular path. In L2 research, we use the term constrained to mean that development over time is pushed along a particular route or path that the learner cannot consciously control; nor can it be controlled by exterior forces such as instruction. It is now accepted that language acquisition is constrained; however, it is not always clear what the source of the constraints is.

One kind of constraint comes from markedness, as we saw earlier. Learners' linguistic systems are constrained by markedness in that more marked structures are more difficult to acquire than less marked structures. In addition, learners are less likely to transfer marked structures from the L1 compared to unmarked structures during L2 acquisition. We can say, then, that markedness guides or constrains language development in particular ways. Acquisition is also constrained by universal aspects of language. In generative theory, for example, language acquisition is said to be constrained by **Universal Grammar**. Universal Grammar or UG is a set of universal features and principles common to all languages. No language may fall outside the scope of the features contained within UG and no language may violate the principles of UG.

Let's begin with a basic notion within UG. Sentences are said to consist of hidden structure involving phrases. Phrases are of two types: lexical phrases and functional phrases. Lexical phrases are the types of phrases many of us are familiar with, such as verb phrases (e.g., *eats veggies*) and prepositional phrases (e.g., *in the kitchen*). Functional phrases are such things as tense phrases and complementizer phrases. Tense phrases are hidden parts of sentences that contain information about past, present, or future, for example. Complementizer phrases are hidden phrases that contain information about what type of sentence or clause we are dealing with, such as declarative versus question versus embedded clause. We cannot easily illustrate a functional phrase here because functional phrases often do not contain lexical material, although lexical material can be inserted into them, as we will see in a minute. UG says that all languages have such phrases. What is more, UG says that all such phrases consist of a head (e.g., in a verb phrase, the verb is the head of the verb phrase; in a prepositional phrase, the preposition is the head of the phrase) and a complement (e.g., in a verb phrase, the object of the verb is a complement; in a prepositional phrase, a noun or noun phrase tends to be the complement of a preposition). So the verb phrase *eats veggies* consists of the head *eats* and the complement *veggies*. The prepositional phrase *in the kitchen* consists of the head *in* and the complement *the kitchen*. Again, all languages must have such underlying structure. What is more, a consequence of phrase structure is that there are only two possible orders: head + complement (like English) and complement + head (like Japanese). Thus, whereas English says *eats veggies*, Japanese says something like *veggies eats*. And UG likes things to be uniform such that all phrases, lexical and functional, in a language follow the same order. So all English phrases are head + complement and all Japanese phrases are complement + head.

Now let's look at a functional phrase. To form a *yes/no* question in English, we insert a form of *do* as in *Do you eat veggies? Do* is the head of the complementizer phrase, and note that the standard head + complement order is followed: *do + you eat veggies*. Japanese uses the particle *ka* to indicate *yes/no* questions and, following its standard phrase structure, the equivalent English question would be *you veggies eat ka?* That is, the complement precedes the head: *you veggies eat + ka*. Research has shown that both child L1 learners of Japanese and adult English speakers of Japanese as an L2 very quickly (after the most minimal exposure) determine that Japanese has complement + head word order. Children demonstrate this from the first time they put two words together, and adult L2 learners know this after about 30 minutes of exposure to basic subject-object-verb sentences. They do not need to hear and see every single instance of a phrase type to know that Japanese is complement + head. Mere exposure to simple sentences with verb phrases "tells" the internal mechanisms that in Japanese the head of a phrase follows the complement. Bill VanPatten and Megan Smith demonstrated this in a study published in 2015. After exposure to just 100 simple sentences in Japanese containing verb phrases and prepositional phrases (which, technically, in Japanese we would call postpositional phrases), 9 out of the 49 participants demonstrated knowledge of Japanese word order in all the domains they were tested on, including some they were not exposed to (i.e., *yes/no* questions, embedded clauses). Another 20 participants demonstrated knowledge of Japanese word order in some domains they were not exposed to (i.e., *yes/no* questions). Something was pushing these learners to "unify" phrase structure and assume that all underlying phrases in Japanese were complement + head – even for phrase types they had not been exposed to – another example of the poverty of the stimulus; learners had come to know something about the language they were learning when they had not been exposed to it yet.

In another approach to **universals** referred to as the typological approach, languages are viewed as having either categorical universals or strong tendencies regarding structure and formal features of language. The name most associated with this framework is Joseph H. Greenberg. In 1963 he published a set of linguistic universals, one of which is Universal 41: *If in a language the verb follows both the nominal subject and nominal object as the dominant order, the language almost always has a case system.* In other words, if a language has dominant subject-object-verb or SOV word order, it is also likely to have case endings indicating subjects and objects. The same is not true for subject-verb-object or SVO languages; these languages tend not to have case endings. Indeed this is borne out in the literature. Matthew Dryer has surveyed over 500 languages. He found that of the 253 SOV languages he studied, 72 percent case-marked nouns in some way. For the 190 SVO languages he studied, only 14 percent case-marked their nouns. This is a very strong tendency. Bill VanPatten and Megan Smith (in a different study) show how this kind of universal guides and constrains language acquisition in adults. They studied 50 participants with no prior knowledge of or exposure to case marking or SOV word order. They divided them into two groups to learn Latin from scratch (Latin is an SOV language with case marking). One group was exposed to only SOV sentences in Latin while the other was exposed to only SVO sentences (all sentences were the same for each group except the word order). What they found after exposure to just 100 simple sentences was that the SOV group demonstrated a very strong sensitivity to case-marking violations (85 percent) while the SVO was at chance (around 55 percent). Thus, the consistent exposure to SOV somehow guided the learners' internal mechanisms to search for case marking during exposure much better than for those in the SVO exposure. Note that in this experiment the participants were not taught anything about Latin or case marking. They simply heard sentences while looking at pictures. Taken together, the VanPatten and Smith studies with beginning learners indicate that something about the way the mind processes language constrains acquisition and guides learners' internal systems in the development of the implicit system. This process is independent of instruction, explicit knowledge of the structure in question, the L1, and the L2 (Japanese and Latin mark case differently).

Other theories impose other kinds of constraints on acquisition. In **usage-based models** of acquisition, acquisition is constrained by a number of factors working together, two of which are frequency in the input (input is discussed in the next chapter) and blocking. In this framework, the human mind contains what we might call a "frequency tabulator." This tabulator keeps track of the relative frequency of things that learners encounter in the language that surrounds them. More frequent things build up faster than others, putting a kind of constraint on when things emerge in the learner's linguistic system; that is, less frequent things don't make it into the linguistic system as fast as more frequent things. This is as true of vocabulary as it is for grammatical structure and formal features of language. To be sure, other factors may combine to attenuate the role of frequency. One of those factors is **salience**. Salience is not a well-defined term in the field of L2 research but it is often understood to mean something like "the degree to which something stands out compared to something else." So in a herd of elephants, a lone zebra would be salient. It would stick out. In language, salience is tied to such things as where something occurs in a sentence (e.g., the beginnings of sentences seem to be more salient positions than the middle parts of sentences). Syllables with strong stress are more salient than syllables with weak stress. There are other attributes to salience, and the idea is that salience may serve as an intervening factor to attenuate frequency (e.g., non-salient items that are frequent may take longer to acquire than salient frequent items). In spite of these caveats, the "frequency tabulator" in the mind is part of the mechanism that guides and constrains acquisition.

Blocking refers to the way that previous knowledge affects how incoming data are handled. The learning mechanism might not let something into the linguistic system if something previously learned "seems to already do the job." The previously learned knowledge could be something from the L2 or something from the L1. As one example, Nick Ellis and Nuria Sagarra, in a 2010 publication, showed how L2 learners of Spanish (with English as L1) relied on previously learned adverbs of time (e.g., *yesterday, last week*) to determine if something was in the past. This reliance blocked their processing of verb endings that also indicated past tense. So a previously learned "cue" (in this case adverbs of time) caused another cue (in this case verb endings) to be ignored. They also showed that Chinese L1 speakers showed difficulty with past-tense endings in English as an L2, presumably because their previous knowledge of Chinese "blocked" their processing of English past-tense verb endings; Chinese has no verb endings to indicate any kind of tense.

Various approaches indicate that language acquisition is constrained by universals, L1 knowledge or already acquired L2 knowledge, frequency, and other factors.

In short, various approaches clearly indicate that language acquisition is constrained by universals, markedness, L1 knowledge or already acquired L2 knowledge (blocking), frequency, and other factors. By and large, learners seem to be in control of the acquisition of formal properties of language acquisition (e.g., morphemes, syntax), albeit uncon-sciously. Internal constraints guide and nudge acquisition down particular paths and not others.

Back to Variation for a Moment

Some scholars have looked at **variation in L2 development**. By variation we don't mean differences between learners but what learners might do at a given stage of development. For example, at Stage 2 of negation in English (see above) the learner is said to be at the stage of subject + negator + phrase, as in *I no like* and *He don't drink beer*. Variation occurs in this stage for a variety of reasons. First, stages aren't so neat that the learner leaves one stage and is 100 percent in the next stage with the following stage being 100 percent absent. Instead, the learner is largely in Stage 2 with some remnants of Stage 1 and some aspects of Stage 3 beginning to creep in. So even though we categorize the learner as being at Stage 2, that learner's production is not entirely made up of Stage 2-like structures. In addition, at Stage 2 the learner may freely interchange *no* and *don't* as negators, each meaning the exact same thing, with the exact same grammatical properties. But as the learner switches between *He no like* and *He don't like*, it seems there is variation in the choice of the negator.

Likewise in the acquisition of morphemes we see variation. A learner in the stages of acquiring the past tense may sometimes use the past-tense ending (*Yesterday he called me*) and may sometimes leave it out (*Yesterday he call me*). At the same time, that learner may sometimes produce nativelike irregular past-tense verbs (*went*) and sometimes non-nativelike irregulars (*wented*).

The source of variation is not clear. What is to be noted is that variation as described here is well documented in child L1 acquisition as well. So it seems that as learners move through a stage of acquisition, regardless of context, they will exhibit variation in control over something in their spontaneous and communicative production.

To be sure, there is some variation across learners as well. Let's go back to Stage 2 of negation in English for a moment. Some learners may use almost exclusively *no*. Some may use almost exclusively *don't*. Others may mix. Again the source of this variation is not clear, and we will discuss individual differences in Chapter 8.

Does variation undermine the ordered development and stage-like development described in this chapter? Not at all. Learners seem to vary within a range of possi-bilities; they do not seem to create completely idiosyncratic linguistic systems that do not resemble each other in some way. We can look at a metaphor using snow-flakes. It is said that each snowflake is different. This is true if we stand back and look from afar. But a close inspection of snowflakes reveals the following. First, all snowflakes are six sided. There are no eight-sided, ten-sided, four-sided or X-sided snowflakes. And there is a reason for this. Digging a little deeper, we see that the crystalline structure underlying snowflake formation follows a universal structure. These universal structures may adhere to each other to give each snowflake a unique appearance, but underlyingly each snowflake is alike. In language acquisition, linguists look beyond the immediate surface manifestations of language to discover the underlying structure of a learner's linguistic system at a given time. For this reason, then, the learner who says *He no like* and the learner who says *He don't like* seem to be doing different things but their underlying grammars are the same: subject + negator + phrase.

What about Social Factors?

Social factors such as identity and who we want to talk with are powerful factors in communication. As such, they influence the kind of language we are exposed to and thus the linguistic data we are exposed to. This in turn influences the way we talk or behave with language. And to be sure, if social factors affect who we talk to and how much, this affects the language we are exposed to and this may accelerate acquisition or it may negatively affect the rate. Imagine, for example, the learner abroad who fiercely clings to his native identity compared to the learner who is open and almost adopts a new identity in the second culture. Such situations can and do affect learning overall. However, they do not seem to affect such things as ordered development and internal constraints on language.

Social factors may influence some of the variation we see in learner performance. Imagine the learner who, consciously or unconsciously, perceives that social context X is different from social context Y and adjusts his or her communication accordingly. It is not clear from the research, however, that such adjustments affect the grammatical components of language in the implicit system. Clearly social factors affect tone, word choice, possibly sentence length, and other "stylistic" aspects of language – all very important aspects of communication. But the focus here is on the actual linguistic (formal) system. It is not clear at all whether social factors affect the variation between *He no like* and *He don't like.* That is, it is not clear whether the use of one or the other of these negative sentences during Stage 2 of negation development indicates the influence of social factors such as perceptions of social context.

Recap

In the present chapter, we touched on the following major ideas and issues.

- The acquisition of formal features of language (grammatical aspects of language) is ordered.

- Learners show evidence of acquiring morphemes in particular orders over time.
- The acquisition of a particular structure (e.g., negation) shows stage-like development.
- U-shaped learning (i.e., starting well with something, getting worse, and then getting better again) has been found for some features of language.
- The acquisition of formal features of language is constrained. Such things as markedness, Universal Grammar, and perhaps general learning mechanisms all work to push and guide acquisition in particular directions.
- The role of the L1 is also constrained.
- Variation is present in learners. That is, when in a given stage of the acquisition of a particular structure, they may show variation in their production of that structure. And learners may vary one from the other in the degree and type of variation within a stage. However, the ordered and constrained development of the formal features of language is not affected by variation.

REFERENCES AND READINGS

- Andersen, R. A. (1983). Transfer to somewhere. In S. Gass & L. Selinker (Eds.), *Language transfer in language learning* (pp. 177–201). Rowley, MA: Newbury House.
- Dryer, M. S. (2002). Case distinctions, rich verb agreement, and word order type. *Theoretical Linguistics*, 28, 151–157.
- Dulay, H. & Burt, M. (1974). Natural sequences in child second language acquisition. *Language Learning*, 24, 37–53.
- Eckman, F. (1977). Markedness and the contrastive analysis hypothesis. *Language Learning*, 27, 315–330.
- Eckman, F. (2004). Universals, innateness and explanation in second language acquisition. *Studies in Language*, 28, 682–703.
- Ellis, N. & Sagarra, N. (2010). The bounds of second language acquisition: Blocking and learned attention. *Studies in Second Language Acquisition*, 32, 553–580.
- Ellis, N. & Wulff, S. (2015). Usage-based approaches to SLA. In B. VanPatten & J. Williams (Eds.), *Theories in second language acquisition* (pp. 75–93). New York: Routledge.
- Greenberg, J. H. (1963). Some universals of grammar with particular reference to the order of meaningful elements. In J. H. Greenberg (Ed.), *Universals of language* (pp. 73–113). Cambridge, MA: MIT Press.
- Hatch, E. M. (Ed.) (1978). *Second language acquisition: A book of readings* (pp. 207–230). Rowley, MA: Newbury House.
- Kellerman, E. (1985). If at first you succeed … In S. M. Gass & C. Madden (Eds.), *Input in second language acquisition* (pp. 345–353). Rowley, MA: Newbury House.
- Krashen, S. D. (1982). *Principles and practice in second language acquisition.* New York: Pergamon Press.
- Krashen, S. D., Houck, N., Giunchi, P., Birnbaum, R., Butler, J., & Srei, J. (1977). Difficulty order for grammatical morphemes for adult second language performers using free speech. *TESOL Quarterly*, 11, 338–341.

- Luk, Z. P. & Shirai, Y. (2009). Is the acquisition of grammatical morphemes impervious to L1 knowledge? Evidence from the acquisition of plural -*s*, articles, and possessive -*s*. *Language Learning*, 59, 721–754.
- Murakami, A. & Alexopoulou, T. (2016). L1 influence on the acquisition order of English grammatical morphemes: A learner corpus study. *Studies in Second Language Acquisition*, 38, 365–401.
- VanPatten, B. (1984). Morphemes and processing strategies. In F. Eckman, L. Bell, & D. Nelson (Eds.), *Universals of second language acquisition* (pp. 88–98). Cambridge, MA: Newbury House.
- VanPatten, B. (1987). Classroom learners' acquisition of *ser* and *estar*: Accounting for the data. In B. VanPatten, T. R. Dvorak & J. F. Lee (Eds.), *Foreign language learning: A research perspective* (pp. 61–76). Cambridge, MA: Newbury House.
- VanPatten, B. & Smith, M. (2015). Aptitude as grammatical sensitivity and the initial stages of learning Japanese as an L2: Parametric variation and case marking. *Studies in Second Language Acquisition*, 37, 135–165.
- White, L. (2003). *Second language acquisition and universal grammar*. Cambridge: Cambridge University Press.
- Wolfram, W. (1991). Interlanguage variation: A review article. *Applied Linguistics*, 12, 102–106.

FOLLOWING UP

1. On your own, you should be able to succinctly describe and offer examples of each of the following:
   - ordered development
   - U-shaped behavior
   - constraints on development
   - variation in staged development.

2. Because of the similarities between ordered development in both English as an L1 and English as an L2 (e.g., morpheme orders, developmental sequences) and because of the way in which development seems to be constrained similarly in both acquisition situations, some researchers concluded early on that L1 acquisition and L2 acquisition were fundamentally the same. This was termed the "L1 = L2 hypothesis." Conduct a search on this hypothesis and report (1) the evidence behind the hypothesis at the time and (2) any criticisms of that hypothesis. Add your own conclusion about what the evidence suggests.

3. Although we will review the effects of instruction on acquisition in a later chapter, review the Exemplary Study in this chapter (R. Ellis, "Are classroom and naturalistic acquisition the same?"). In that study, he found that learners in a classroom showed the same developmental trajectory or path as learners without any classroom experience. What is your reaction to this? Do you expect that instruction would "override" ordered development?

4. In this chapter, we have minimized the role of the L1 (i.e., transfer) in L2 development. We do not mean to imply that L1 transfer is non-existent, but instead that it is constrained. Read either Andersen, "Transfer to somewhere" or Eckman, "Markedness and the contrastive analysis hypothesis" (see References and Readings) and summarize in 1,000 words or less (or the equivalent in a PowerPoint presentation!) how L1 transfer is said to be constrained. Note: Both readings contain technical jargon here and there.

5. One of Greenberg's universals is this: In languages with dominant order VSO (i.e., verb subject object, such as Irish, Classical Arabic), an inflected auxiliary always precedes the main verb. In languages with dominant order SOV (e.g., subject-object-verb, such as Japanese, Turkish), an inflected auxiliary always follows the main verb. What predictions would you make about acquisition based on this universal? In other words, how would acquisition be constrained by this universal? Do you expect learners of a VSO language to have consistent problems with word order when learning an SOV language? Do you expect learners of an SOV language to have consistent problems with word order when learning a VSO language? Or do you think something internal to the learner will push that learner along a particular path because of Greenberg's universal?

6. Review the poverty of the stimulus (POS) situation described in this chapter. See if you can summarize in simple terms what the POS is. In your answer, pay particular attention to ungrammaticality; that is, how learners come to know what is impossible or ungrammatical in a language. If you need to, conduct an internet search on "poverty of the stimulus in language acquisition" to see more examples.

What Are the Roles of Input and Output?

As L2 research quickly emerged in the 1970s and early 1980s, scholars pondered the ordered development we reviewed in Chapter 2. Clearly something was going on in the minds and brains of L2 learners regardless of context and regardless of language being learned. Current theories in the field of SLA argue about what the learner brings to the task of acquiring another language and how this imposes order on acquisition. But there is consensus in the field about something very basic: what the data are that learners use to create a linguistic system. Most teachers and classroom learners assume the data to be the rules they learn in textbooks and the practice they engage in (see Chapter 6 for discussion of the role of instruction). But we see ordered development in and out of classrooms and they look the same. The reader may recall the study by Rod Ellis presented in Chapter 2 in which the ordered acquisition of German sentence structure is identical for learners in classrooms in the United Kingdom and for learners of German not in classrooms in Germany. Non-classroom learners don't get rules and don't get the practice that classroom learners get. How is this possible?

As scholars began to peel back the layers of classroom and non-classroom comparisons and the nature of ordered development, they zeroed in on the hypothesis that the data for acquisition must be something other than textbook rules and practice. What scholars concluded was that the data must be what is now called *input*. Because input is a ubiquitous term in common everyday language (e.g., "I'd like your input on this," "Where's the video input slot in the back of the TV?") we will need to define input as it is used in the acquisition literature (for both L1 and L2). So we begin with a definition of input followed by discussion of its role and necessity in acquiring a language.

The Nature of Input

Input refers to the language (in spoken, written, or signed forms) the learner is exposed to in communicative contexts. It is language that learners hear, read, or see that carries some sort of message. For example, in child L1 acquisition when a parent says to a two-year-old "Get your teddy bear, honey. We're going to Grandma's now," this stretch of speech is input to that child because the parent is communicating a message that the child is supposed to respond to (e.g., by going to get the teddy bear). In an L2 classroom in Denmark, when the instructor says to a first-year learner in French, "Where's your homework? Did you do your homework?" this stretch of speech is input to that learner because the instructor is communicating a message that the learner is supposed to respond to (e.g., by saying "I don't have it" or pulling out the homework and showing it). In a Starbucks in Chicago, the clerk might ask the L2 learner of English at the counter "What size would you like? We have tall, grande, and venti" while showing the cups. This stretch of speech is input to that learner because the clerk is communicating a message that the learner is supposed to respond to (e.g., by pointing or saying "tall").

What all of the previous scenarios have in common – whether L1, L2 classroom, or L2 non-classroom – is that input is language embedded in some kind of communicative event. Learners are actively engaged in trying to comprehend meaning. Because the focus of the learner with input is on comprehension, input is not limited to oral or interactive language. As alluded to earlier, input can be written (street signs, ingredients on a label, stories, newspaper articles, websites), it can be non-interactive (movies, radio, songs), and of course it can be signed when communicating with hearing-impaired persons.

Scholars have distinguished different kinds of input. There is input in general (any language that is embedded in communication intended for a learner to comprehend) but there are also **comprehensible input** and **modified input**. Comprehensible input is usually associated with the scholar Stephen Krashen and is a construct he developed in the late 1970s. In essence, Krashen claimed that for input to be useful for language acquisition it must be comprehensible. After all, if language is not comprehensible in some way, it is mere noise. Lurking behind this idea is that during the act of comprehension, learners are engaged in mapping meaning onto form. The internal mechanisms are working on the data found in the input to create language in the head. The mechanisms can't do this if nothing in the speech stream is comprehensible.

Modified input is a term first coined by Michael Long in the early 1980s and refers to what speakers do when they encounter a communication problem with a language learner. For example, a speaker might say to a learner "Do you have any siblings?" When the learner looks puzzled or attempts to say "siblings" with rising intonation to show she doesn't understand the word, the speaker might then say, "Yes. Siblings. Brothers and sisters. Do you have any brothers and sisters?" The speaker has just modified the original stream of speech and elaborated on it in an attempt to help the learner comprehend. As in the case of comprehensible input, modified input is related to the idea that acquisition happens when learners comprehend messages coded in the input.

Evelyn Hatch, among others, has attempted to describe what happens to modified input or input made comprehensible to learners. In her 1983 essay, Hatch compares language addressed to learners with that addressed to natives. She discusses such things as slower rate and more pauses in the input. She also identifies the use of higher-frequency vocabulary and fewer uses of pronouns in addition to more simplified syntax and shorter sentences. In addition, Hatch describes how input to learners contains more repetitions and restatements, how the discourse is adjusted, for example by offering options (e.g., "Do you want tall, grande, or venti?") rather than leaving things completely open-ended (e.g., "What size do you want?"). This is just a partial description of what Hatch outlines in detail about how speakers go about modifying input for learners.

The definition of input as language embedded in a communicative event (what we might call **communicatively embedded input** or **CEI**) suggests, then, that acquisition is a by-product of learners actively trying to comprehend language. Acquisition is not a product of learning textbook rules and practicing them. Thus, textbook rules and lists of verbs and their conjugations are not input for acquisition. Again, we will discuss the role of instruction and any effects it has on acquisition in Chapter 6. For now, we want to be sure we delimit and make clear just what is meant by input. For this reason, we think the term communicatively embedded input is a good way to think about input. As a reminder to the reader, communication has a definition used in L2 research and teaching. First offered by Sandra Savignon and then elaborated on by others and more recently by Bill VanPatten in his 2017 book, *While We're on the Topic*, communication is defined as the expression and interpretation of meaning in a given context with a given purpose. From this definition, it falls out that CEI falls on the side of the interpretation of meaning. We will touch on the expression of meaning later in this chapter.

> Input as language embedded in a communicative event suggests that acquisition is a by-product of learners actively trying to comprehend language.

Consider this ...

Input must be communicatively embedded and it must, in some way, be comprehensible for it to be of use for language acquisition. If such data are required for language acquisition (as scholars have concluded), the outcome of this claim is that whatever language-creation mechanisms exist in the mind of the student can only operate on one kind of data. What general implications does this have for language teaching? What general implications are there for comparing L1 and L2 acquisition?

Learners are exposed to vast amounts of input over time. The child L1 acquirer at the age of 1.5 years might hear hundreds of sentences during a typical day. The L2 learner might hear, see, or read hundreds of sentences in a given week.

Yet acquisition is slow. The child L1 learner does not get a fully developed adult-like system for years. For the L2 learner, given limited contact with the L2, even more time (in terms of years) is involved. Why is acquisition so slow if input is so abundant? In a seminal 1967 essay, S. Pit Corder coined the construct **intake**. Intake is that subset of the input that a learner can actually make use of at a given time. Scholars vary slightly on the exact definition of intake, but one definition we think works best is this: Intake is that subset of the input for which a learner can connect form and meaning during real-time comprehension. For example, in the earliest stages of learning English, a learner might hear "The professor gives way too much homework." Using context and other non-linguistic cues, the learner attaches meaning to "professor," "give," and "homework." The rest is mere noise. It can't form part of intake. Later in acquisition, the learner might hear the same sentence and this time process not just "professor," "give," and "homework" but also "too much." Later, the learner might hear the same sentence but this time process not only those same words but also "the." In this simple example, we see that something internal to the learner constrains what part of the input the learner can actually process while trying to comprehend a speech stream. While the outside world largely (but not exclusively) controls the kind of input learners receive, learners are the ones who control the intake – what actually gets processed at any given point in time and becomes available for acquisition. And to be sure, the internal mechanisms and constraints on acquisition discussed in Chapter 2 may further narrow what actually becomes part of the developing linguistic system.

> While the outside world largely controls the kind of input learners receive, learners are the ones who control the intake – what actually gets processed.

Interestingly, while intake is a concept accepted by most if not all scholars of SLA, little research has been conducted to determine what factors and what mechanisms are involved in the "conversion of input to intake." Some scholars have considered the role of working memory – just how much information people can process at any given moment – and how that affects what parts of the input learners "get." Others have looked at linguistic constraints such that learners can't process B until they can already process A (e.g., in our example, learners tend not to process determiners like *the* and *a/an* until they can readily process nouns like *professor* and *dog*). And to be sure, there are a few other ideas about constraints on the processing of input and we have listed some suggested readings in the conclusion of this chapter. The point is that scholars *know* that learners don't process all of the input they are exposed to at a given point; they just have not converged on clear explanations of *why*.

We have mentioned the word **process** several times and also mentioned **form–meaning connections**. Before continuing, it might be a good idea to touch on the complexity of these notions. Above we used simple vocabulary items like linking *professor* to its intended meaning and later *the professor* to its intended meaning. One reason the creation of intake is so complex is that there is a lot of hidden "stuff" going on in linking form to meaning. The simple word *the*, for example, has a number of features associated with it that must get "tagged" and incorporated into the word for it to be fully represented in the learner's mind/brain. For example, it must be tagged with the feature "D" which stands for "determiner." This feature restricts where the word can be used in a sentence; that is, it can only occur where determiners are allowed. Without this feature attached to it, the word could show up anywhere in a sentence! But we know it can't. So the learner's mechanisms have to tag it with this syntactic feature. The learner's internal mechanisms must also tag it with the feature "specific." This abstract feature is what distinguishes *the* from *a/an* as well as the lack of any determiner in sentences such as *Dogs make good pets* (as opposed to *The dogs make good pets*). Another abstract feature that has to get tagged with *the* is "known to the speaker and hearer." This is the feature that allows the person to understand the difference between *The dogs sure are good with the kids* and *Dogs sure are good with kids*. In the first sentence, the entities (particular dogs and kids) are known to the speaker and the hearer. We can't say that for the second sentence. So a simple morpheme such as *the* is not so simple as we might first think when we begin to peel back the linguistic layers surrounding it. It could be, and probably is, that intake is partly constrained by all the features and behind-the-scenes "stuff" that have to be mapped onto words and parts of words. Learners just can't tag everything at once. And imagine the learner's mechanisms trying to process an entire sentence such as *The story Anne liked is very good* during the earliest stages of language acquisition.

So far, we have touched on the idea that learners are in control of intake, that mechanisms internal to their minds constrain what parts of the speech stream get processed at any given point in time. Some scholars have focused on factors external to the learner that affect the "conversion of input to intake." Scholars like Brian MacWhinney, Nick Ellis, and others focus on factors such as frequency. More frequent things in the input tend to make it into intake before less frequent or infrequent things. In ordered development, we see that *-ing* is much more frequent in input than third-person *-s*. This might be one (and only one) reason why *-ing* is acquired before third-person *-s*. Another factor is reliability. Does a particular thing always serve the same function and have the same meaning in the input? If so, it is highly reliable and is more likely to make it into intake compared to something that is less reliable (e.g., has multiple functions or meanings). In the end, because of the complexity of language acquisition, it is likely that factors both internal and external to learners work in tandem in the creation of intake from input.

> **Consider this ...**
>
> Input that learners of languages like Spanish and French receive contains abundant examples of gender of nouns as well as gender agreement with adjectives. For example *la casa/la maison* 'the house,' *el libro/le livre* 'the book' and thus *la casa blanca/la maison blanche* 'the white house' and *el libro blanco/le livre blanc* 'the white book.' Yet we know that learners first "get" masculine and singular and only later "get" feminine. What do you think is happening during the processing of input by learners of these languages? Do you think somehow they are not processing gender and gender agreement? Do they skip it in the input?

The Necessity of Input

As we said earlier in this chapter, the role of input in acquisition began as a hypothesis in the 1970s as researchers struggled to make sense of the ordered development they were seeing in and out of classrooms and by all ages of learners. Since the early 1980s, the role of input as a fundamental ingredient in language acquisition has moved from hypothesis to accepted fact. Learners don't build linguistic systems in their minds without CEI. Even those who claim "Well I learned all the grammar and stuff and this is how I learned language" would be hard pressed to discount the role of input as they consider what else they did other than learn rules and memorize verb forms (e.g., read, hear instructors talk, study abroad, watch movies, seek out speakers of the language). No advanced speaker of a language has become advanced without extensive interaction with CEI. All current mainstream theories in both L1 and L2 research accept input as the data for language acquisition.

The question for us, then, is why is input necessary? Why can't people learn a language simply by memorizing rules and verb forms and then practicing them? The answer is relatively simple: That's how the mind/brain is wired. Regardless of one's theoretical position (and we will explore two of the more widely used theories in a moment), learners are not blank slates when it comes to language acquisition. Learners come equipped with internal mechanisms that can only act on communicatively embedded input when it comes to creating a linguistic system. There are two broad categories of theories that we can briefly examine to understand this idea. Those categories are the nativist and the non-nativist theories.

The most well-known nativist theory is the **generative tradition**, based on the work of Noam Chomsky. In the generative tradition, people are genetically endowed to learn language (as opposed to bees, dogs, and chimpanzees).

Language is defined as a complex and abstract system that, for example, allows a learner of Spanish to know very early on in acquisition that explicit subject pronouns ('he,' 'she,' 'it') must have antecedents whereas null-subject pronouns (subject pronouns are not required in Spanish) do not require antecedents. Thus, in Spanish, both *Ella habla* and *Habla* are grammatical and mean 'She speaks.' Very early on, even if the learner can barely eke out a sentence in Spanish, that learner knows that *Ellos me robaron* 'They robbed me' means specific people committed a robbery and that the speaker knows who they are. The subject pronoun *ellos* must have an antecedent. That same learner also knows that *Me robaron* 'They robbed me' can mean the perpetrators are unknown and there is no antecedent. Thus only the second sentence can be used to mean "I was robbed" and not the first. This underlying knowledge is linked to another aspect of Spanish that learners know early on and that is that when there is no antecedent, null-subject pronouns are required, as in weather expressions (*Está lloviendo* 'It's raining'), time expressions (*Es la una* 'It's one o'clock'), impersonal expressions (*Es imposible* 'It's impossible'), and existential statements (*Hay café* 'There's coffee'). In these examples, English requires what are called expletive subjects ('it' and 'there'), but in Spanish such subject pronouns are prohibited, hence the lack of any expletive subject pronouns in those sentences. What the theory says is that these properties of null and explicit subject pronouns are part of Universal Grammar (UG) and available to all learners of language before they ever hear a word of a language (both L1 and L2). UG shapes and constrains the kinds of unconscious "hypotheses" the learner can make about how languages work. This is why the syntactic properties of null and explicit subject pronouns come in so quickly in language acquisition. In this view, language is what is called modular: It is special and is learned with mechanisms that are particular to language (i.e., UG and language processing mechanisms). Because the linguistic system is modular, it can only operate on the kind of data it regulates: language embedded in communicative contexts. It can't operate on explanations or rules provided by a textbook. And for the record, the properties of null and explicit subject pronouns are never taught to either L1 or L2 learners yet both types of learners quickly "get" these properties. What happens to learners is that as soon as they begin to interact with communicatively embedded input from the environment, "UG goes to work" to determine if the language allows both null and explicit subject pronouns or only explicit subject pronouns. Once it does this, the relevant properties are "kicked in" without the learner even knowing.

An example of a non-nativist tradition is **usage-based approaches**. Usage-based approaches agree that what winds up in the head is a complex and abstract array of "stuff" that we call *language*, but usage-based approaches do not posit a role for something like UG. Instead, usage-based approaches claim that general learning mechanisms (the same kind that, for instance, allow a child to know that a pelican is a bird and not a rodent when seeing a pelican for the first time) are used in language acquisition. However, to create a linguistic system in the mind/brain, those general learning mechanisms need access to basic linguistic data for all the "categories" and "patterns" associated with language. In short, the learning mechanisms need communicatively embedded input for language to grow, examples of birds embedded in real-life events for the notion of "bird" to grow, and so on. Each area of abstract knowledge in the head of a learner is dependent on an interaction of real-world examples with general learning mechanisms.

The point in this brief exposition is that differing theories about what underlies language acquisition converge on what the basic data are for acquisition. Whether you believe

> Differing theories about what underlies language acquisition converge on what the basic data are for acquisition: communicatively embedded input.

that language is special and therefore language acquisition is special or whether you believe that language acquisition is the result of the same processes as something like category learning (e.g., a bird is not a rodent), you would still believe that acquisition happens as a result of internal mechanisms operating on CEI: communicatively embedded input.

In Chapter 5 we will explore the issue of whether nativelikeness is possible in language acquisition. For now, let's accept a general observation that many L2 speakers are non-nativelike. They have accents. They sometimes produce sentences or use words that don't sound the way native speakers make sentences or use words. Such observations have led some scholars to ask whether CEI is sufficient for L2 acquisition. It is clearly sufficient for L1 learners or they'd never become native speakers. But because L2 acquisition appears to be "incomplete" for many learners, some scholars have made the claim that while input is necessary, it isn't sufficient. This has led them to posit a role for instruction, for example – the idea being that input needs to be supplemented by some kind of explicit focus on the formal properties of language. Again, we will take up the role and effects of instruction in Chapter 6, but as a preview we say here that the effects of instruction on language acquisition tend to be exaggerated. But even if there are positive and beneficial effects of instruction, these results do not necessarily suggest that input is not sufficient for acquisition. Let's look at the logic of this position for a moment.

One problem with the input-is-not-sufficient claim is that there are learners who become nativelike (Chapter 5). If non-nativeness is a central criterion for claiming that input is not sufficient, then those learners who do become nativelike pose a problem for the argument – especially those that do so when all they have is exposure to input over time. What is more, being nativelike is not an either/or proposition. A learner could be nativelike in some parts of the language and not nativelike in others (again, see Chapter 5). This situation, too, poses problems for the fundamental claim of the input-is-not-sufficient argument. But let's just assume for the moment that L2 learners generally don't become nativelike. It could be that this is just the way it is and that nothing can make an L2 learner nativelike. Although we don't necessarily agree with this position, it is a possible claim. If so, then the input-is-not-sufficient argument goes out the window: Input is sufficient and it's just that L2 acquisition tends to result in non-nativeness for reasons that researchers have yet to articulate in a convincing way. Again, these issues are taken up in Chapter 5.

Another problem with the input-is-not-sufficient claim is that it tends to focus on time on task based on years. In a later chapter we will demonstrate that the way to view the time on task for acquisition is hours and not years. For example, by the age of five, a child L1 learner has amassed thousands and thousands of hours of inter-action with CEI. An adult, on the other hand, who begins learning Japanese in the classroom does not – and cannot – match the thousands of hours of interaction with input during a five-year span. What this observation suggests is that it's not that input is not sufficient, it's that most L2 learners just don't spend the time interacting with input that first-language learners do. One final problem with the input-is-not-sufficient argument is that the research on instruction – teaching learners language explicitly to help them along – has not borne the fruit of its efforts. It's not clear that instruction really does anything. We will take up that matter in Chapter 6.

In short, although it could be the case that some kind of evidence or research may someday show us that input is not sufficient, at this point the argument is specu-lative at best. It is based on the observation that many L2 learners do not become nativelike. Our position is that the default hypothesis should be that input is both necessary and sufficient and that one goal of L2 research is to determine why most L2 learners don't become nativelike or why some parts of the linguistic system don't become nativelike. Once more, some of this research is discussed in Chapter 5.

Consider this ...

If we take the default position that communicatively embedded input is both necessary *and* sufficient for language acquisition, what do you think might be the reasons for L2 learners tending to be non-native in the long run compared to L1 learners? Here are some possibilities for you to ponder: motivation, the learner already has an L1, quality of input, working memory deteriorates with age, social factors.

Output

There is the claim floating around in some teaching circles and in the general pub-lic that you have to speak in order to learn a language. The idea is that you can't learn Arabic or Spanish unless you practice speaking these languages. What does the research say, if anything, about this position? Before we explore the role of speaking (or signing or writing) let's be sure what we mean by speaking, referred to as **output** in the L2 literature.

Output is generally defined as any attempt by an L2 learner to produce language in spoken, written, or signed form – although most L2 research on output deals with oral output. When learners produce output, they are not engaged in comprehension as they are with input. They are doing something else. One kind of output is what we might call "practice," in the traditional sense of the term. This is the kind of output that many language learners encounter. Learners repeat something after the instructor (or the voice on the software program they are using). Learners translate a sentence from the L1 to the L2. Learners are asked to make a sentence in the past tense to show they can make the past tense. Learners are asked to write full sentences as answers to particular prompts (e.g., "Where do you live?" "I live in London."). Learners are asked to describe their daily routines using reflexive verbs in Spanish or pronominal verbs in French. What all of these output events have in common is that learners are producing language for the sake of producing language. This is **output as practice**.

The other major kind of output can be termed **communicative output** or **communicatively embedded output**. The reader may recall our definition of communication from earlier: the expression and interpretation of meaning in a given context for a given purpose. Context is defined by participants and setting, and purpose refers to why meaning is exchanged (e.g., social reasons, to learn something, to remember something later, as when we repeat a phone number). So communicative output refers to the kind of language learners produce in order to express meaning to someone else in a given context for a given purpose. When a learner approaches someone at a bus stop and asks, "Does bus number 25 come here?" that learner is engaged in communicative output. When a learner says to an instructor "Professor, I don't understand this word" and points to a word on a page, that learner is engaged in communicative output. When a learner witnesses an accident and the police interview that learner-witness, the learner engages in communicative output during the interchange. What all of these scenarios have in common is *communicative purpose* and not practice; that is, learners are speaking not because they are practicing sentence structure, verb forms, or vocabulary – they are speaking because some kind of meaning-making is relevant to the task or situation at hand. Those learners need information, are seeking help, or are asked to supply some kind of information for a given task, for example.

So the question that confronts L2 research is whether output as practice, communicative output, or both play a role in L2 acquisition. If so, what is that role? Because output as practice is largely confined to classrooms and explicit learning environments, we believe any role it plays is part of instruction. We thus will not address the role of practice here and direct the reader to Chapter 6 on the effects of instruction on acquisition. Our focus in this chapter will be on the role of communicative output.

There are three possible ways to view the role of communicative output in L2 acquisition. The first is that it is necessary. The second is that it is not necessary but is somehow beneficial. The third position is that it is neither necessary nor beneficial; in essence, it does not affect L2 acquisition. Before exploring these positions, let's be clear what we mean by acquisition: the creation of a linguistic system in the mind/brain of the learner. The question here is the role of communicative output in how language grows *inside* the learner. We are not focused on how learners *make use of* language during communication, what is called by any number of terms (not all meaning exactly the same thing): skill, proficiency, interactional ability, communicative ability, among others.

Output Is Necessary

Most theories and perspectives in contemporary L2 research do not hold that communicative output is necessary for L2 acquisition. The one exception is skill theory. Under skill theory, there is no concern for what grows in the mind/brain of the learner but instead the focus is on how particular abilities *to deploy language in real time* develop. A major proponent of skill theory is Robert DeKeyser. Borrowing from research in cognitive and educational psychology, DeKeyser has argued that some kind of output is necessary during acquisition so that declarative knowledge (knowledge of) can become procedural knowledge (doing), which in turn can become automatized (be done without thinking) for the purpose of speaking (or signing). It is important to underscore here that DeKeyser and those working within skill theory are not concerned with how language grows in the mind/brain; they are concerned with the development of skill, as the name of the theory clearly suggests. In a sense, then, it is not fair to claim or imply that skill theorists believe that communicative output is necessary for a linguistic system to develop; their position is that it is necessary for skill to develop.

Consider this …

In the 1970s, Sandra Savignon made the claim based on her research that learners learn to communicate by engaging in communicative events. This notion has been supported by research since then. In a sense, she was suggesting that the skill of using language to express and interpret meaning develops because learners are constantly put in situations in which they have to express and interpret meaning. How do learners who are at the lower levels of proficiency communicate? Can you describe what they do? Here are some ideas to consider: How dependent are they on the other speaker for the construction of the conversation? How easily do they initiate topics or ask questions of the other speaker?

How well do they elaborate in an answer to a question? Consider the following fictitious example of a newly arrived exchange student to the United States with minimal ability. B is the exchange student and A is a native speaker at the school where B will be taking classes.

A: Are you new to the United States?

B: Sorry?

A: New. Are you new to the United States? Did you recently arrive?

B: Oh, yes.

A: When? When did you arrive?

B: Uh, two weeks.

A: Two weeks ago?

B: Yes. Two weeks.

In 1985, Merrill Swain launched what she called "The Output Hypothesis." Swain was interested in the outcomes of elementary school immersion programs in Canada – programs in which learners didn't have language classes per se but instead learned language by studying content matter such as history and science. What Swain and her colleagues documented was that learners in immersion programs were far from being nativelike in their abilities. While better than learners in traditional language programs, they were far from being "perfect" in using the L2. This situation caused Swain to ponder what was going on in immersion classes and what the learners were doing. She concluded that while communicatively embedded input was necessary or essential to L2 acquisition, there was something missing (i.e., input is necessary but not sufficient). What was missing was communicative output: the constant opportunity to express one's own meaning in the L2. Swain argued that the role of such output was threefold: (1) to allow the learner to develop skill (again, we will touch on this later); (2) the opportunity to try out "hypotheses" about how the language works while making meaning; and (3) having to make meaning in the L2 could trigger the learner to focus more on how to say something (what Swain called moving from "semantic processing to syntactic processing"). Later, in 1998, Swain would also discuss how having to make output has a metalinguistic function in getting learners to talk about language.

Since Swain's hypothesis, a good deal of research has been conducted in and out of classrooms to examine the role of output. Unfortunately, some of the research has strayed from Swain's original intent of communicative output such that some scholars lump output as practice along with communicative output. The research that best captures Swain's original intent would be that research that focuses on actual interactions between L2 speakers and others in which meaning-making is at the center of what the interlocutors are doing. However, it is very difficult to isolate variables in such research and to actually show that communicative output is necessary for language growth. As we will see, such research falls more into the camp that communicative output is beneficial.

Output Plays Little to No Role

At the extreme end of output is necessary is the position that output plays (essentially) no role in the acquisition of language. In other words, output has no effect on linguistic development itself. It is difficult to find scholars who would agree with this position wholesale. We can, of course, find scholars who would agree with the idea that output as practice does little to nothing for the development of the linguistic system; that is, that you don't internalize a linguistic system by practicing. We might even find that a majority of scholars agree with this position in one way or another. But that is not the focus of this chapter. We are focused on communicative output – when learners speak to express meaning and interact with someone else. So we conclude this very brief subsection by stating that the idea that communicative output plays absolutely no role (either direct or indirect) in the development of a linguistic system is the least tenable position of the three outlined in this chapter.

Output Is Beneficial

In between the positions that output is necessary and output does little to nothing for acquisition is the position that communicative output is somehow beneficial but not necessary. By engaging in interactions with others, learners benefit in some way. Most scholars would agree with this, but there are different positions on just what parts of acquisition output might positively affect.

One position is that when learners engage in interactions with other speakers, their participation as meaning-makers creates more input for them – and possibly better input in that the input might be adjusted for their level. We caught a glimpse of this in the section on input when we reviewed the concept of modified input. Michael Long, Stephen Krashen, and others have tended to align with this position. As we said earlier in this chapter, how a learner responds to another speaker may trigger adjustments in how that other speaker talks. That speaker might slow down, repeat, rephrase, pause more, and so on (see the discussion above of Evelyn Hatch's description of input to non-native speakers). Michael Long has argued that such adjustments can increase comprehension. When comprehension is increased, acquisition is fostered. That is, modifications increase what Stephen Krashen has called comprehensible input. What is more, by engaging with another speaker, that learner is getting that person to talk more, which simply increases the amount of input as well. So the idea here is that a learner engaged in making meaning through communicative output gets more conversational input from other speakers. The more input, the better – and the more the input is comprehensible, the better.

Another position is similar to one of Swain's ideas, namely that by engaging in communicative output, a learner can be pushed to be more precise and that this may trigger some kind of learning (although it is not made clear in the literature just what that learning is or the underlying psycholinguistic processes involved). Unlike the position that such processes are necessary, those in this camp tend to claim it is beneficial or facilitative. Names associated with this position include Susan M. Gass, Alison Mackey, and others. Many in this research tradition claim that when learners produce output, they can then somehow "check it" against input to see where there are gaps in their knowledge. This is called **noticing the gap**. Here is a sample interchange from Mackey's research that shows how, during the meaning-making process, the learner comes upon a new and more appropriate way to talk about a particular concept (see the 2012 reading at the end of this chapter for the source). Note that NS stands for native speaker and NNS stands for non-native speaker.

NNS: And in hand in hand have a bigger glass to see.
NS: It' err. You mean, something in his hand?
NNS: Like spectacle. For older person.
NS: Mmmm, sorry I don't follow, it's what?
NNS: In hand have he have has a glass for looking through for make the print bigger to see, to see the print, for magnify.
NS: He has some glasses?
NNS: Magnify glasses he has magnifying glasses.
NS: Oh aha I see a magnifying glass, right that's a good one, ok.

In this interchange, we see that the learner does not have the word *magnifying glass* at the outset. Through the course of interaction, the NS keeps giving indications that the NNS is not being clear. This pushes the NNS to keep talking until in the end the NNS hits upon the word *magnifying glass* and there is an "aha moment" for the NS. Communication is successful. What this interchange exemplifies is a classic **negotiation of meaning** scenario. Although communication is defined as the expression and interpretation of meaning in a given context for a given purpose, communication is not always successful – in an L1 or an L2. When it is clear to one or more of the parties that something is not understood or not understood as it was intended, the interlocutors may enter into a negotiation phase. In this sample interchange, negotiation is first seen in the NS query "You mean, something in his hand?" The NS is seeking confirmation about what he or she *thinks* the other person is saying. Such negotiations may push learners to search for alternative ways to say something, perhaps to be more precise. Or they may push the other speaker to say something like "Oh! You mean a magnifying glass!" In either case, the idea in such interactions is that learners may benefit by learning something about language because of their own participation in the conversation. They "notice the gap" in what they want to say and whether or not they can say it.

The astute reader may have noticed that in the above interchange, the focus was on a lexical item. That is, the problem in communication was a particular word the NNS did not know, and what the learner arrived at in the end was a new word: *magnifying glass*. But what about formal parts of the linguistic system such as word endings, sentence structure, the sound system, and so on? In 2003, Susan Gass stated that interaction might only have an effect on what she termed "low-level phenomena" such as some aspects of pronunciation and the basic meanings of lexical items. At the time of her writing, there was no research to claim that interaction affected the formal parts of language (except see the Exemplary Study in this chapter). We do not see that such evidence has emerged since 2003, at least not compelling evidence. Interaction seems to affect precisely what Gass suggested it might: non-formal phenomena that affect meaning-making and successful communication. To put it in "notice the gap" terms, the research does not show very strong evidence that learners notice gaps between their sentence structure or word formation, for example, and that of their interlocutors. As we have seen elsewhere in this book, acquisition of the formal elements of language is constrained in multiple ways, so it may not be so surprising that the formal elements of language are the last to receive any "notice the gap" treatment by learners during interaction.

To be sure, some of those involved in interaction research would claim that the research has shown effects for sentence structure and more formal elements of language. The problem with this conclusion is that the research relies on what is called **uptake** as well as **explicit learning**. Uptake refers to that moment in an interaction when a learner repeats something he or she just heard. This interchange comes from Bill VanPatten, who has reported this interchange before; it is one he overheard in the locker room after his men's tennis league was done with its doubles matches for that week. Bob, the native speaker, is asking Tom, the non-native, about his doubles partner.

BOB: So where's Dave?
TOM: He vacation.
BOB: He's on vacation?
TOM: Yes. On vacation.
BOB: Lucky guy.

In this interchange, Tom demonstrates that he does not have the preposition phrase *on vacation* in his repertoire yet. When Bob confirms what he hears through what is called a conversational **recast** (saying what the learner said but in a nativelike way), Tom repeats what Bob says to mean "yes, that's what I meant."

When Tom uses *on vacation* at this moment, this is called uptake. Uptake is not the same as intake in that researchers do not know if what is "taken up" during the conversation actually goes anywhere (i.e., is "taken in"). Most research claiming that interaction affects formal elements of language tend to rely on uptake data. As researchers such as Susan Gass and María Pilar de García Mayo have suggested, however, these kinds of "snapshot" studies are unable to speak to whether anything is actually acquired and if there are long-term effects of a particular interaction or even sets of interactions. In other words, the theoretical status of uptake and how it interacts with acquisition is unclear. What is more, it would be almost impossible to design research to show a connection between uptake and acquisition in spite of some attempts to do so. Most research on uptake during interactions is based "on the moment" and not on long-term effects (e.g., going back months later to see if learners now have something in their linguistic systems that they didn't have before).

Exemplary Study

Mackey, A. (1999). Input, interaction, and second language development? An empirical study of question formation in ESL. *Studies in Second Language Acquisition,* 21, 557–587.

Participants

- 34 learners of ESL at different developmental levels
- L1 included Korean, Mandarin, Cantonese, Indonesian, Thai, Japanese, Spanish
- location: Sydney (Australia)

Major Target Item

- *wh*-question formation in English
- previous research on ESL has revealed the following developmental stages
    1. subject-verb-object: *It's a monster? Your cat is black? I draw a house here?*
    2. fronting of *wh-/do/*Q word: *Where the cats are? Does in this picture there is a cat?*
    3. pseudo-inversion: *Have you got a cat? Had you drawn the cat?*
    4. auxiliary verb in second position: *What do you have? What have you got in your picture?*
    5. non-inversion in subordinate clause: *Can you tell me where the cat is?*

tag questions: *It's on the wall, isn't it?*
Neg Q: *Doesn't your cat look black?*

Materials and Procedure

- participants engaged in tasks such as story completion, picture sequencing (discovering the order of a pictures in a story), spot-the-difference, picture drawing
- participants were divided into five groups: interactionally modified input through tasks (n = 7); developmentally unready (n = 7); observers (unlike the first two groups, they watched but did not participate in interactions) (n = 7); premodified scripted group (a speaker read a script but no meaning was negotiated) (n = 6); control (n = 7)
- participants engaged in tasks for 10–15 minutes per day during week 1, the same one week later, and the same three weeks later
- spot-the-difference tasks were used as a pre-test and a post-test instrument
- pre- and post-test tasks were coded for developmental stage of the participants and for different stages of questions produced

Results

- A majority of participants showed an increase in stage development except for the control and scripted group.
- The changes in production of question types for the other groups all proved to be significant (e.g., these participants produced more questions from stages 4 and 5, see above).

Conclusion

- Conversational interaction seems to facilitate L2 development.

Finally, there is an underlying assumption in the research on interaction and learner output that has gone largely unstated – and that assumption is that somehow explicit learning is linked to acquisition. Explicit learning refers to consciously focusing on something in the language. We will touch on the potential role of explicit learning in Chapter 7, but here we will simply state that there is no clear link between explicit learning and acquisition. This creates questions for research on interaction and output because so much of the research reports a very explicit focus on surface features of language. Returning to the example from Alison Mackey cited above, it should be obvious to the reader that there is an explicit focus on the right word *magnifying glass*. But let's look at another example regarding a surface feature of language. This example comes from research by

María Pilar García Mayo published in 2002 and is exemplary in that we find many such examples, partly in response to Merrill Swain's claim that output serves a metalinguistic function.

LEARNER 1:   *men are less incline* ... it has to be an adjective ... inclined to confess, you are inclined to do something
LEARNER 2:   to confession ...
LEARNER 1:   to confess
LEARNER 2:   but after a preposition ...
LEARNER 1:   to confess ... what?
LEARNER 2:   to is a preposition
LEARNER 1:   yeah ...
LEARNER 2:   so it should be followed by ing
LEARNER 1:   inclined to confessing
LEARNER 2:   yeah
LEARNER 1:   no, because to is part of the second verb ... inclined to confess ... yeah
LEARNER 2:   ok I trust you

This interchange typifies what researchers call a **language-related episode** in which learners engage in explicit discussion about language itself and how it works – almost like a mini-lesson. As the reader can see, there is a very explicit focus here, with use of words such as adjective, preposition, part of the second verb, and so on. While teachers may delight in such an interchange and researchers may find it interesting, the claim that such interchanges foster acquisition depends on some kind of hypothesis within a theory of language acquisition that such explicit learning can "turn into" or "foster" the development of an implicit underlying linguistic system, what we have called in this book mental representation. As we will see in Chapter 7, it is not at all clear that such a connection between explicit learning and acquisition can be made.

With the above said, there is one seemingly clear piece of evidence that interaction might affect the development of formal elements at the level of the sentence. This evidence is illustrated in the Exemplary Study in this chapter, the study by Alison Mackey published in 1999. However, we note here that although we find this study intriguing and hopeful in terms of what it suggests about the effects of interaction, it is an isolated study and short term in nature (see comments in Chapter 6 about the problems of short-term studies). From the excerpts provided by Mackey, the interactions suggest that learners who are participating in the tasks are getting higher-quality and perhaps "targeted" input. Here's an example from Mackey's 1999 study.

NNS: What the animal do?
NS: They aren't there, there are no bears.

NNS: Your picture have this sad girl?

NS: Yes, **what do you have in your picture**?

NNS: What my picture have to make her crying? I don't know your picture.

NS: Yeah ok, I mean **what does your picture show? What's the sign?**

NNS: No sign? ... No, ok, What the mother say to the girl for her crying?

NS: It's the sign "no bears" that's making her cry. **What does your sign say?**

NNS: The sign? Why the girl cry?

This sample comes from one of the treatment interactions (not the pre- or post-tests). We have highlighted here what the native speaker is doing during the task. Notice the consistent and constant use of *what* questions. If we assume that this kind of interaction happened consistently during all phases of the study, we might easily conclude that the learner was getting modified input that repeatedly used this kind of question. We also note that this is a stage 5-type question and production of stage 4 and 5 questions was of particular interest to Mackey. Two things could have occurred in this study (and others like it): (1) the learner got mini-massive doses of *wh*-questions in the input that pushed acquisition along; (2) learners began "copying" *wh*-questions from what they were hearing and using them for communication without the internal system having actually progressed in terms of the underlying complexities regarding the features and operations required to make *wh*-questions. In other words, they could have explicitly learned something and then applied it during interactions in this particular study yet their underlying mental representation for how *wh*-questions actually work has not changed. This possibility becomes greater when we look at another treatment interchange provided by Mackey.

NNS: You have girl too?

NS: Yeah I do, **how many** girls in yours?

NNS: I have a one girl my picture. **How many** girl?

NS: I've got three girls in my picture.

NNS: Ok two difference. Another one. **How many**?

NS: **How many** what?

NNS: **How many** bird birds in you picture?

NS: Birds? There are lots of birds ...

NNS: Ok, same. **How many** tree?

(two lines later) NNS: **How many** flower in your picture?

(two lines later) NNS: In your picture, **how many** blue sky?

(two lines later) NNS: **How many** small animal?

(two lines later) NNS: **How many** sun?

(several lines later) NNS: **How many** lines ... sun lines?

In this interchange, it seems that the NNS picked up on the "how many" to ask about numbers after the NS says "How many girls in yours?" and then a bit later "How many what?" From then on, the NNS keeps using *how many* + sentence, almost in a formulaic way. Although this may be a productive and useful communicative strategy, we don't know from this if there is any change in the underlying syntax of how *wh*-operators work in English. It would remain to be seen what their spontaneous non-experimental speech would look like, say, outside the classroom and outside the experiment as well as what their underlying competence looked like when probed with non-speaking tasks.

Returning to Susan Gass's 2003 claim, it remains to be seen whether interaction research and thus the contribution of learners' commu-

> It remains to be seen whether interaction research and thus the contribution of learners' communicative output actually affects the development of formal features of language in the mind/brain.

nicative output actually affects the development of the formal features of language in the mind/brain. As we hinted earlier, when learners are engaged in interactions or use output to communicate meaning, they develop important communication skills. But that is not the focus of our discussion here. For now, we end this section saying that one of the clearly beneficial roles of learners engaging in meaning-making via output is that it gets them more input. Given the critical role of input in language acquisition and given that learners may incidentally push other speakers to modify their input, this is not a trivial benefit.

What about Social Factors?

Social factors must clearly impact how learners interact (or don't) with speakers of the language they are learning. And part of these social factors may be cultural conditioning. For example, if interaction pushes learners to "notice the gap" as suggested above, how do learners react to such things as other speakers asking for clarification or even providing feedback? Do they see it as challenging or do they see it as helpful and a normal part of the communication process? And are learners more accepting of questions and feedback from certain kinds of people as opposed to others? Scholars like Jenefer Philp and Alison Mackey, along with Elaine Tarone, among others, suggest that the identity and social roles of interlocutors in L2 situations may indeed play a role in interactions and how learners perceive what the other speaker is doing. This would, of course, somehow affect the degree to which learners actually learn from interactions and perhaps what they learn.

Recap

In this chapter we have reviewed the following major ideas.

- the nature of input as communicatively embedded input as well as the constructs of comprehensible input and modified input

- the fundamental and essential role that input plays in the acquisition of a linguistic system
- the nature of communicative output as part of meaning-making
- three perspectives on the role of output in language acquisition:

  o two not widely accepted positions, that output is necessary or that output contributes little or nothing to language acquisition
  o that output embedded in interactions is beneficial to language acquisition

- the benefits of interaction and output are short term/in the moment and tend to rely on episodes of explicit learning (such as uptake), and it is not clear what aspects of language as part of mental representation are actually affected by interaction
- interaction and output can and often do result in modified and more comprehensible input, which in turn can foster language acquisition given the fundamental role of input.

REFERENCES AND READINGS

- DeKeyser, R. M. (2015). Skill acquisition theory. In B. VanPatten & J. Williams (Eds.), *Theories in second language acquisition: An introduction*. 2nd edition (pp. 94–112). Mahwah, NJ: Lawrence Erlbaum.
- Ellis, N. C. (2012). Frequency-based accounts of SLA. In S. M. Gass & A. Mackey (Eds.), *Handbook of second language acquisition* (pp. 193–210). New York: Routledge.
- García Mayo, M. P. (2002). Interaction in advanced EFL pedagogy: A comparison of form-focused activities. *International Journal of Educational Research*, 37, 323–341.
- García Mayo, M. P. & Alcón Soler, E. (2013). Negotiated input and output/interaction. In J. Herschensohn & M. Young-Scholten (Eds.), *The Cambridge handbook of second language acquisition* (pp. 209–229). Cambridge: Cambridge University Press.
- Gass, S. M. (1998). *Input, interaction, and the second language learner*. Mahwah, NJ: Lawrence Erlbaum Associates.
- Gass, S. M. (2003). Input and interaction. In C. Doughty & M. H. Long (Eds.), *The handbook of second language acquisition* (pp. 224–255). Oxford: Blackwell.
- Gass, S. M. & Mackey, A. (2015). Input, interaction and output in second language acquisition. In B. VanPatten & J. Williams (Eds.), *Theories in second language acquisition*. 2nd edition (pp. 180–206). New York: Routledge.
- Hatch, E. M. (1983). Simplified input and second language acquisition. In R. W. Andersen (Ed.), *Pidginization and creolization as language acquisition* (pp. 64–86). Cambridge, MA: Newbury House.
- Krashen, S. (1982). *Second language acquisition and second language learning*. Oxford: Pergamon.
- Krashen, S. (2009). The comprehension hypothesis extended. In T. Piske & M. Young-Scholten (Eds.), *Input matters* (pp. 81–94). Bristol: Multilingual Matters.

- Leeser, M. J. (2008). Pushed output, noticing, and development of past-tense morphology in content-based instruction. *Canadian Modern Language Review/La Revue canadienne des langues vivantes*, 65, 195–220.
- Long, M. H. (1983). Linguistic and conversational adjustments to non-native speakers. *Studies in Second Language Acquisition*, 5, 177–193.
- Long, M. H. (1985). Input and second language acquisition theory. In S. M. Gass & C. G. Madden (Eds.), *Input in second language acquisition* (pp. 377–393). Rowley, MA: Newbury House.
- Mackey, A. (1999). Input, interaction, and second language development: An empirical study of question formation in ESL. *Studies in Second Language Acquisition*, 21, 557–587.
- Mackey, A. (2012). *Input, interaction and corrective feedback in second language learning.* Oxford: Oxford University Press.
- MacWhinney, B. (1987). The competition model. In B. MacWhinney (Ed.), *Mechanisms of language acquisition* (pp. 249–308). Hillsdale, NJ: Lawrence Erlbaum Associates.
- Philp, J. & Mackey, A. (2010). Interaction research: What can socially informed approaches offer to cognitivists (and vice versa)? In R. Batstone (Ed.), *Sociocognitive perspectives on language use and language learning* (pp. 210–228). Oxford: Oxford University Press.
- Savignon, S. (1998). *Communicative competence: Theory and classroom practice.* 2nd edition. New York: McGraw-Hill.
- Swain, M. (1985). Communicative competence: Some roles of comprehensible input and comprehensible output in its development. In S. M. Gass & C. G. Madden (Eds.), *Input in second language acquisition* (pp. 235–253). Rowley, MA: Newbury House.
- VanPatten, B. (2004). On the role(s) of input and output in making form–meaning connections. In B. VanPatten, J. Williams, S. Rott, & M. Overstreet (Eds.), *Form–meaning connections in second language acquisition* (pp. 29–47). Mahwah, NJ: Erlbaum.
- VanPatten, B. (2015). Input processing in adult SLA. In B. VanPatten & J. Williams (Eds.), *Theories in second language acquisition.* 2nd edition (pp. 113–135). New York: Routledge.

FOLLOWING UP

1. Review the recap that concludes the formal part of this chapter. Can you expand on each idea and explicate it in your own words?

2. Read Hatch, "Simplified input and second language acquisition" in References and Readings. Create a check sheet of features of simplified input that she discusses. Then collect 10 minutes of native-to-native speech of a language you are familiar with and 10 minutes of that same language but native (or teacher) to non-native (preferably novice or intermediate learner). Which of Hatch's characteristics can you isolate and exemplify? Prepare a brief presentation on your findings.

3. In this chapter we have distinguished between output as practice and output as part of communication (i.e., communicative output). Under this distinction, output as part of communication has to have a purpose other than practice; that is, learners don't produce language because someone has asked them to. They produce language because meaning-making is at the core of an event. With someone else, review the following questions. What ideas surface in your discussion?

   a. What is the purpose of communication? Why do people communicate?
   b. What does "meaning" mean?
   c. If a teacher asks a student "What color is this pen?" and the student says "It's red," is this an example of communication? How does it compare to what people do outside of the classroom?

4. Underlying much of the discussion in this chapter is the notion of communication: the expression and interpretation of meaning in a given context for a given purpose. Both input and output must be embedded in communication for either of them to be of use. What factors do you see influencing a learner's access to communicative events? With someone else make a list and present it. Can you categorize or typify the factors in any way (e.g., how many of them are related to "social" ideas and factors?)?

5. A reasonable conclusion to this chapter would state that communicatively embedded input is necessary for language acquisition and the door remains open that communicatively embedded output may play an indirect role in acquisition. Yet many people, including teachers, believe that you have to speak in order to "learn the grammar" or "learn the language." Where do you think this belief comes from? Is it a belief that you subscribe to? If so, come back and visit this belief after reading this book and decide if it has changed at all.

6. Read either Long, "Linguistic and conversational adjustments to non-native speakers" or Leeser, "Pushed output, noticing, and development of past-tense morphology in content-based instruction" (see References and Readings) and prepare a summary similar to the summary of the Exemplary Study in this chapter.

4 What Is the Initial State?

In his bestselling book, *The Language Instinct*, Steven Pinker makes the compelling case that children do not begin language acquisition with a "blank slate." Prior to the revolution of linguistics in the 1960s and the work in child language acquisition that was initiated around the same time (see Chapter 1), many people believed that children were empty vessels upon which the environment could make its imprint once they were born. As "blank slates" babies came into the world with nothing, so to speak, and were at the mercy of the environment for learning. In short, babies aren't hard wired for anything. Although there is no doubt that the environment shapes learning, we now know that in a variety of domains, children seem to come into the world equipped with special learning mechanisms that help them sort out the environmental stimuli they are exposed to. One of those mechanisms is claimed to be Universal Grammar, at least by those working in the Chomskyan tradition. (We touched on Universal Grammar in Chapter 2 and will revisit it here.) We might say that the "initial state" for child L1 acquisition is Universal Grammar and not a blank slate.

The question in this chapter is the nature of the **initial state** for L2 learners. What do they begin the task of acquiring language with? Clearly, L2 learners cannot be blank slates if it is the case that children are not. L2 learners must begin the process of acquiring another language with something. But what is that something? In this chapter we will explore three possibilities based on the generative tradition:

- the initial state is Universal Grammar
- the initial state is the L1
- the initial state contains parts of the L1 but not all.

As we will see, even with the second two positions, Universal Grammar is operative in the L2 context. That is, regardless of the starting point, Universal Grammar is constraining acquisition all along the way as it does in L1 acquisition. We will begin with a brief overview of Universal Grammar in order to provide background for this chapter.

Universal Grammar

As noted in Chapter 2, **UG** is part of the generative tradition in linguistics. The nature of UG has changed somewhat as the theory has progressed over the years (the construct has been around since the early 1960s) and in its current form the characteristics of UG are the following:

- it is human specific and innate (i.e., no other animals have UG)
- it consists of a finite set of abstract features and principles (or constraints)
- it guides and constrains language acquisition the minute a human begins to hear (or see) language in a communicative context.

It should be clear to any reader that animals do not have language. They do have systems of communication, to be sure, and some are quite complex. But animals do not have such things as syntax, morphology, and so on (i.e., the formal and abstract components of language). Even "signing apes" such as Koko the gorilla were found to be able to communicate with signs but lacked the formal system that governed it. So we won't belabor here that UG (which underlies language) is human specific.

So what does UG consist of? First, UG consists of a finite set of abstract features related to language from which individual languages may choose. For example, Case and Tense are abstract features. Languages like Classical Latin and Modern Turkish select for these features. Once selected, UG dictates that certain things must "play out" in the language regarding the features – namely, that the feature has to have an overt expression (e.g., a marking on a noun or noun phrase in some way, marking on a verb in some way) and that the feature has to get "checked" during sentence computation to make sure the sentence is grammatical. Languages like Chinese do not select for Case or Tense. It is the selection from this finite set of features that causes languages to look different from each other while sometimes looking similar.

At the same time, UG consists of a finite set of principles or constraints that all languages must obey. One such example is called phrase structure. The principle that governs phrase structure states that all languages must contain phrases and that these phrases consist of a head and a complement. Familiar to most readers is something like a noun phrase. In English *professor of linguistics* is a noun phrase. *Professor* is a noun and is the head (which gives the phrase its name – noun phrase) and *of linguistics* is the complement. Phrases are very important in how languages work, in part because although we can hear and see something like a noun phrase, there are hidden phrases called functional phrases such as a tense phrase. Even though we can't hear or see these phrases, they are well motivated theoretically and empirically. These hidden functional phrases play important roles when it comes to abstract features such as Case, Tense, Number, and others. Because phrases consist of a head and a complement, only two orders are permitted: head + complement and complement + head. These two options are what make, say, English have one kind of typical word order and Japanese another. Thus, in English prepositional phrases are head + complement (as all phrases are in English) and we get *in the kitchen*. In Japanese, phrase order is the opposite: complement + head. So the equivalent of *in the kitchen* in Japanese is *kitchen in*. The same is true for the hidden functional phrases. There is a functional phrase called a complementizer phrase, with complementizer referring to the head of an entire sentence (where a complement like *that, which,* or *who* would appear if the sentence were embedded, for example). Because English is head + complement, we get *that acquisition is complex* (as in 'I know that acquisition is complex') and because Japanese is complement + head, we get *acquisition complex is that*.

So the nature of phrase structure constrains the shape of languages. All languages must have phrase structure; this is a "law" of UG. And because there are only two orders available, languages wind up being either head + complement or complement + head. There are other principles and constraints that work like "laws" in languages. In Chapter 5 we will review the overt pronoun constraint when we talk about how subject pronouns work and, given our limited space, we will not offer more examples here.

The third feature of UG is that it constrains and guides acquisition. It does this because it sets limits on what languages can do. At every

> Universal Grammar constrains and guides acquisition. This does not mean that during L1 acquisition the child's representation is adult-like; it means the representation is language-like.

stage of language acquisition, the mental representation for language is evolving. Because it is still language at every stage of evolution, it must conform to whatever the contents of UG are. Thus a stage of language acquisition may not invent a new abstract feature but must select it from the inventory in UG. Likewise, at every stage, the developing language must obey the principles of UG. This does not mean that during child L1 acquisition the child's mental representation is adult-like; it means that the mental representation is language-like. It obeys the properties of language that all human languages must obey.

The claim in child L1 acquisition is that the starting point of L1 acquisition is UG. Children are not blank slates but instead come equipped with the contents of UG that subsequently guide and constrain the unconscious hypotheses that they can make as language unfolds in their minds/brains. From the UG perspective, the ability to learn a language successfully is independent of intelligence, personality, and social environment. Of course, UG is not the entire picture. Children learn the language they are exposed to and it is the input data they hear or see that pushes the mental representation to select this feature or that feature and for this principle or that principle to be triggered.

> **Consider this ...**
>
> A common misunderstanding about Universal Grammar is that it guarantees acquisition. What is the difference between guaranteeing acquisition and constraining it? Can you think of other areas where something constrains or guides development but doesn't guarantee it? Note: This will become important later in this chapter when we discuss L2 acquisition and will be especially important in Chapter 5.

Against this backdrop of UG and its role in language acquisition we will review the three possible scenarios listed at the beginning of this chapter, namely, whether UG is the starting point as it is in L1 acquisition, whether the starting point is the L1, or whether the starting point is "partial transfer" of the L1.

Universal Grammar as the Initial State

There are two basic perspectives on UG as the initial state. We will begin with what is called No Transfer.

No Transfer

The first position about the initial state we will review is **the Initial Hypothesis of Syntax** as developed by Christer Platzack in 1996. The basic claim of this hypothesis is that the initial state of acquisition for L1 and L2 is the same; that is, that both L1 and L2 learners begin the process of acquisition with just UG. Thus, L2 learners go about the business of building a mental representation of the L2 based on UG and the input they are exposed to. There is no influence from the L1 at the outset (or along the way). What this means, then, is that a Japanese speaker acquiring English as an L2 does not unconsciously assume at the outset that English selects for Tense as a feature (even though both Japanese and English do) and does not unconsciously assume that English is complement + head. Instead, the learner starts out with all the features from UG available (including Tense) and only assumes that the language has phrases. From the input data, the learner will determine whether to select Tense or not for English and whether the language is head + complement or complement + head.

The Initial Hypothesis of Syntax has not received a lot of attention in the L2 literature. Platzack provided some support for his hypothesis in looking at the acquisition of word order. He provided some evidence that learners of an L1 in which the inflected verb is required to be in "second position" as in Swedish do not seem to transfer this to learning an L2 which also requires the same (e.g., a language like German). In German, there is a hidden feature that requires that inflected verbs move out of their underlying position and to a spot higher up in a sentence in order to get that hidden feature checked. (We will see what "higher up" means and looks like a bit later.) This is why Swedish and German get word orders such as 'Every day take the employees a break' whereas in English we would say something like 'Every day the employees take a break.' *Take* has moved from its original position to a position higher up, which in serial order means closer to the front of the sentence. This is called V2 for short because the verb is in "second position" in the sentence. What Platzack argued was that data show that learners who speak a V2 language don't transfer V2 order right away into learning another V2 language. Instead, they might assume something like English, where the verb stays in its original spot. According to Platzack, this means that learners are open to options (provided by UG) and don't assume L1 values for features at the outset. Again, they are operating much like child L1 learners.

Another piece of evidence that Platzack cites is that L2 learners tend to use the order negation + verb at the outset of acquisition even when their L2 order is verb + negation. The prediction here is that a speaker of French with post-verbal negation (e.g., *Je n'aime pas ça* 'I don't like that' where *pas* is the negator) would first produce sentences such as '(I) no like that.' Platzack cites evidence from learners of Swedish and German, in which negation is post-verbal; yet in their early production of language, learners produce negation + verb-type structures. In essence, what Platzack claims is that if there is no transfer of the L1 at the beginning, the initial state must be UG. We will evaluate this hypothesis after we review the next one.

The Full Access Hypothesis

The Full Access Hypothesis was posited by Suzanne Flynn and her colleagues in the early to mid 1990s. Although the authors never really claim that UG is the initial state, their hypothesis functions in a similar fashion to the Initial Hypothesis of Syntax. Under the Full Access Hypothesis, L2 mental representations are constrained by UG at every stage of development. What is more, the authors explicitly claim that the L1 cannot be the initial starting point; that is, the learner does not transfer all of the L1 features and values of those features at the outset of acquiring an L2. If this is the case, then by default UG must be the initial state, especially if it constrains acquisition at every stage – including the beginning stage. Flynn and her colleagues do not rely on the same kind of evidence that Platzack does for his Initial Hypothesis of Syntax. They conducted experiments with learners using tasks such as elicited imitation and grammaticality judgments. In elicited imitation, learners are given sentences to repeat, and presumably how they repeat those sentences is reflective of their underlying grammars. The sentences are, of course, not easy two- or three-word sentences but more complex sentences (e.g., 'The happy janitor does not want the new television' and 'Which secret message does the young girl find in the basket?'). When learners repeat them with alterations, Flynn and her colleagues check to see what those alterations represent and how different they are from when children learning English try to imitate the sentences. They claim their results suggest that learners aren't transferring properties of the L1 into L2 acquisition but instead their alterations reflect basic UG constraints on sentence structure. To be sure, Flynn and her colleagues rely on other evidence as well, but the idea here is that where Platzack tends to rely on production data gathered from various research projects, Flynn and her colleagues tend to rely on experimental data.

It is fair to say that the position that UG alone is the initial state of L2 acquisition is not the dominant "paradigm" for thinking about how learners begin the process of acquisition. First, not much evidence has emerged from this perspective and much more evidence has emerged from other perspectives. Second, some scholars have been critical of the methodologies used and the interpretation of the data. Indeed, Platzack admits at various points that there are other interpretations of some of the data he examines. A major criticism of the Flynn et al. research is that they tend not to use beginning learners, which means that the data may not be the best to talk about the initial state. We turn our attention now to the opposite position about the initial state.

The L1 Is the Initial State

Full Transfer/Full Access

The major paradigm from the generative perspective is what is called **Full Transfer/Full Access**, launched by Bonnie Schwartz and Rex Sprouse in the 1990s. Adherents of this position basically argue that the initial state of L2 acquisition is the L1 mental representation. That is, learners begin by unconsciously assuming that the L2 contains all the features, operations, and so on that make up the L1. So English L1 learners of Japanese would assume that Japanese is just like English. While they might correctly assume that Tense is a feature in Japanese, they would incorrectly assume that Japanese is head + complement or that Japanese has the feature that moves *wh*-elements out of their original position and into a higher position in the sentence – which it doesn't. In Japanese you would say something like "Bill what wants?" Remember that Japanese is complement + head. Instead of *wants what?* in Japanese we would say *what wants?* because *what* is the object of the verb *wants* and *wants* is the head of the verb phrase. As another example, Spanish-speaking learners of English would assume that English has a feature that moves verbs out of their place of origin, which is what gives word orders like *¿Qué quiere Pablo?* 'lit: What wants Pablo' for 'What does Pablo want?' and *Alessandro lee a menudo la ciencia ficción* 'lit: Alessandro reads often science fiction' for

'Alessandro often reads science fiction.'). On the other hand, English speakers of Spanish L2 would assume the opposite, that verbs don't move and the word order would be like English.

So full transfer means that the initial state is made up of the L1 mental representation for the formal components of language (and perhaps for all of language). Learners start with the L1 and basically have to "rewrite" or "overwrite" what is there as they gain experience with the language. The Full Access part of the name means that UG is fully available during L2 development and both constrains and guides acquisition especially when the L2 input suggests that the L2 is different from the L1. So the English speaker learning Spanish who hears questions like *¿Qué quiere Pablo?* over and over in the input gets cru-

> Full Transfer means that the initial state is made up of the L1 mental representation for the formal components of language. Learners start with the L1 and basically "overwrite" what is there.

cial data that verbs move and that there is an underlying feature causing this. That feature is part of UG, and how it operates is subsequently constrained by the content of UG. Traditionally, this restructuring (i.e., switching something from an L1 "value" to an L2 "value") is called **parameter resetting**. A parameter refers to the consequences of a particular value of a feature (e.g., a strong Tense feature forces verbs to move out of the verb phrase whereas a weak Tense feature does not) or to the consequences of a particular principle (e.g., the parameters for phrase structure are head + complement and complement + head). For the reader unfamiliar with what we mean by "move out of the verb phrase" we offer this rough description. *Alessandro lee a menudo la ciencia ficción* 'Alessandro often reads science fiction' "starts out" as something like *Alessandro a menudo lee la ciencia ficción.* The strong Tense feature of Spanish forces the verb out of its verb phrase so that it winds up in the Tense phrase under the Tense feature itself. A linguist would capture it this way, with details excluded: [TP [T] [ADVP a menudo] [VP Alessandro [v lee] [NP la ciencia ficción]]] → [TP Alessandro [T lee] [ADVP a menudo] [VP – [v –] [NP la ciencia ficción]]]. The dashes indicate the empty spots left behind by movement.

The main argument for Full Transfer or for the L1 as the initial state comes from the observation that at all levels of acquisition (beginner, intermediate, advanced) there seems to be L1 influence on learner performance. If there is L1 influence at the intermediate and even advanced levels, it is assumed that the L1 influence was there at the beginning.

Of course, the best evidence for Full Transfer would be to see L1 influence in the earliest stages of development. Few studies along these lines exist, but one study from the 1990s has been influential. That study comes from Belma Haznedar. She investigated a child L2 learner with Turkish as L1. For the first two months that child lived in a Turkish-only environment in the United Kingdom. However, during the third month the child began nursery school with English-speaking children. Haznedar was able to study the child in those initial stages of development.

Two pieces of evidence are relevant for Full Transfer at the outset and both are a result of "headedness." Let's recall that languages can be head + complement (like English) or complement + head (like Japanese). Turkish is a complement + head language. Like Japanese it has object + verb order instead of verb + object order for verb phrases. For negative phrases Turkish has complement + negator instead of negator + complement. The child in Haznedar's study began producing basic sentences following Turkish word order. Here are some examples:

I something eating (SOV, like Turkish, instead of SVO, like English)
Finish no (verb + negator, like Turkish, instead of negator + verb, like English)

These examples suggest the learner assumed that English was complement + head like Turkish. However, it did not take long for the relevant input to push the child toward English head + complement direction, and within a month, Haznedar reports examples such as:

You eating apple (SVO order, like English)
I not eat cornflake (negator + verb, like English)

Although the data are not abundant in that Haznedar does not report lots and lots of examples, what she does report is consistent in that the child used Turkish word order 100 percent of the time at the outset. This kind of evidence is strongly suggestive that the child unconsciously assumed that English would be like Turkish.

Consider this ...

The child in Haznedar's study was learning English in a non-instructed environment. In addition, the child was a pre-schooler. Do you think it is possible to get this kind of free and spontaneous data from adult immigrants? What about beginning classroom learners of an L2? Do you think it would be a good idea to try to get different kinds of data?

As stated above, the idea is that if there is L1 transfer evident in intermediate and more advanced stages, then it is assumed that the L1 was the starting point and that transfer has simply persisted. The vast majority of research regarding Full Transfer looks at non-beginners. There is considerable research on this so we will offer just one typical study and encourage the reader to consult additional readings. Boping Yuan conducted a study that tested whether the L1 influences acquisition. This study is summarized in the Exemplary Study. He focused on learners of Chinese as L2. What is critical about his study is that he used learners from two different L1s: Japanese and English. For the target structure Yuan was interested in, these two languages were necessary as their L1s functioned differently. The target structure in question was the reflexive pronoun *ziji* in L2 Chinese.

As the summary in this chapter indicates, Yuan's results suggest that L1 influence was present in that it helped the Japanese speakers but hindered the English speakers. Once again, because the influence is seen at both intermediate and advanced levels, L1 transfer is assumed to be there at the beginning.

As suggested earlier, there are many more studies such as Yuan's suggesting L1 transfer than there are studies that support no transfer as outlined in the previous section. In the next section, we turn our attention to a third possibility for the initial state.

Consider this ...

If the initial state of L2 acquisition is the L1, this clearly makes L2 acquisition different from L1 acquisition. In what way? Does this mean that the underlying processes of acquisition are different? Does it mean that the roles of input and output are different (see Chapter 3)? Or does it simply mean the starting point is different but everything else might be the same?

Exemplary Study

Yuan, B. (1998). Interpretation of binding and orientation of the Chinese reflexive *ziji* by English and Japanese speakers. *Second Language Research*, 14, 324–340.

Participants

- 81 participants
- 24 Japanese speakers learning Chinese as L2
- 57 English speakers learning Chinese as L2
- 24 Chinese native speakers who served as a control group
- Location: China

Major Target Items

- In English, reflexive pronouns can only be interpreted as referring to the closest possible antecedent. By closest possible antecedent we mean an antecedent that is in the same clause. In the sample sentence (1) below, the reflexive *himself* can only refer to Bill, which is in the same clause. It is barred from referring to John. In Chinese, the equivalent pronoun can be interpreted as referring to either Bill or John; it is not restricted to only antecedents in the same clause. This is shown in (2). (Note that the subscript letters $_i$ and $_j$ indicate what items can refer to, with an asterisk meaning that co-reference is not possible.) Crucially, Japanese functions just like Chinese; the reflexive pronoun is not restricted to taking an antecedent only in its own clause.

(1)   John$_j$ said that Bill$_i$ trusts himself$_{i/*j}$. (English)

(2)   John$_j$ renwei Bill$_i$ xiangxin ziji$_{i/j}$ (Chinese)
      John think Bill trust self
      'John thinks Bill trusts himself.' Or 'John thinks Bill trusts him.'

Material and Procedure

- The participants were given a proficiency test and the English learners were split into two groups: intermediate and advanced. The Japanese group as a whole was intermediate and not split into two groups.
- The participants took a paper-and-pencil interpretation test to determine how they were interpreting the pronoun *ziji*. The test included sentences that were pragmatically biased for one antecedent over the other. If learners were following a purely syntactic constraint on interpretation of the pronoun, they would not be led astray by the pragmatic bias.

Results

- The English-speaking and Japanese-speaking groups treated *ziji* differently, even when the groups were matched for proficiency. That is, the intermediate Japanese learners were better at interpreting *ziji* than were their English-speaking counterparts.
- The L1 English groups tended to interpret *ziji* as referring to a local antecedent, even in contexts that favored another antecedent further away. The English learners with advanced proficiency were more likely to accept a long-distance reading for *ziji*, but they did so less consistently than the L1 Japanese group.
- In most cases, the Japanese L1 group – even though it was only at the intermediate level – behaved like the Chinese L1 control group. The English speakers tended to be different from the Chinese L1 control group.

Conclusion

- Because of the difference between the English groups and the Japanese group, Yuan concluded that transfer was the main variable. It slowed down the English speakers but helped the Japanese speakers. Because these

results were seen at the intermediate level, Yuan concludes that transfer was present from the beginning.
- In spite of transfer, enough advanced English speakers showed similarity to the Chinese L1 group that Yuan concluded that UG was still operative in adult L2 learners.

Partial Transfer of the L1 in the Initial State

Situated between no transfer in L2 acquisition and full transfer of all features and formal elements of the L1 at the outset lies the idea of partial transfer. We will examine two proposals that gained wide circulation in the 1990s.

Minimal Trees Hypothesis

In a series of publications in the mid to late 1990s, Anne Vainikka and Martha Young-Scholten launched what is called **the Minimal Trees Hypothesis**. The use of the word trees is purposeful because the idea behind the hypothesis is related to how linguists visualize syntax as "syntactic trees." To give you an example, here is a basic sketch of any simple sentence (with much detail removed) as a linguist would see it.

First, the letters refer to phrases and their elements. VP stands for verb phrase and inside this VP we see its head (V) and its complement (XP). XP is a shorthand way of saying various different kinds of phrases could be the complement of V (a noun phrase, a prepositional phrase, even another sentence, which would be a CP). Things such as VP, NP, PP, and so on are what linguists call lexical phrases because the heads of the phrases are actual lexical items such as verbs, nouns, prepositions, and so on. Above the VP are functional phrases. These are the "hidden" parts of sentences where syntactic information is encoded in the form of abstract features.

TP stands for tense phrase (the head is a T "element" and its complement is the VP). CP stands for complementizer phrase, which basically means "clause/sentence". C is the head of the phrase and TP is its complement. The reader will note that there is also a Spec embedded in each head. This abbreviation stands for specifier and, for right now, we will ignore what it is. What the reader should see so far is that a sentence contains lexical phrases and functional phrases. Something else the reader should note is that phrases exist in a hierarchical order and are "stacked." That is, sentences do not consist of linear ordering (although we may hear and read them that way) but instead have a hidden internal structure in which phrases build up, one upon the other.

In syntactic theory, functional phrases may motivate structural operations depending on the features embedded in them. For example, in languages like Spanish and English, questions have a strong Q feature residing in the CP. This motivates the movement of a *wh*-element up into the CP as illustrated below. Languages like Chinese and Japanese lack a strong Q feature and so the *wh*-elements don't move out of their original positions.

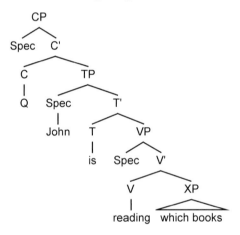

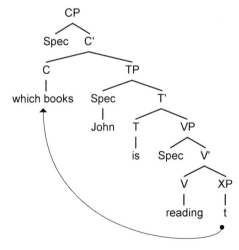

What Vainikka and Young-Scholten have argued is that learners transfer only the **lexical categories** from the L1 at the outset, but not the **functional categories**. What this means, then, is that learners begin L2 acquisition only with VPs, NPs, PPs, and so on but not CPs, TPs, and other functional phrases. Their underlying syntactic trees are minimal, hence the name. The sentence above would be represented as something like this under the Minimal Trees Hypothesis:

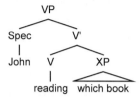

Indeed, beginning L2 learners of English produce sentences such as this one, suggesting that there is no movement and there are no functional categories (note the lack of *is* for *is reading* because there is no TP in which the *is* can be inserted).

Vainikka and Young-Scholten's initial support for Minimal Trees came from research on various groups of L1 learners acquiring German as an L2 in

> The Minimal Trees Hypothesis claims that lexical categories and phrases transfer from the L1 at the outset but functional features and phrases do not.

Germany. Those L1s included Turkish, Korean, Spanish, and Italian. What the researchers keyed in on was what we have seen repeatedly in this chapter: the order of elements in a phrase. In particular, the order of heads and complements. German is a complement + head language, as are Korean and Turkish. Spanish and Italian are head + complement languages. Thus, Korean and Turkish basic word order for verb phrases is object + verb whereas for Spanish and Italian it is verb + object. Vainikka and Young-Scholten collected various kinds of oral data and noted that the Turkish and Korean speakers readily produced OV order in German from the outset while the Spanish and Italian speakers produced VO order and only later switched to OV. What is more, they noticed an absence of functional words in their speech (e.g., auxiliaries, modals) and a lack of *wh*-movement, suggesting that functional phrases and features were not there, even though in Spanish and Italian such features are. Their conclusion was that the lexical phrases transfer at the beginning of L2 acquisition but not the functional phrases.

Consider this ...

The absence of auxiliaries and modals and a lack of *wh*-movement suggest to Vainikka and Young-Scholten that there is no CP in their participants' early representations. But we know that with *yes/no* questions, *do* winds up where a *wh*-element would go. Example: *He wants*

> *to go? → Does he want to go?* Suppose an early-stage learner produces something like *Do he want go store?* Would you take this as evidence that the learner has a CP and therefore Minimal Trees is wrong? Hint: Consider looking at all the instances of *do* used by the learner to see exactly how they are used, e.g., *Do he can go? Do you like? Do I can eat this one?*

The Minimal Trees Hypothesis is appealing given the data examined, but as a number of scholars have pointed out, we cannot rely exclusively on oral production data. Why is this? It is possible that learners may know more than what they can do. That is, their production does not necessarily match their underlying competence. This is a given in the child L1 literature, in which children are sometimes shown to have underlying abstract features in their syntax that are not realized in their speech. The same is certainly possible in L2 acquisition. Just because a learner doesn't produce, say, an auxiliary or show evidence of *wh*-movement does not necessarily mean that TP and CP are absent from their underlying competence or that they haven't transferred the features associated with these phrases from their L1 into the L2 at the outset. It could be, for example, that learners just haven't heard enough auxiliaries and modals for them to be part of their lexicon. There are other methodological issues with how Vainikka and Young-Scholten determined whether something is present or absent in learner speech but we will not belabor those here. Readings and references at the end of the chapter will allow the reader to explore these and other topics in this chapter in more detail.

Valueless Features Hypothesis

The Valueless Features Hypothesis, also called "weak transfer," was proposed by Lynn Eubank around the same time as the Minimal Trees Hypothesis. Unlike the Minimal Trees Hypothesis, the Valueless Features Hypothesis claims that L1 lexical and functional categories are indeed transferred to the L2 and they are present in the earliest mental representations of learners. However, despite the fact that the functional categories are available, the strength of the features associated with L1 functional categories does not transfer. In short, the functional phrases are hanging around in the syntax with little to do because they are, in essence, devoid of anything that would cause syntactic operations involving movement (see above with the *wh*-example and the strong Q feature).

Curiously, Eubank claims that a consequence of Valueless Features is that learners may sometimes show evidence of L2 word order and sometimes evidence of L1 word order. Given that nothing is forcing compliance with L2 word order and nothing is forcing compliance with L1 order in the functional phrases, then learners may produce whatever they wish, in a sense. So as not to rely on production data alone, Eubank tested the hypotheses derived from Valueless Features in several studies involving sentence matching and truth-value. In sentence matching, participants read a pair of sentences and have to determine if they match or not. Response times are tracked and recorded. Critical are the response times comparing pairings of grammatical sentences and pairings of ungrammatical sentences. It should take longer to match the ungrammatical sentences if an underlying representation prohibits such sentences. Here are sample pairings from this kind of study:

Paired grammatical:	The woman often loses the books.
	The woman often loses the books.
Paired ungrammatical:	The woman finds sometimes the pencils.
	The woman finds sometimes the pencils.

In truth-value tasks, learners read a scenario and then determine whether the sentence that follows logically flows from what they just read. Here is one example from a Eubank study.

Tom likes to draw pictures of monkeys in the zoo. He likes his pictures to be perfect, so he always draws them slowly and carefully. All the monkeys jump up and down really fast.
True or false? Tom draws slowly jumping monkeys.

The target sentence can be read one of two ways: that the monkeys are jumping slowly (which is the typical English reading) or that Tom draws slowly and what he draws are jumping monkeys (i.e., *slowly* modifies what Tom does and not how the monkeys jump). The latter might be a reading if your L1 is Spanish or French, for example, and you transferred verb movement from your L1 (e.g., Spanish and French both allow sentences like "Tom drinks slowly his coffee" whereas English allows "Tom slowly drinks his coffee").

What Eubank found out in a series of experimental studies was that the predictions of the Valueless Features Hypothesis did not hold up. At the very least, the data are not conclusive but, as some scholars have suggested, they tend to point to disproving the hypothesis rather than supporting it. For example, in the sentence-matching task, while the native speakers of English performed as expected, the L2 learners did not and their response patterns did not coincide with what the hypothesis would predict.

Not much work is done any longer with the Valueless Features Hypothesis for a variety of reasons. It is safe to say that as of the writing of this book, it is a proposal that has not received strong empirical support and the methodology associated with it has been heavily critiqued. We no longer see many references to this hypothesis but we have included it here for historical reasons.

Quick Recap

Before continuing, we should recap where the generative field is now in terms of the three positions presented. Both the UG-only and the Partial Transfer positions have tended to be overwhelmed by the bulk of evidence suggesting there is L1 transfer all along the way. In other words, the dominant generative position today is that the initial state is the L1. In a 2016 publication, for example, Roumyana Slabakova says that there is almost universal consensus that although UG is operative in L2 acquisition as it is in L1 acquisition, in the L2 context, learners begin acquisition with an L1. One would be hard pressed to find a publication at this date that takes a non-L1 transfer perspective within the generative tradition. This does not mean that there are not some who hold on to the other two positions, but, as we have suggested, they now form a very small minority of scholars. Within the generative tradition, most scholars simply assume L1 transfer from the outset and we no longer see research testing competing proposals such as the three different perspectives just presented.

> **Consider this ...**
>
> Although the evidence strongly tips in favor of L1 as the starting point, to what extent might this be an artifact of trying to get learners to show something early on? Imagine you are asked to perform a task after two months of being in an L2 environment. That task could be a grammaticality judgment, a truth-value test, an oral production task. How do you do the task if what it asks you to do is beyond your current underlying mental representation? Could it be that we use our L1 to perform tasks when our L2 is not up to snuff?

Other Perspectives

In this chapter we have taken a generative approach to the question of the initial state largely because this field originally motivated the question and has tended to dominate the discussion. However, there are several other approaches that we will review briefly so that the reader understands that an initial state may refer to something other than underlying mental representation.

In usage-based models of acquisition in which there is no UG and no special mechanism(s) for language, it is widely assumed that there is L1 influence from the beginning. Because usage-based models tend not to talk about mental representation but underlying connections that are related to performance (e.g., the presence of *the* is strongly connected to something "nouny" as in *the dog* and not strongly connected to something "prepositional" as in **the with*), they differ from a generative perspective in terms of what might get transferred. Currently, the predominant position in usage-based models is that the L1 connections are present from the beginning of L2 acquisition and may actually block new connections from forming (or might help, depending on the L1/L2 pair). Nick Ellis and Stefanie Wulff, for example, discuss this in a 2015 publication in which they say that the initial state for L2 acquisition is not a "plastic system" as it is for L1 acquisition. Instead it is a system that is "tuned and committed" to whatever the L1 is. So even though usage-based models are predicated on non-linguistic learning mechanisms, the consensus among the researchers is that the initial state is the L1. In this framework, the initial state is the L1 plus general learning mechanisms that are involved in everything from language acquisition to learning what a dog is and how it isn't a cat.

Another perspective on the initial state is **Input Processing** as articulated by Bill VanPatten in a series of publications from the 1990s until the present day. Input Processing is less concerned with underlying representations at the outset and instead is concerned with how learners process input sentences during comprehension. Theoretically, there are three choices (much like above): (1) the learner uses a set of universal processing strategies and procedures that are not derived from the L1; (2) the learner uses well-worn L1-based processing strategies to try to comprehend the L2 from the outset; (3) the learner has some universal and some L1-based processing strategies that work during comprehension. The third position is not widely accepted and in fact it is almost impossible to find any research or theory on it so we won't dwell on it here. VanPatten has taken the position that all learners, regardless of L1, possess a set of universal processing strategies they take to the task and that it is not an "L1 processor" that attempts to compute sentence structure during comprehension. To be sure, these universal strategies have nothing to do with Universal Grammar. For example, one such processing strategy is that learners come to the task knowing that words exist and that there are ways to "label" meaning with language. A consequence of this, according to Input Processing, is that at the earliest stages, learners search for content lexical items to try to comprehend what they hear and they may "skip" function words and other small things in the input for the time being. At the same time, they rely on what is called the first-noun strategy (or principle), which says that as long as there is no contextual or semantic evidence to the contrary, learners assume the first noun or pronoun they encounter is the subject/agent of the sentence. So let's imagine the learner hears a simple sentence such as "The dog is chasing the cat." The learner knows that someone is talking about a dog and cat and what they're doing because it's happening in front of the learner or there is a picture or some other way the learner connects the input string to some event. At the earliest stages of acquisition, the learner may process only "dog," "cat," and "chasing." Now let's imagine that learner knows these words but hears a new sentence: "The dog was chased by the cat." Here the learner once again processes "dog," "chase," and "cat" and assumes the same meaning as the first sentence. This is because the learner assumes that "dog" is both subject and agent. Words such as "was" and "by," for example, aren't processed – meaning the learner doesn't link them to any meaning or function. They are just "noise." This would happen even if the L1 and the L2 both have the same sentence structure for a passive sentence such as "The dog was chased by the cat."

> Input Processing predicts that the input processors filter out data from the input. The way the filtering happens is universal.

What the model of Input Processing predicts, then, is that the input processors filter out data from the input and deliver structural information to the internal mechanisms that build representation (e.g., UG). The way the filtering happens is universal. Some scholars disagree with this position, believing that the L1 processor is active at the outset. VanPatten has recently suggested that the L1 processor can "kick in" at some points during acquisition but that at the outset, it is the universal set of strategies that learners take to the task of comprehending input at the very beginning.

Yet another perspective on the initial state can be found in **Processability Theory**. Processability Theory was formulated by Manfred Pienemann and is a theory not about input processing or what is in the mental representation but instead about universal constraints on how learners process output. In other words, how learners put words together in real time to make sentences. The theory claims that output processing starts with and is constrained by a universal set of output processing procedures that are hierarchically ordered. What this means is that learners must acquire one processing procedure before they can acquire another processing procedure, which in turn they must acquire before acquiring yet another processing procedure. The theory is much more complex than this, but for now we will illustrate it with just a subset of these procedures.

Central to Processability Theory is the idea that when stringing sentences together, there may need to be an exchange of grammatical information. A classic example is subject–verb agreement for languages that have such agreement. If a subject is, say, 2nd-person plural, that information has to be exchanged with the verb so that the verb is also 2nd-person plural. Another example is noun–adjective agreement for languages that have this agreement. If a noun is feminine and singular then the adjective that goes with that noun must also be feminine singular (i.e., the grammatical information needs to be exchanged between noun and adjective). Also central to the theory is the idea of syntactic boundaries. The exchange of grammatical information is easiest when there is no information to exchange, while the most difficult is when grammatical information has to be exchanged across sentence or clause boundaries, with various difficulties in between depending on whether the grammatical information has to cross a boundary or not. In English, producing "the rat" is not a problem because no information is exchanged between the determiner and *rat*. However, "The rat hates cheese" requires grammatical information to be exchanged between the noun phrase *the rat* [3rd-person singular] and the verb in the verb phrase. This involves crossing a syntactic boundary.

Now let's look at an example from Spanish that helps us understand the boundary and distance issue a bit better. In Spanish, nouns and adjectives have to agree in number and gender. A single word such as *casas* 'houses' does not exchange grammatical information with anything if it's not part of a sentence. Now let's put it into a noun phrase with an adjective: *casas blancas* 'white houses.' Here grammatical information has to be exchanged between a noun and an adjective but the information remains in the same phrase, the NP. Now here's another sentence: *casas son blancas* 'houses are white.' Here the grammatical information has to travel outside the NP over to the VP. In these three examples we see three distinct grammatical information procedures:

- plain word: no information exchanged
- within a phrase: information is exchanged between two words in the same phrase
- across a phrase boundary: information is exchanged between two words in two different syntactic phrases.

Processability Theory says that these three procedures (part of a set of seven) are ordered as we see them from easiest to more difficult. In turn, this means learners will

> Processability Theory claims that there is a universal and hierarchically ordered set of output processing procedures that are acquired over time and not influenced by the L1. Instead, they constrain the influence of the L1.

need to develop these procedures in the order in which we see them. They are universal and not influenced by the L1. Whether you are an English speaker learning Spanish (English does not have adjective agreement) or a speaker of French learning Spanish (French does have such agreement), you will have to progress through the development of the procedures in the same way. However, and this is important, this does not mean that there is no transfer. What it means is that L1 transfer is constrained in that things can transfer only when a learner is developmentally ready for those things to transfer. A learner with French as L1 acquiring Spanish as L2 can only transfer agreement between a noun and an adjective across an NP into a VP after that learner has first been able to do the same inside the NP. Pienemann has suggested that when such transfer does happen, it may accelerate or benefit acquisition. But again, a learner cannot simply transfer all the procedures of the L1 from the outset. In a sense, transfer may be "triggered" at points when there is a match between what the learner creates based on universal procedures and what the L1 looks like.

We have been brief in this section to demonstrate other non-generative and non-representational approaches to the nature of the initial state. In the first – usage-based – we see something that resembles full transfer. The other two, both related to processing but one focused on input processing and the other focused on output processing, do not posit the L1 as a starting point. Instead, L1 processing procedures or strategies may be triggered at particular times during development.

Consider this ...

We have seen perspectives on the initial state that are related to underlying representation. That would be in the generative tradition. We have also seen three perspectives outside of the generative tradition: usage-based, input processing, and output processing. Is it possible that some of these perspectives are compatible? For example, could it be that learners' internal representation begins with an assumption that the L2 is like the L1 but learners process input using universal strategies? Consider the various combinations.

Recap

Here are some major ideas and topics covered in this chapter.

- The generative tradition has led the "debate" on the initial state. There are three positions that have emerged within this framework:
  - the initial state is UG by itself
  - the initial state is the L1 (with UG still constraining and guiding)
  - the initial state includes only partial, non-functional aspects of the L1 (with UG still constraining and guiding).
- Of the three positions, the one with the most empirical research behind it is the second: The initial state is the L1 plus UG.
- There are other frameworks that make claims about the initial state:
  - usage-based approaches converge on the idea that L2 learners come to the task with an L1 system as the starting point
  - input processing posits that independent of underlying representations, learners begin input processing at the outset with universal strategies for comprehending sentences
  - Processability Theory focuses on output processing and claims that L1 transfer is constrained by universal output processing procedures and that the L1 thus is not the starting point for how learners develop the ability to string words together to make sentences.

What about Social Factors?

As the reader might guess, the issue of the initial state for L2 acquisition is viewed as an internal, cognitive/linguistic matter. That is, the focus is on formal properties of language and how and when they transfer, if at all, as well as the presence of something like UG at the outset. But there is a role for social factors in how the learner approaches the entire process of L2 acquisition. Let's consider the question of learner identity, for example, and that learner's perceived relationship to the world around him or her. Elizabeth Miller and Ryuko Kubota, for example, discuss the issue of how learners construct a "second language identity." The question becomes, how do they do this and what is the starting point for the construction of that identity? Do learners begin the task of identity construction with an "open mind," a sort of socio-personality version of UG? Or do they begin identity construction based on their own L1 community (or communities) identity? Identity construction is as complex as acquisition of language itself, and scholars like Miller and Kubota review scholarship on everything from social, to cultural, to political aspects of identity. Other scholars speak of something called socialization – defined largely as integration into a particular society or social group. How do learners begin this process? These are good questions but most research in this area focuses on factors and contexts that affect identity and socialization. So is it possible to think of an "initial state" for socialization and identity construction?

REFERENCES AND READINGS

- Dube, B. (2000). Where are the minimal trees? Evidence from early Zulu second language subordination. *Second Language Research*, 16, 233–265.
- Ellis, N. & Wulff, S. (2015). Usage-based approaches to SLA. In B. VanPatten & J. Williams (Eds.), *Theories in second language acquisition* (pp. 74–93). New York: Routledge.
- Eubank, L. (1993). Sentence matching and processing in second language development. *Second Language Research*, 9, 253–280.
- Eubank, L. & Grace, T. (1998). V-to-I and inflection in non-native grammars. In M.-L. Beck (Ed.), *Morphology and its interfaces in second language knowledge* (pp. 69–88). Amsterdam: John Benjamins.
- Hawkins, R. (2001). *Second language syntax: A generative introduction*. London: Blackwell.
- Haznedar, B. (1997). Second language acquisition by a Turkish-speaking child: Evidence for L1 influence. In E. Hughes, M. Hughes, & A. Greenhill (Eds.), *Proceedings of the 21st annual Boston University conference on language development* (pp. 245–256). Somerville, MA: Cascadilla Press.
- Miller, E. R. & Kubota, R. (2013). Second language identity construction. In J. Herschensohn & M. Young-Scholten (Eds.), *The Cambridge handbook of second language acquisition* (pp. 230–250). Cambridge: Cambridge University Press.

- Pienemann, M. & Kessler, J.-U. (Eds.) (2011). *Studying processability theory.* Amsterdam: John Benjamins.
- Platzack, C. (1996). The initial hypothesis of syntax: A minimalist perspective on language acquisition and attrition. In H. Clahsen (Ed.), *Generative perspectives on language acquisition: Empirical findings, theoretical considerations, crosslinguistic comparisons* (pp. 369–414). Amsterdam: John Benjamins.
- Radford, A. (2004). *Minimalist syntax: Exploring the structure of English.* Cambridge: Cambridge University Press.
- Schwartz, B., & Sprouse, R. (1996). Second language cognitive states and the full transfer / full access model. *Second Language Research,* 12, 40–72.
- Slabakova, R. (2016). *Second language acquisition.* Oxford: Oxford University Press.
- Vainikka, A. & Young-Scholten, M. (1994). Direct access to X′-theory: Evidence from Korean and Turkish adults learning German. In T. Hoekstra & B. Schwartz (Eds.), *Language acquisition studies in generative grammar: Papers in honor of Kenneth Wexler from the 1991 GLOW Workshops* (pp. 265–316). Amsterdam: John Benjamins.
- Vainikka, A. & Young-Scholten, M. (1996). Gradual development of second language phrase structure. *Second Language Research,* 12, 7–39.
- VanPatten, B. (2015). Input processing in adult SLA. In B. VanPatten & J. Williams (Eds.), *Theories in second language acquisition* (pp. 113–134). New York: Routledge.
- White, L. (2003). *Second language acquisition and universal grammar.* Cambridge: Cambridge University Press.
- Yuan, B. (1998). Interpretation of binding and orientation of the Chinese reflexive *ziji* by English and Japanese speakers. *Second Language Research,* 14, 324–340.

FOLLOWING UP

1. Explain in your own words what the three positions are on the initial state for L2 acquisition.

2. Before the contemporary era of linguistics and acquisition research, children were thought to come into the world with a "blank slate." Do some internet and bibliographic research on this term and the debate surrounding it. You might wish to consider looking at Steven Pinker's book published in 2003 titled *The Blank Slate: The Modern Denial of Human Nature.*

3. Most non-researchers (including teachers) would argue that "Of course, the L1 influences L2 acquisition and probably does so from the outset." (1) What do you think such people mean and what kind of examples would they offer? (2) Based on what you've read, what might you tell them?

4. In the 1980s, Bill VanPatten established the first stage of copular (linking verbs) in Spanish to be an absence of copular verbs. (Spanish has two verbs to mean 'be': *ser* and *estar*.) In the earliest stages of acquisition, VanPatten reported utterances such as *Juan alto* 'John tall' and *Juan no aquí* 'John no here' for *Juan es alto* and *Juan no está aquí*, respectively. These data came from

classroom learners of Spanish with English as L1. Knowing that English has the word *be* and that it is required (e.g., *John is tall/*John tall*), do you think these data speak against L1 transfer at the outset? Why do you think the learners in this early stage don't have a copular verb in Spanish L2 when they have one in English L2? Note: Since VanPatten's early research, the phenomenon has been found to be widespread and also with speakers of Chinese as L1 who are learning Spanish. Chinese has no copular verb equivalent to 'be.'

5. Under the Full Transfer approach, what does it really mean to have the L1 as the initial state? Under this proposal, learners have to "overwrite" what's in the L1 to build an L2 representation. What does this actually mean? Clearly, the L1 does not disappear, so the learner doesn't really rewrite the L1. Does the L2 learner "create a copy" of the L1 and write that over? Can you think of some other way to talk about this idea?

6. If we assume that the L1 is the starting point for learners, should this assumption inform teaching materials in any way? Why or why not? Note: You may want to come back and revisit this question after Chapter 6.

5 | Can L2 Learners Become Nativelike?

In this chapter, we consider whether adult L2 learners can achieve the same knowledge and facility with an L2 that native speakers of that language have. At first blush, the answer to this question seems obvious: No. After all, conventional wisdom and experience both tell us that people who learn an L2 as adults still speak with accents and make grammatical "mistakes." This is true even of people who function at a professional level and live their adult lives in the country where the language is spoken. We also assume that the younger people start to learn an L2, the better their odds of becoming nativelike. While this experiential evidence is important, it's not the whole story. Consider the language classroom experience of one of the authors of this book for a minute. In high school, Megan studied both French and Japanese. Her French teacher was a native French speaker. Her Japanese teacher was a native English speaker who had worked in Japan for several years, married a Japanese woman, and, at the time, was finishing a Ph.D. in Japanese literature. Both of these teachers were qualified to teach the language classes, but one was a native speaker, and one was not. That we hire non-native speakers as language teachers suggests that at least some adults can acquire an L2. Similarly, you may have had professors who, though not being native English speakers, live, work, and generally manage their professional lives in English. That means that they have acquired an English proficiency that allows them to handle all of the tasks that native English speakers do. Anecdotally, then, we have two answers to the question of whether L2 learners can become nativelike. On the one hand, we have some evidence that the answer is no, and that the age at which someone starts acquiring a language has a relationship with their final proficiency level. On the other hand, we also have evidence that some people manage to acquire an L2 well enough to live and work in that language. We'll come back to these observations at the end of the chapter, but before we do, we'll first define "nativelikeness." We'll also discuss three possible answers to the question of whether L2 learners can become nativelike: (1) L2 learners cannot become nativelike, (2) L2 learners can become nativelike in some domains but not others, and (3) nativelikeness is possible.

What Is Nativelikeness?

In Chapter 1, we suggested that the question behind all of the questions in the field of SLA is whether L1 acquisition and L2 acquisition are the same thing. **Ultimate attainment** – basically, how far in language acquisition learners get – is no different. If we had definitive evidence that learners can't become nativelike, that would suggest a major difference between L1 and L2 acquisition. So we need to take a step back and think about what nativelikeness is. Nativelikeness typically refers to the implicit representation of a language that someone who has grown up speaking that language has. This includes pronunciation, vocabulary, and what most of us would call "grammar." In short, adult native speakers know what's possible in the target language. They also come to know what is *impossible* in the target language. To see this, let's consider the sentences in (1). Sentences (1a) and (1c) are declarative sentences, and sentences (1b) and (1d) are questions based on those declarative sentences.

(1)   a.   John said Bill left.
     b.   Who did John say left?
     c.   John wondered whether Bill left.
     d.   Who did John wonder whether left?

Does (1b) sound better – more like English – to you than (1d)? If you're a native English speaker (and even if you're not a native English speaker), you should have had a little bit of a "what?!" moment when you read (1d). This is because your underlying English competence tells you that (1d) is not a possible English sentence. Given that (1d) is formed in exactly the same way as (1b), the impossibility of the sentence is surprising. The precise reasons why a sentence like (1d) is impossible are beyond the scope of this book, but the general point is that part of an adult's steady-state mental representation of language (i.e., a representation that is no longer in development) includes this kind of knowledge. That is, not only do you know what the grammar of your language allows, you also know what is not permitted in the grammar – and it may not be clear where this knowledge comes from.

This mental representation for language is what people usually have in mind when they ask whether someone knows a language. Researchers and language teachers are concerned with the formal properties of language: for example, pronunciation, grammar, and vocabulary. The mental system for language is really important, but it's not the only thing that is necessary for communication to be successful. Part of growing up in a culture means learning how to use your language in ways that communicate in that culture. This includes, but is not limited to, knowing how to start and participate in a conversation, knowing how to make requests, and knowing how to shift between informal and formal modes of speech. It also includes learning how to read and write. These skills can develop unevenly, so that people are capable in one domain but not another domain. That adult native speakers of a language may have different types of linguistic skills is important for how we conceive of nativelikeness. Does it mean being able to do everything with language that an adult native speaker who works in a professional job can do? Or does it mean something else? If we consider educated adults our benchmark for nativelikeness, then we conflate underlying linguistic knowledge with linguistic skill (communication). It's important that we keep them separate – communicative skills depend on having the corresponding linguistic knowledge, and these skills develop in the communicative contexts in which they are used. This isn't to say that communicative skill isn't important for L2 learners – being able to write a professional email is very important in work contexts, for instance – but it means that skill development is secondary to our concern in this chapter. We are primarily concerned with the development of a mental representation for another language.

> Nativelikeness means having a mental representation for the target language that more or less matches that of adult native speakers of that language.

So we will define nativelikeness as having a mental representation for another language that more or less matches that of adult native speakers of that language. This means that we will focus on the underlying and implicit (unconscious) knowledge that non-native speakers acquire and the processes by which they acquire that knowledge.

Consider this …

It is very common for children acquiring English as their native language to go through a period of time in which they overgeneralize regular verb endings to irregular verbs, so that *went* becomes *goed/wented* and *brought* becomes *bringed* in the child's speech. Similarly, one of the authors of this book has a friend whose 3-year-old daughter couldn't say the *sp-* cluster and turned words like *spoon* and *Sparty* (the name of the author's dog) into words like [sun] and [sarti]. This is not an adult system for English. Does this mean that the child is not a native English speaker? Why or why not? Given that these non-adult-like utterances are normal in child language development, what does it mean if we see similar patterns in adult L2 development? Is there a point in adult development when non-nativelike forms would be more problematic? What point would that be?

Second Language Acquisition

Now that we've defined *nativelike* as having a mental representation for the target language that more or less matches that of native speakers, we can consider three possible answers to the question of whether L2 learners can become nativelike. The first possibility is that L2 learners cannot become nativelike. The second possibility is that nativelikeness is possible in all domains of the L2 system, and the third possibility is that nativelikeness is possible in some domains, but not in others. We will explore each of these possibilities below. Although learners need to be able to put their linguistic competence to use in real-world situations, again we will limit our discussion in this chapter to the development of L2 mental representation. There are two reasons for this: First, most of the major hypotheses and questions in this area deal with underlying knowledge or mental representation only, and second, communicative skill depends, in part, on linguistic knowledge.

L2 Learners Cannot Become Nativelike

This position is fairly self-explanatory. The main claim is that the processes – and therefore the outcomes – of L2 acquisition are different from those of L1 acquisition, and therefore L2 learners cannot acquire a mental representation for the target language that matches that of the native speakers of that language. In this section, we discuss two major proposals: the Fundamental Difference Hypothesis and the Critical Period Hypothesis.

The Fundamental Difference Hypothesis

The Fundamental Difference Hypothesis (FDH) was proposed by Robert Bley-Vroman in two articles, one published in 1989 and the second published in 1990. Bley-Vroman argued that, because of observed differences between child L1 acquisition and adult L2 acquisition, the two processes – and therefore the two outcomes – are distinct from each other. Bley-Vroman took the standard generative position that child language acquisition is the result of Universal Grammar and **domain-specific learning mechanisms**. These mechanisms are specific to language, and children use them to construct a mental representation for their L1 using input (see Chapter 3) as their data. Both Universal Grammar and these learning mechanisms push the child to construct an L1 mental representation that more or less matches that of adults in their community. Given this account of L1 acquisition, Bley-Vroman builds his argument for a fundamental difference between L1 and L2 acquisition on four key observations about adult L2 acquisition.[1]

The first of these observations is that adult L2 acquisition is much more variable than child L1 acquisition. L2 acquisition is variable in several ways. First, most adults do not achieve high proficiency levels in their L2 and they fall on a broad range of levels (i.e., some stop learning and are intermediate-like while some go on and are advanced-like). Second, even relatively accomplished adult L2 learners do not seem to have the same kind of mental representation that native speakers do. L2 pronunciation seems to be particularly prone to divergence from native-speaker

---

[1] Bley-Vroman (1989) lists nine observations; we have condensed them here for ease of reading.

norms. Third, adults, unlike children, adopt different strategies and goals in language learning, and seem to be content with that. Some people take several weeks of language classes in preparation for a trip overseas; other people learn diplomatic and political language but would have a hard time ordering a beer or reading a children's book. None of these observations is characteristic of child L1 acquisition.

The second observation is that adult L2 acquisition often seems to **fossilize**. Fossilization happens when a specific form or structure in the L2 is only partially acquired and does not seem to become more target-like over time. For example, a learner could fossilize with respect to English past-tense marking in that they do not consistently supply a past-tense verb in required contexts. This is, of course, in contrast to native speakers who, if they fail to supply the appropriate form of the verb, are assumed to have had performance problems but are not assumed to have a deficient mental representation (i.e., they made a momentary mistake but their underlying system is intact). Fossilization is not a construct in child L1 acquisition.

The third observation is that adult L2 mental representations are often marked by indeterminate intuitions. **Indeterminate intuitions** refers to the relative strength of the unconscious knowledge people have about the language that they speak. Let's start with native speakers' intuitions. Native speakers tend to have pretty strong intuitions about what is grammatical and what is ungrammatical in their language. To see this, take a minute and indicate whether the following sentences are possible, slightly strange, or impossible. When you do this, think about what you might say or have heard other people say – don't worry about whether the sentence conforms to rules from an English class.

(2) a. David likes to talk about politics.
     b. What does David like to talk about?
     c. About what does David like to talk?
     d. Sally turned the television on.
     e. What did Sally turn on?
     f. On what did Sally turn?

Native English speakers usually rate the sentences in (2) as follows: (2a), (2b), (2d), and (2e) are totally possible and sound like good English sentences. Judgments might differ for (2c); at the very least, it should sound less natural than (2b) but it is generally accepted as possible. The example in (2f), however, should sound very strange – and, any interpretation you give it is not related to (2d). Regardless of what your judgments were, the knowledge that you relied on to make them is part of your mental representation for English. Bley-Vroman's argument is that non-native speakers' intuitions about their L2 aren't as strong as native speakers' intuitions. Non-native speakers may not have a strong feeling one way or another. Or, they might judge something grammatical in one instance and ungrammatical in another instance. This is why these intuitions are called indeterminate. Bley-Vroman argues that indeterminate intuitions reflect clear differences in the type of mental representations that native and non-native speakers have. Bley-Vroman claimed that because native speakers typically have clear-cut intuitions about grammaticality, indeterminate intuitions indicate that non-native speakers have a different kind of mental representation than native speakers.

The fourth observation is that L2 acquisition often involves explicit instruction and often includes **negative evidence**. Negative evidence is information about what is not possible in a given language. To see this, consider the example in (3), which presents a contrast between English and French related to the way *wh*-questions are formed with prepositional phrases.

(3) a.   John talked to Mary.
    b.   Who did John talk to?
    c.   To whom did John talk?
    d.   Jean a parlé à Marie.
    e.   *Qui a Jean parlé à?
    f.   A qui a Jean parlé?

In English, as in French, the *wh*-word replaces the object, *Mary* in this case. English has two options for question formation: Either only the *wh*-word is moved to the front of the sentence, as in (3b), or both the preposition and the *wh*-word are moved, as in (3c). The example in (3c) sounds more formal than that in (3b), but both sentences are possible. In French, however, only the equivalent of (3f) is possible. To form a question, French moves both the preposition and the *wh*-word; it is not possible to move only the *wh*-word. If L1 English learners of French transfer the English options to French, they will have an L2 grammar for French that has more options than the native French grammar has. They will have to learn that only one of the options – and it's the less common option in English – is the only possible option in French. If L1 English speakers are told that sentences like (3e) are not possible in French or if they are corrected when they produce something like (3e), they are provided with negative evidence for that structure. In other words, negative evidence is information about what is *impossible* in the target language, usually in the form of error correction. So if an L1 English speaker produces a sentence like (3e) and is corrected, that learner is receiving negative evidence. Child language acquisition is assumed to take place without negative evidence because there is a significant amount of research that shows that parents usually don't correct grammatical errors in their children's speech, and that if they do, the child typically ignores the correction (see Chapter 1 for some examples and discussion). Because negative evidence doesn't seem to play a role in L1 acquisition, a significant role for negative evidence in L2 acquisition would point to a major difference between L1 and L2 acquisition.

> ### Consider this ...
>
> It is true that L2 acquisition often involves explicit instruction and negative evidence for many adults and teenagers. It is also true that language classes are often set up to prioritize explicit instruction and negative evidence. Do those two facts necessarily mean that L2 acquisition *has to* involve explicit instruction and negative evidence? Does this way of structuring L2 instruction suggest that a larger assumption about the nature of L2 acquisition is at work in how we think about language curricula? If so, what is that assumption? Note: We will explore the role of instruction in Chapter 6.

Based on these four observations, Bley-Vroman argued that L2 acquisition looks more like general skill acquisition than it does like child L1 acquisition. In other words, Bley-Vroman suggests that the domain-specific language-learning mechanisms available to the child are no longer available to the adult. Instead, adults rely on **general learning mechanisms**, which are the only mechanisms available to them. General learning mechanisms are the cognitive mechanisms that allow us to acquire new skills and new knowledge. They are not specific to any one domain, skill, or knowledge area. Because these are the only mechanisms available to adult learners, L2 linguistic systems will necessarily be different from L1 linguistic systems. Concretely, Bley-Vroman proposes that L1 acquisition is the result of input, domain-specific learning mechanisms, and Universal Grammar. In contrast, L2 acquisition is the result of input, general learning mechanisms, and the native language. We'll evaluate the FDH in a minute, but before we do, let's think about what it predicts, and what we might expect to see in the data. The FDH makes two predictions: (1) adult L2 acquisition does not depend on the same mechanisms as L1 acquisition, and (2) it results in a qualitatively different system. These predictions can be tested. If, for instance, it can be shown that adults rely on the same mechanisms and progress through the same stages of development as children, then the first prediction would be falsified. Similarly, if it can be shown that adults acquire mental representations for an L2 that look like native speakers' mental representations, then the FDH would be falsified on the second prediction.

The Fundamental Difference Hypothesis predicts that L2 acquisition depends on different mechanisms than L1 acquisition and that it results in a different kind of linguistic system than L1 acquisition does.

The FDH is problematic on both logical and empirical grounds. On logical grounds, the FDH rests on observations about L2 acquisition that sound plausible but actually have very little to do with the nature of the developing linguistic system itself. For example, the observation that adult L2 acquisition usually involves explicit instruction and negative evidence is an accurate one. At the very least, it describes most language classrooms we are familiar with. That doesn't mean that L2 acquisition *has* to happen with explicit instruction and negative evidence. People have been acquiring L2s without having access to classroom instruction for millennia, and this still happens today. For example, some anthropologists, linguists, and missionaries move to remote parts of the world to work with groups of people whose language has no writing system and for which there are no text-books and there is no formal instruction. It takes time, but these adults do manage to acquire the target language. Similarly, another observation that the FDH rests on is that L2 learners differ from children in terms of outcomes: Children are guaranteed to converge on a system for their native language that matches the adults in their community, while many L2 learners fail to acquire even the ability to order a cup of coffee in the target language. This observation does, indeed, match our experience. It does not necessarily mean, however, that adults and children rely on different systems for language acquisition. It could be due to other factors, such as differences in the quantity and quality of input that children and adults receive, or it could be due to non-linguistic factors, such as motivation. (See Chapter 8 for a longer discussion of motivation.)

In addition, the FDH doesn't provide good coverage of the empirical data. One of the predictions that it makes is that adults should not acquire implicit knowledge of what is impossible in the L2, especially if the L1 and the L2 work differently. We have seen examples of these constraints already: The ungrammaticalities in sentences (1) and (2) above are based on subtle constraints on English. The FDH predicts that non-native English speakers will not have the same judgments for these sentences as native English speakers do. In fact, there is evidence that these kinds of subtle constraints are acquirable in an L2. This evidence comes primarily from research that investigates **poverty of the stimulus** situations. Poverty of the stimulus (POS) situations are those in which a particular syntactic structure is impossible in a language, but there is nothing about the input that would tell the learner that the structure is impossible. Nor is there any information that the learner could transfer from the L1. There are particular L1 and L2 pairs providing clear test cases for knowledge related to POS situations. For example, English and Japanese differ in terms of whether every sentence requires an overt subject. In English, every sentence requires a subject, and this is true even in cases where the subject really has no semantic content (i.e., when we can't link the subject to a person or thing in the real world), as in (4c). The word *pro* is used in this example and in (5) to indicate an unpronounced pronoun. When we talk about these differences, we refer to overt subjects (subjects and subject pronouns you can hear or see) and null subjects (subjects and subject pronouns you can't hear or see but are hidden in the syntax).

(4) a. Megan drinks too much coffee.
     b. *pro drinks too much coffee.
     c. It's ten o'clock.
     d. *pro is ten o'clock.

Unlike English, Japanese permits null subjects, and there are some cases in which an overt subject is actually ungrammatical, as in (5d). (Note to the reader: The second line in these examples is called a 'gloss.' Glosses are how linguists provide syntactic and morphological information to the reader in a "literal" rendering of the sentence in English. The third line in each example is how we would normally render the sentence in English. For the reader unfamiliar with glosses, the abbreviations are these: TOP = topic; NOM = nominative; ACC = accusative; *pro* = null-subject pronoun; COP = copular verb like 'be'.)

(5) a. Hanako-wa koohii-o   nomi.sugi.ru.
         Hanako-TOP coffee-ACC   drink.too much.NON-PAST
         'Hanako drinks too much coffee.'

     b. *pro* koohii-o   nomi.sugi.ru.
         pro coffee-ACC   drink.too much.NON-PAST
         'I/you/he/she/we/they drink too much coffee.'

     c. *pro* jyuji   desu.
         pro ten o'clock   COP
         'It's ten o'clock'

     d. *Kare-wa jyuji   desu.
         He/it-TOP ten o'clock   COP
         'It's ten o'clock.'

Essentially, the difference between Japanese and English is as follows: English always requires that something (a word, a phrase) occupy the subject position. In some cases, there is no semantic subject. In these cases, English requires *it* or *there* to occupy subject position as in *It's raining* or *There's fresh coffee in the kitchen*. In these sentences, there is no *it* or *there* to point to; they don't refer to anything (as opposed to *him* in *I saw him yesterday*, which presumably refers to some guy the speaker and hearer both know). In Japanese, overt subjects are optional in many cases. In addition, they are prohibited in cases where there is no person or thing in the real world for the subject to refer to. (You may recall that we discussed this in relation to Spanish in Chapter 2. Note how UG puts restrictions on how null- and overt-subject pronouns work even in languages as different as Spanish and Japanese.) To see this, compare the sentences in (4c) and (4d) with those in

(5c) and (5d). The English pattern and the Japanese pattern are the reverse of each other. For the most part, this difference between English and Japanese can be acquired on the basis of the input to which learners are exposed. L1 English speakers learning Japanese as an L2 will hear sentences like those in (5a–c) on a regular basis. Those sentences provide evidence that Japanese permits null subjects.

Languages like Japanese are called null-subject languages, and languages like English are called non-null-subject languages. Things get more interesting when we look at how non-null-subject and null-subject languages handle pronouns in embedded clauses. Let's look at some data from English first. Consider the sentence in (6) and think about what the pronoun *he* can refer to.

(6) John$_i$ said that he$_{i/j}$ would be late.

In English, *he* can refer to either John or to someone else. So, sentence (6) can mean that John would be late, or it can mean that someone else would be late. By itself, the first interpretation, where *he* refers back to *John,* is probably more natural, but both interpretations are possible. This ambiguity is shown by the little letters *i* and *j* attached to the pronoun *he.* Note that *John* also has a subscript letter *i* attached to it. The subscript *i* on *he* matches the one on *John,* so *he* refers to *John.* The word *he* has a second subscript, the letter *j,* that doesn't have a match in the sentence. This indicates that the pronoun can refer to someone not mentioned in the sentence. Now let's see how the same sentences work in Japanese. Recall that Japanese allows both a null pronoun (*pro*) and an overt pronoun. The example in (7) shows two sentences; (7a) has a null pronoun and (7b) has an overt pronoun.

(7) a. Taro$_i$-ga   *pro$_{i/j}$*   mou   tabe.ta   to   it.ta.
        Taro$_i$-NOM   *pro$_{i/j}$*   already   eat.PAST   COMP say.PAST.
        'Taro$_i$ said that *pro$_{i/j}$* already ate.'

    b. Taro$_i$-wa   kare-ga$_{i/j}$ mou   tabe.ta   to   it.ta.
        Taro$_i$- TOP   he$_{i/j}$ -NOM   already   eat.PAST   COMP say.PAST.
        'Taro$_i$ said that he$_{i/j}$ already ate.'

In both of these sentences, the pronouns work like they do in English. In (7a) *pro* has a subscript *i,* indicating that it can refer back to Taro, so that the sentence means that Taro ate. It also has a subscript *j,* which doesn't have a match in the sentence, and indicates that the pronoun can also refer to someone outside the sentence so that someone other than Taro ate. The same pattern is there in (7b): The pronoun *kare* can refer to either Taro or to someone other than Taro. So far, it looks like null and overt pronouns work the same way in both English and in Japanese.

Now let's look at what happens when the subject of the main clause is a word like *everyone, who,* or *no one.* Again, we'll look at English first.

(8) Everyone$_i$ said that he$_{i/j}$ was hungry.

The pronoun *he* in (8) works the same way it does in (6): It can refer to *everyone* or it can refer to someone not mentioned in the sentence. In formal English, *he* is used as a neuter pronoun while in spoken English *they* is more popular. Even with *they* the sentence would work the same: The pronoun could refer back to *everyone* or it could refer to people outside of the sentence. Now let's look at the Japanese equivalent of (8), given in (9). Again, because Japanese has both a null and an overt pronoun, we will look at two sentences. The sentence in (9a) has a null pronoun, and the sentence in (9b) has an overt pronoun.

(9) a. Minna$_i$-ga   *pro*$_{i/j}$ mou   tabe.ta   to   it.ta.
         Everyone$_i$-NOM *pro*$_{i/j}$ already   eat.PAST COMP   say.PAST
         'Everyone$_i$ said that *pro*$_{i/j}$ already ate.'

     b. Minna$_i$-wa   kare-ga$_{*i/j}$ mou   tabe.ta   to   it.ta.
         Everyone$_i$-TOP   he-NOM $_{*i/j}$ already   eat.PAST COMP   say.PAST.
         'Everyone$_i$ said that he$_{*i/j}$ already ate.'

The sentence in (9a) works the same way as the examples we've already seen. When the pronoun is null, the sentence is ambiguous and can mean either that each person has already eaten or that someone not mentioned in the sentence has already eaten. This pattern is broken in (9b), however. In (9b), when the pronoun is overt, the sentence can only mean that some other person, not included in *everyone*, has eaten. In other words, the only possible interpretation of (9b) in Japanese is that everyone who was asked said that another person (Taro, or Kenji, or someone else) already ate. It cannot mean that each person who was asked said that they themselves ate. This difference in the interpretation of null and overt pronouns is a property of null-subject languages more generally – the same thing happens in languages as different from each other as Spanish, Turkish, Korean, Italian, Mandarin, and Portuguese – and it's called the overt pronoun constraint (OPC). The important thing about the OPC is that there is no way to acquire it from the input alone. Instead, once learners of null-subject languages unconsciously determine that the language they are learning is a null-subject language, the OPC kicks in without anyone knowing. This is a classic poverty of the stimulus case: The OPC cannot be learned based solely on the input, and yet it's something native speakers have very clear intuitions about.

Now let's consider what this means for language acquisition. Remember that the FDH predicts that L2 learners will not have very strong intuitions about syntactic constraints in the L2, and that this indicates that the L2 system is qualitatively different from the L1 system. Let's think about what this means for a native English speaker learning Japanese as an L2. English speakers come to

Japanese with a non-null-subject mental representation, which means that they must acquire a different representation for Japanese. They will get evidence from the input that Japanese does not require subjects; some of it comes from time expressions like those in (5). More will come from exposure to sentences without subjects, which are very common in Japanese. In addition, classroom learners will probably be told early on that subjects are optional in Japanese. So the fact that Japanese permits null subjects is not a particularly difficult thing to acquire; the evidence is there in the input. The question is whether these Japanese learners also show evidence of the interpretive constraints on null and overt pronouns exemplified in the OPC. Because the ambiguous interpretations in (7) and (9a) are the same in Japanese as they are in English, English learners of Japanese might transfer their knowledge that pronouns are ambiguous from English to Japanese. If they do this for sentences like (9b), however, they will also interpret the pronouns in these sentences as ambiguous. Thus, the crucial question is whether L2 learners know that sentences like (9b) have to be interpreted following the OPC, and are therefore not ambiguous. There is nothing about English or the Japanese input that provides evidence for the interpretation in (9b). It's also not something that is discussed in language classes. The research has shown that native English speakers are sensitive to the OPC, and that this sensitivity kicks in relatively early in the acquisition process. Kazue Kanno tested a group of fourth-semester L2 Japanese learners with English as an L1 and found that the L2 learners gave the same interpretation for sentences like (9b) as native Japanese speakers. Again, to underscore the point, these learners could not have deduced the OPC from the input. They could not transfer it from the L1. But the OPC is part of UG. How did the learners show evidence of the OPC if they don't have access to UG as the FDH predicts?

In addition to Kanno's research with learners of Japanese, other researchers have investigated whether non-native speakers of Italian, Spanish, Turkish, and Portuguese are sensitive to the OPC in those languages. Overall, study after study has found what Kanno did: L2 learners are sensitive to the interpretive constraints captured in the OPC. In addition, this sensitivity starts to show up very early; it's usually apparent in classroom learners during their second year of college-level study of the language. Studies such as these, which describe clear POS situations in L2 acquisition, run contrary to the predictions of the FDH. The FDH predicts general failure on subtle constraints like the OPC, but the empirical evidence actually suggests that these subtle constraints show up in L2 learners' unconscious mental representations. To be sure, there is research on other constraints and other non-OPC phenomena that point to a greater picture of UG working in adult L2 acquisition. We have focused here on the OPC to offer a more detailed description of this kind of research.

The Critical Period Hypothesis

One of the authors of this book worked in Japan for several years. She had American co-workers who moved to Japan when their children were three and five years old. Her co-worker said that he expected his children to pick up Japanese easily, whereas he and his wife would have to work hard to learn it. This person's beliefs about the ease with which his children would acquire Japanese reflect something known as **the Critical Period Hypothesis** (CPH). In this section, we examine the CPH and the evidence for and against it.

> The Critical Period Hypothesis proposes that a linguistic system can only be fully acquired if people are exposed to it before a certain age.

The CPH proposes that there is a **critical period** for language acquisition. What this means is that for a linguistic system to be fully acquired, it must be acquired by a certain age. The term critical period comes out of biology and what we know about how certain aspects of biological development take place. For instance, there is a critical period for imprinting in ducklings. When ducklings are born, there is a certain window of time in which they will bond with the mother duck, and whatever animal they see during that critical period is the animal that they imprint on. Similarly, there is a critical period for vision in kittens. If kittens are not exposed to certain visual stimuli within a certain period after they are born, they will never develop the ability to see as accurately as they would otherwise. In both cases, it's important to note that these functions are input dependent (they depend on access to a specific kind of stimuli in the real world), and that a lack of access to the critical stimuli does not entail no ability whatsoever. Instead, it means that ducklings might look to a member of another species to be their caregivers, and that kittens won't develop the full range of visual acuity they would otherwise have done.

The CPH for language acquisition comes from Eric Lenneberg's 1967 book, *The Biological Foundations of Language*. On the basis of the neurological correlates for human language, evidence from children who do not succeed in learning an L1, and because child language acquisition takes place during a period of time that is marked by a lot of neurological activity, Lenneberg argued that L1 acquisition is subject to critical period effects. Specifically, Lenneberg argued that if children are not exposed to an L1 by the age of about five, they will not acquire language. Although most proponents of a CPH for adult L2 acquisition cite Lenneberg, he limited his proposal to child L1 acquisition. He mentions L2 acquisition almost in passing, stating that if someone is of average intelligence, that person can learn another language after the beginning of what he calls "their second decade." He adds that the incidence of "language-learning blocks" increases after puberty. He ends by saying that because natural languages tend to resemble each other in so many ways, the ability to acquire another language is present in humans.

Although Lenneberg says nothing directly about a critical period for L2 acquisition, there is some circumstantial evidence for a critical period for child language acquisition. One piece of evidence comes from the case of Genie. Genie was locked in a closet by her step-father at a young age and was deprived of any linguistic input. When she was discovered by child protective services, she was 13. Despite receiving intensive interventions to teach her English, she never developed the ability to speak fluently. Although she acquired some vocabulary, her language production lacked syntactic structure and also lacked systematic morphological marking. We should avoid drawing too many conclusions from the case of Genie, though. The fact is, Genie's childhood was marked by severe and lengthy emotional and physical abuse, part of which included linguistic deprivation. In short, her language deficits could be related to the cognitive and emotional problems stemming from the abuse she endured. Other pieces of evidence for a critical period for L1 acquisition come from feral children. Feral children are children who are abandoned and spend their early years living away from human communities. When they are discovered, they face a long road to be reintegrated into society. These children often do not acquire the language of their communities completely, but, again, these outcomes cannot be separated from the neglect they endured. This is one of the major problems with directly testing the CPH: Most of the cases we have of people who lack exposure to language do so because they have been deprived of the social environment necessary for all kinds of healthy human development, including the development of human language. In fact, it is impossible to directly test the CPH because to do so would essentially involve depriving infants and children of human contact. Thus, although the evidence for critical period effects in L1 is suggestive, it is impossible to test the CPH directly.

Consider this ...

Assume for a minute that we had definitive evidence for a critical period for child L1 acquisition. Does this necessarily mean that there would be a critical period for adult L2 acquisition? Why or why not? What are some of the other ways in which the L1 and the L2 could interact? What are some other differences between L1 and L2 acquisition that might influence how far learners get?

Many L2 researchers adopted Lenneberg's hypothesis as a possible explanation for the observed lack of success in L2 acquisition. The first papers to investigate age effects in L2 acquisition were done by Jacqueline Johnson and Elissa Newport. In one of these papers, Johnson and Newport investigated whether native Chinese and Korean speakers living in the United States had nativelike knowledge of a range of English syntactic structures. Johnson and Newport gave their participants a task that asked them to listen to English sentences and indicate whether the sentences were grammatical or ungrammatical. Participants had different **ages of arrival**; some had moved to the United States to do their graduate work, and others had moved in childhood. Johnson and Newport found that participants who had moved to the United States between the ages of 3 and 7 performed like native English speakers on the judgment task. The older participants were when they arrived in the United States, the more their judgments differed from those of native English speakers. Johnson and Newport argued that these results support the hypothesis that L2 acquisition is subject to critical period effects.

As other researchers have pointed out, there are a number of confounding factors that may have influenced the results that Johnson and Newport reported. One of these factors is that age of arrival correlates strongly with other variables that we know influence L2 acquisition, such as quantity and quality of input, motivation to integrate, and so on. Researchers have also pointed out that evidence that many L2 learners do not perform like native speakers on tests like those given by Johnson and Newport is not necessarily evidence that L2 learners cannot acquire a nativelike mental representation of language. This means that if there is evidence that some people do attain an L2 competence that is virtually indistinguishable from that of native speakers, this is counter-evidence to the CPH. One study that presents counter-evidence is a case study that was conducted by Georgette Ioup and her colleagues. This study presents evidence from two native English speakers who acquired Egyptian Arabic as adults. It is presented in more detail in the Exemplary Study.

One participant, Julie, learned Egyptian Arabic by interacting with native speakers in Egypt. She did not receive any explicit instruction. Despite having lived in Egypt for 26 years at the time of the study, she could not read or write Arabic. The second participant, Laura, had had some formal instruction in Arabic before moving to Egypt. She was literate in Arabic, and taught Arabic at the University of Cairo. Both women married Egyptian men and spoke Arabic at home. Ioup and her colleagues collected speech samples and syntactic judgments from their participants. Native Arabic speakers rated the speech samples for nativelikeness. Both women were rated as native speakers, and performance on the syntactic judgment task was consistent with native-speaker judgments in all but a handful of cases. Those cases were cases in which native speakers also demonstrated some variability in their judgments. Research results such as these are difficult to explain under the CPH.

Work on the CPH has continued apace since the early 1990s, but the basic challenges in conducting this research are still present. Researchers have added measures, such as length of residence (as distinct from age of arrival) and aptitude scores, as well as created criteria for inclusion in these studies that require participants to be perceived as native speakers. For instance, Niclas Abrahamsson and Kenneth Hyltenstam tested L1 Spanish speakers on their L2 Swedish competence. To be included in the participant pool, participants had to be rated as native speakers by L1 Swedish speakers. Participants then completed tasks that tapped lexical and morphosyntactic knowledge at the upper range of native-speaker proficiency levels. The L1 Spanish speakers did not perform like L1 Swedish speakers, so the authors concluded that critical period effects are active in adult L2 acquisition. Studies like those conducted by Abrahamsson and Hyltenstam are important because they show that nativelikeness is quite rare. Even these studies, though, have a hard time isolating age itself from other factors that we know influence L2 attainment, such as access to sufficient input. What is clear from critical period studies is that most L2 learners stop acquiring their L2 somewhere short of nativelike knowledge. These studies have not, however, definitively shown that this is due to the age at which one begins acquiring an L2. In addition, there is evidence that, in some cases, L2 learners do develop nativelike knowledge of their L2.

Exemplary Study

Ioup, G., Boustagui, E., El Tigi, M., and Moselle, M. (1994). Reexamining the Critical Period Hypothesis: A case study of successful adult SLA in a naturalistic environment. *Studies in Second Language Acquisition*, 16, 73–98.

Research Questions

- How does the linguistic competence of a naturalistic L2 learner compare to that of native speakers?
- Are there differences between tutored and untutored near-native speakers in terms of grammatical competence?

Participants

- Two L1 English speakers with Egyptian Arabic as an L2:
  - One participant, Julie, moved from the UK to Egypt when she married an Egyptian. She acquired Arabic entirely through naturalistic exposure to the language. At the time of the study, she was working as an ESL teacher/trainer at the university level and had lived in Egypt for 26 years. She could speak Arabic but could not read or write it.
  - The other participant, Laura, was an American who studied standard Arabic in college and earned an M.A. and a Ph.D. in standard Arabic. She moved to Egypt while working on her Ph.D., married an Egyptian, and stayed in Egypt. At the time of the study, she was teaching standard Arabic at the university level and had lived in Egypt for ten years. She was fully literate in Arabic.

Linguistic Domains Investigated

- speech production
- accent identification
- grammatical intuitions

Materials, Method, and Procedure

- Speech production
  - o elicited spontaneous speech samples from both L2 speakers
  - o intermixed with speech samples from native and non-native speakers
  - o a separate group of native speakers categorized the speech samples as native or non-native
- Accent identification
  - o participants identified regional Arabic dialects and regional Egyptian dialects
  - o participants classified speech samples from Egyptian and non-Egyptian Arabic speakers
  - o participants classified speech samples from speakers from different parts of Egypt
- Grammatical intuitions

  - o translation task from English into Arabic containing relative clauses, *yes/no* questions, *wh*-questions, and noun phrases joined by words like *and*
  - o grammaticality judgment task that included Arabic-specific constructions and UG-constrained constructions
  - o anaphora interpretation task that tested participants' pronoun interpretation preferences in different syntactic contexts

Results

- Both participants were rated as native speakers by most of the judges in the speech production task.
- Both participants accurately discriminated between Egyptian and non-Egyptian accents.
- Julie performed more closely to native speakers in her ability to distinguish between Egyptian accents; Laura could not distinguish between them.
- Both participants scored perfectly on the grammatical contrasts tested in the translation task, including with respect to morphology.
- Both participants performed close to native speakers on the structures tested in the grammaticality judgment task, including with respect to

relativized questions, headless relative clauses, resumptive pronouns, and multiple *wh*-questions.

- Both participants performed like native speakers with respect to anaphora resolutions in most contexts. The exception was Julie, who did not perform like native speakers on items testing for interpretation of pronouns in texts.

Conclusion

- With the exception of one kind of anaphora, little distinguishes tutored and naturalistic L2 learners at the end state of language acquisition.
- These results provide counter-evidence to the Critical Period Hypothesis: Both participants began acquiring Arabic as adults, and both perform like native speakers on multiple measures.

Learners Can Become Nativelike in Some Domains, But Not Others

The proposals that fall under this category differ in terms of scope and where they place the locus of divergence between L1 and L2 grammars. We deal with two major proposals here: representational deficit hypotheses, which deal with the underlying mental representation, and the Shallow Structure Hypothesis, which deals with language processing.

Representational Deficit Hypotheses

This section is called "Representational Deficit Hypotheses" because there are several proposals that all fall under a general category. Rather than treat each one separately, we'll sketch out the broad outlines of the proposal. Throughout this book, we have been talking about what it means for learners to have a mental representation for language. Part of that representation includes morphology, the units of sound and meaning that encode grammatical information. This grammatical information can include agreement information, such as agreement between subjects and verbs or between nouns and adjectives. If a language has overt agreement, such as when a verb has a different ending depending on whether the subject is singular or plural, both the subject and the verb have to share the same **features**. In this case, the subject would have a [+plural] feature and so would the verb. If the features on a subject and a verb don't match, they can't be used together. To see how this works, let's look at the example in (10), from French.

(10) a.　Je　　　joue　　au　　tennis
　　　　I　　　play.1SG　DET　tennis
　　　　'I play tennis.'

b. Nous   jouons   au   tennis.
   We   play.1PL   DET   tennis.
   'We play tennis.'

c. *Je   jouons   au   tennis.
   I   play.1PL   DET   tennis.
   *'I play tennis.'

Proponents of representational deficit hypotheses argue that if a learner's L1 lacks certain functional features, learners will not be able to represent those features in an L2.

The basic idea in syntactic theory is that if something is marked overtly, either through a word or a bound morpheme (i.e., an ending or prefix that is attached to a word; literally the morpheme is bound to another morpheme and can't appear by itself, such as *-s* for plural), there has to be something in the syntax that reflects that difference. Overt morphology is the result of something called **functional features**. These indicate syntactic information such as person marking, tense marking, or gender agreement. Agreement happens because the noun and the verb, in the case of subject–verb agreement, have to match. So in (10b), for example, both the pronoun and the verb ending have a feature for first person plural. The verb also has a feature for present-tense marking.

Representational deficit hypotheses rest on a fairly robust observation of a major difference between L1 and L2 acquisition. Children generally do not have a hard time acquiring the morphology of their native language. Adults, in contrast, do seem to have a hard time with L2 morphology, and this is despite the fact that language classes tend to emphasize accurate morphology, such as subject–verb or gender agreement. Even though classroom language learners receive instruction and practice with morphology, they often do not produce it accurately and do not rely on it for comprehension until they are very proficient. And, in many cases, L2 speakers never demonstrate nativelike mastery of morphology in their second language. This difference between native and non-native speakers can't be due to a lack of explicit instruction. Instead, some researchers have proposed that it is due to a systematic deficit in the underlying competence of L2 speakers. In particular, the claim is that L2 learners do not or cannot represent new functional features in their mental representation. Their mental representations can only contain abstract features that already exist in their L1. So, for instance, native English speakers who learn Spanish or French do not acquire gender marking in these languages because these features are new and not present in their L1. Because Spanish and French both mark gender, these hypotheses further predict that native Spanish speakers who learn French should be able to represent the feature for gender in French. These learners still have to acquire French vocabulary, which takes time. Crucially, however, native Spanish speakers who learn French will be more accurate with gender marking than native English speakers.

Representational deficit hypotheses share an important commonality with the FDH. Both of them predict that L2 mental representations will lack the syntax or morphology that governs native speakers' representations. Representational deficit accounts are more limited than the FDH because representational deficit accounts limit non-nativelikeness to aspects of the grammar that depend on abstract functional features. In order to evaluate representational deficit accounts, we need to know whether it is true that L2 speakers do not represent features in their mental representation for the target language. A lot of the research that has investigated this question has looked at whether L2 speakers accurately produce morphology and whether L2 speakers are sensitive to violations of agreement relationships (e.g., whether they know that sentences like *John drink coffee* are ungrammatical in English). The limitation of this research is that both subject–verb agreement and gender agreement depend on words being well represented in learners' mental dictionaries for the target language. That is, for subjects and verbs to agree, verbs must be strongly situated in the mental dictionary. For nouns and adjectives to agree, both nouns and adjectives must be strongly situated in the mental dictionary. So it's not always clear whether non-nativelike performance on these tasks is due to a representational problem or whether it's due to a vocabulary problem (e.g., slowness in retrieving lexical items from the mental dictionary). Morphology is not the only aspect of language governed by features, however. Features also govern **movement**. Movement is a process by which a word or a phrase is generated in one position of the sentence and is moved to another position as a result of a syntactic operation, such as question formation (we touched on this in Chapter 4 with the example *Alessandro lee a menudo la ciencia ficción* 'Alessandro often reads science fiction.'). Moving a word from one place to another leaves a trace in the word's original position and creates a link between that position and its final position.

For example, the standard analysis of English *wh*-questions involves movement. Let's look at the sentences in (11). The first one is a declarative sentence, and the second is a *wh*-question that targets the object in (11a).

(11) a.   Bill drinks wine while he makes dinner.
     b.   What$_i$ does Bill drink e$_i$ while he makes dinner?

Intuitively, there is a semantic relationship between the sentences in (11a) and (11b). To see this, make a list of possible answers to the question in (11b). They should all be able to replace the word *wine* in (11a). In other words, the sentence in (11b) starts out as *Bill drinks what for dinner*, and then the word *what* moves to the front of the sentence (actually, up higher into the sentence, as we saw in Chapter 4) to get the final word order. This is called *wh*-movement, and it's the primary way that English forms *wh*-questions. In syntax, words can't move around in a sentence without good reason. Words can move due to the presence of strong features. In English, there is a position at the beginning of the sentence that determines whether the sentence is a statement or a question. When it is a question, it is associated with [+Q] features that indicate that the sentence is a question. In addition, the word *what* is tagged with the same [+Q] features. The word *what* then moves to the front of the sentence so that its [+Q] features will match the features in the initial position in the sentence. Although some languages move the question word to the front of the sentence to form a question, other languages, such as Japanese and Mandarin, form questions without moving the *wh*-word. In these languages, the *wh*-word simply replaces the part of the sentence the question is about. In other words, *wh*-questions in these languages look like *Bill drank what?* These languages lack the strong [+Q] features that allow the movement to take place. Because representational deficit hypotheses predict that L2 learners cannot acquire new features in the L2, they predict that native speakers of languages like Japanese and Chinese will not acquire nativelike knowledge of question formation in L2 English.

Most of the work that has investigated representational deficit hypotheses has focused on the acquisition of verbal morphology (e.g., verb endings) and gender marking. There is significant evidence that both of these are difficult for L2 learners. Less work has investigated the acquisition of *wh*-movement, but the work that has been done tends to find that certain properties (if not all) of *wh*-movement are acquirable. *Wh*-movement is similar to null subjects in that there is robust positive evidence available to learners in the input (e.g., learners hear sentences with *wh*-movement in them every time they encounter questions like *What does Bill drink?* and *Where does Megan live?*). There are also subtle properties of language that are related to *wh*-movement but are not obvious from the input. For example, consider the sentences in (12).

(12) a. John said Sally left.
     b. Who did John say left?
     c. John said that Sally left.
     d. ?/*Who did John say that left?

Sentences (12a) and (12c) show two possible options for embedded clauses in English; the **complementizer** that introduces the clause is optional (complementizers are words like *which, that,* and *who* that introduce a subordinate clause). The sentence in (12b) indicates that it is possible to ask questions about the subject of an embedded clause in English; that is, Sally is the subject of the verb *left* in the embedded clause and *who* refers to Sally. Given that, it's not clear why the sentence in (12d) should be ungrammatical or at least sound weird – the only difference between this sentence and the sentence in (12b) is the presence of the word *that*. It's not clear why keeping the complementizer *that* should make the *wh*-movement from the subject of the embedded clause questionable in (12d). This is not a syntax textbook, so we won't dwell on why (12d) is ungrammatical here. For our purposes, what's important is that contrasts like those in (12) can be used to test intuitions about *wh*-movement in English. Research that has investigated this has found that native speakers of languages without *wh*-movement are sensitive to these contrasts (and to many others that involve *wh*-movement) in learning an L2 like English, but that these intuitions can take a while to develop. Based on what we have seen so far, it is not clear that the hypotheses about representational deficits hold up. Learners can develop mental representations with new features and new operations that don't exist in their L1.

The Shallow Structure Hypothesis

Representational deficit hypotheses deal specifically with the linguistic system. The Shallow Structure Hypothesis (SSH) deals with the parser. The **parser** is the mechanism in the mind/brain that mediates between the input (language that we hear or read) and our mental representation of language. During sentence comprehension, the parser constructs a moment-by-moment (actually, millisecond by millisecond) computation of sentence structure. As such, the parser is integral to language comprehension, and because language acquisition is input dependent, some kind of parsing is implicated in language acquisition. L1 parsers for fully competent speakers rapidly integrate information from a variety of modules – syntax, semantics, pragmatics, and real-world knowledge – as the input stream is encountered. Native speakers often construct rich, detailed syntactic representations for the sentences that they read or hear. Consider the example in (11b) again, repeated here as (13).

(13) What$_i$ does Bill drink e_i while he makes dinner?

As we discussed earlier, this sentence is formed by replacing the object with a *wh*-word and moving that word to the front of the sentence. Movement creates a link between the space occupied by the original position of the *wh*-word and the position where it winds up. For now, let's call the original position represented by e_i "a gap" as in "there is a gap here because something is missing." Research has shown that native English speakers who read sentences like those in (13) slow down on the word immediately following the gap; in this case, they would slow down when reading the word *while* compared to environments where *while* is not precede by a gap (e.g., *John played the piano while Mary sang*). This slowdown in reading times indicates that the parser is integrating the function of the *wh*-word with its original position in the sentence before the next word is encountered; in other words, the parser is processing the gap itself even though we can't see it or hear it.

Although the L1 parser relies on a variety of sources – semantics, syntax, and pragmatics, among others – in order to compute the L1 input, it depends heavily on syntactic information. In fact, there is some evidence that syntactic information is primary, which leads to **garden-path effects**. Garden-path effects happen when the parser originally assigns a syntactic representation that turns out not to match the intended meaning of the sentence, as in (14).

(14) The cotton clothing is made of grows in Mississippi.

In this sentence, the parser initially interprets *cotton* as an adjective that modifies *clothing* and interprets the string *the cotton clothing* as the subject of the sentence. This parse works until the parser encounters the word *of*, at which point it can no longer make the structure work. At this point, it has to go back and reanalyze the sentence so that *clothing is made of* is in a separate clause that modifies *the cotton*. This is illustrated in (15) where RC stands for relative clause.

(15) The cotton [$_{RC}$ clothing is made of] grows in Mississippi.

In short, the parser heads down a "garden path" only to find out later it is on the wrong path. The presence of garden-path effects in native speakers indicates that the L1 parser relies heavily on syntactic information to parse sentences.

Harald Clahsen and Claudia Felser have proposed that even highly proficient L2 speakers do not rely on the same type of syntactic information to parse sentences in the L2 that native speakers of that language do. Clahsen and Felser base this proposal, in part, on evidence of differences in how native and non-native English speakers process sentences containing *wh*-movement in English. The SSH also predicts that the inability to parse sentences like native speakers is true even when the L1 and the L2 share the same syntactic structures. Thus, native speakers of Spanish, which is a *wh*-movement language, and native speakers of Korean, which is not a *wh*-movement language, should perform more similarly to each other on *wh*-movement structures in English than either group will to native English speakers. In other words, at least when it comes to parsing *wh*-movement sentences, L1 Spanish speakers will not have an advantage over L1 Korean speakers. Specifically, both may fail to slow down and process gaps the way native English speakers do.

The SSH has generated a significant body of research in recent years, and results are mixed. Some researchers have found that non-native speakers consistently rely on parsing strategies that differ from those of native speakers. This finding is particularly robust when it comes to the processing of certain kinds of *wh*-gaps. For example, work by Theodore Marinis and his colleagues investigated whether four groups of non-native English speakers – L1 German speakers, L1 Greek speakers, L1 Japanese speakers, and L1 Chinese speakers – processed sentences like those in (16) in the same way as native speakers. German and Greek are *wh*-movement languages, and Japanese and Chinese lack *wh*-movement. If the L1 makes a difference, the Greek and German participants should perform more like L1 English speakers than the Japanese and Chinese speakers.

(16) The captain *who*$_i$ the officer decided *e*$_i$ that the young soldier had displeased *e*$_i$ will write a formal report next week.

There are two possible origins for *who* in the sentence in (16). The first one is the object of *decide*, and the second is the object of *displease*. For the sake of efficiency, the parser looks to the first possible position (the object of *decide*) to resolve where the *wh*-element originated. If it can't do it there, it keeps looking until it reaches *displease*. Native speakers demonstrate longer reading times at both *that* and *will* in sentences like (16). Marinis and his colleagues found that all four of their L2 groups had longer reading times at *will*, which is where the *wh*-word actually originates, but that there was no evidence of longer reading times at *that*. (Again, keep in mind the researchers compare reading times of words like *that* and *will* to sentences where gaps aren't involved.) The researchers concluded that this was evidence that the L2 parser doesn't process this type of *wh*-movement in the same way as the L1 parser.

At the same time, however, there is some evidence that quantity and quality of exposure to the target language make a difference for L2 parsing. For instance, in 2013 Christos Pliatsikas and Theodoros Marinis tested two groups of L1 Greek speakers on sentences like those in (16). The groups were matched for proficiency, but one group had not spent a significant time in an English-speaking country, and the other group was living in the United Kingdom at the time of testing. The group that was living in the United Kingdom was indistinguishable from L1 English speakers, whereas the group that had not lived outside of Greece did not process the intermediate gap. The results of this study suggest that L2 speakers can rely on the same syntactic information to process sentences in the L2 as native speakers, but that it takes a significant amount of input and exposure to the L2 to do so.

Consider this ...

Representational deficit hypotheses focus on the nature of the mental representations L2 speakers have. The Shallow Structure Hypothesis focuses on language processing, which involves whether speakers can use linguistic knowledge efficiently as their parsers compute sentence structure during comprehension. Is it possible that L2 speakers could have *knowledge* of a particular structure but not be able to use that structure while processing language? If not, can you imagine a reason why?

Nativelikeness Is Possible

The last position we consider in this section is that nativelikeness is possible. As we do this, it's important to keep in mind that even researchers who argue that nativelikeness is possible do not argue that nativelikeness is *guaranteed* for all learners. Rather, they suggest that when non-native speakers do not perform like native speakers at advanced proficiency levels, this is due to factors other than systematic differences between the processes of L1 and L2 acquisition. In this section, we consider two main proposals. The first proposal is Full Transfer/Full Access, which deals primarily with the process of L2 acquisition. Under the broad category of Full Transfer/Full Access, we briefly introduce non-representational deficit accounts. The second proposal is the Interface Hypothesis, which is about what speakers know about the L2 when they have stopped acquiring it.

Full Transfer/Full Access

> Full Transfer/Full Access proposes that L2 learners assume the grammar of their L1 when they begin acquiring an L2. Because they still have access to Universal Grammar, it is possible for them to acquire a mental representation for the L2 that matches that of native speakers.

We introduced the **Full Transfer/ Full Access** (FT/FA) hypothesis in Chapter 4. But it's not a bad idea to review it in some detail here. Proposed by Bonnie Schwartz and Rex Sprouse, the FT/FA attempts to account for the following observations: (1) there is evidence for L1 influence on L2 mental representation, particularly at early stages; (2) L2 learners can and do move away from L1 influence; and (3) L2 representations show poverty of the stimulus effects similar to those found in L1 acquisition. FT/FA also tries to answer two questions: what L2 learners start with and how the L2 representation changes over time. In answer to the first question, Schwartz and Sprouse propose that the initial state (see Chapter 4) of L2 acquisition is the L1. In other words, L2 learners will initially use their mental representation for their L1 to process L2 input and develop a linguistic system. This means, for instance, that native English speakers acquiring Spanish as an L2 will start with a representation for Spanish that does not allow null subjects, contrary to the actual properties of Spanish. Even though learners start with the abstract features of their L1, they restructure their mental representations for the L2 when the existing representations are not sufficient to process the target language input. We can illustrate with null subjects. As English speakers begin to learn Spanish as an L2, they process Spanish-language input. In this input, they are forced to process sentences that don't have overt subjects such as *Juan no está aquí. ¿Está enfermo?* 'John isn't here. *pro* is sick?' and *No es cierto* '*pro* is not true.' As the result of multiple encounters with these kinds of sentences, their mental representations for Spanish posit that the language must be null subject (i.e., that there is such a thing as *pro*, even though this doesn't exist in English). So the *full transfer* part of FT/FA refers to where learners begin. In the scenario just described above, L1 English speakers fully transfer the properties and features of a non-null subject to Spanish at the outset and soon these Spanish L2 learners accept and produce sentences that don't have overt subjects.

The *full access* part of this scenario is a little bit more difficult to see. As we discussed above in the section on the Fundamental Difference Hypothesis, null-subject languages allow both null and overt pronouns. They also place subtle restrictions on what overt pronouns can refer to. Null pronouns can refer to nouns and to words like *everyone, no one,* and *who.* Overt pronouns can refer to nouns but not to words like *everyone, no one,* and *who.* This is called the overt pronoun constraint (OPC) and it is part of UG (we reviewed this in detail above in the examples from Japanese). Because the properties that govern the OPC are abstract and not available from the input alone, the only way that learners could be sensitive to the OPC is if they still have access to UG. And there is a significant amount of evidence that L2 learners are sensitive to the OPC (again, see the discussion above). This is the *full access* part of FT/FA: just as in L1 acquisition, UG constrains and guides the mental representation of L2 acquisition. It has not gone away.

Proponents of FT/FA argue that, in principle, nativelikeness is *possible*; they do not argue that it is guaranteed. To acquire nativelike representation is dependent on access to sufficient quantities of the relevant input (among other things). At the same time, the L1 may influence the way the mental representation for the L2 develops, and in some parts of the language this may be persistent over time. Simply put, FT/FA claims that the mental representation for the L2 will be consistent with UG combined with the input learners receive. This consistency is true at all stages of acquisition. In short, learners don't develop mental representation willy-nilly. Whatever exists in their heads must demonstrate the properties of UG.

Finally, FT/FA applies only to the aspects of language that are constrained by UG. So, for example, the OPC in null-subject languages is part of UG, which is why we consistently see it emerge in learners of null-subject languages so early. But the difference between something like regular and irregular past-tense verbs is not. Even though most learners might eventually learn regular and irregular past-tense verbs, this is not because UG is involved. And just to be sure, we add here that learners might indeed develop nativelike representations for various aspects of the L2, but performance factors and processing demands may mask this underlying knowledge. Indeed, Donna Lardiere has made exactly this argument based on longitudinal data from an L1 Chinese speaker. In her research, she demonstrated that her subject, Patti, had all of the syntactic representation for tense and finiteness in English, but did not consistently inflect verbs for past tense, for example.

The Interface Hypothesis
The Interface Hypothesis was formulated by Antonella Sorace and is based primarily on non-native speakers' knowledge and use of null and overt pronouns in

null-subject languages. As we have seen, native speakers of null-subject languages, such as Italian, Spanish, Japanese, and Chinese, have a mental representation that allows for both null- and overt-subject pronouns. They also have an unconscious knowledge of how to interpret null and overt pronouns. People develop interpretive preferences based on their experience with the language. These preferences are not governed by UG (except for those related to the OPC) and are generally assumed to be language specific. The Interface Hypothesis proposes that properties of language governed by UG are ultimately acquirable, but it also proposes that interfaces between different parts of language may cause long-term non-nativeness. What's an interface? An interface refers to when two different parts of language must work together in sentence formation or comprehension. In the case of null- and overt-subject pronouns, there are syntactic properties of these pronouns and then there are discourse properties of the pronouns used in comprehension and production. We have seen the syntactic properties of these pronouns earlier. Discourse refers to that part of language that connects sentences to each other to ensure cohesion. For subject pronouns, discourse is involved in that a pronoun can take an antecedent outside its own sentence or clause. So, on the one hand, a subject pronoun has syntactic "stuff" it needs to obey, and then there are discourse options for that pronoun when it comes to linking it to an antecedent (except for the OPC). Proponents of the Interface Hypothesis argue that the syntactic properties of null and overt subjects in a language like Spanish or Italian should be no problem for learners but the discourse properties may be. Why? Because the discourse properties have to be learned from the input and speak to speaker preferences and not to hard-and-fast "rules." Very often, these preferences require lots and lots of input. Let's illustrate with an example. Consider the sentences in (17), for English, and (18), for Italian.

(17) Bill$_i$ called Walter$_j$ when he$_{i/j}$ returned from California.
(18) a. Bill ha telefonato Walter quando *pro* è arrivato da California.
      b. Bill ha telefonato Walter quando lui è arrivato da California.

The embedded clause pronoun in (17) is technically ambiguous in that either Bill or Walter could have been in California. In practice, native English speakers prefer to interpret the pronoun *he* as referring to Bill, and not Walter. In other words, the preference in English is for the pronoun in the embedded clause to refer to the subject of the main clause. There is nothing in the mental representation that dictates that it has to be this way; this is just a preference, and there is wiggle room in that native speakers show variability in their interpretations. Similarly, context and real-world knowledge can override these preferences. If, for instance, the speaker and the hearer both know that Walter was in California, then the pronoun would clearly refer to Walter. Interpretative preferences are evident when the context is neutral or disambiguating knowledge isn't available. In Italian, the interpretive preferences change depending on whether the pronoun is null or overt.

In (18a), the embedded clause pronoun is null (*pro*), and it behaves the way it does in English. It can technically refer to either Bill or to Walter, but native speakers prefer to interpret it as referring to the subject of the sentence (research suggests upwards of 80 percent of the time). In contrast, in (18b), Italian speakers prefer to interpret the overt pronoun *lui* as referring to Walter, or the non-subject of the main clause. The idea here is that null subjects are part of "topic continuity" (i.e., the topic of the first sentence is Bill and it is expected to continue being the topic of the next sentence or clause). Overt subjects are part of "topic shift" (i.e., the topic of the first sentence is Bill but the use of *lui* suggests the speaker is changing topics in this new sentence or clause). Topic continuity is a feature of discourse, not syntax.

A number of studies have investigated L1 English speakers' ambiguity resolution preferences in L2 Spanish and Italian. This research finds that, at advanced proficiency levels, L1 English speakers know that Spanish and Italian are null-subject languages – they are indistinguishable from native speakers on tests of the grammatical properties of null subjects, such as the OPC and when null subjects are required or overt subjects are forbidden. However, L1 English speakers tend to diverge from native speakers when it comes to interpretive preferences for ambiguity resolution. L2 Italian and Spanish speakers tend to resolve ambiguities like those in (18) in favor of the main clause subject; that is, regardless of pronoun type, there is a tendency among these learners to assume no topic shift from one clause to the other. This lines up with native-speaker preferences in (18a) but not in (18b). In short, work that has investigated the Interface Hypothesis has found that L2 learners show nativelike representation for syntactic aspects of pronouns but that they do not necessarily develop nativelike abilities when it comes to interpreting and using pronouns. It is worth pointing out that some L2 learners do, however, resemble native speakers on both syntactic and discourse aspects of subject pronouns. This suggests that nativelikeness is possible. But these learners tend to be in the minority. The question is why this is so. The answer probably lies in the fact that discourse preferences involving such things as topic continuity/shift with pronouns requires lots and lots of exposure. There is some research on Spanish L1 acquisition, for example, that suggests this is the case. Children learning Spanish as an L1 do not show adult-like preferences for subject pronoun interpretation until around puberty. It is not surprising, then, that L2 learners would take a long time as well, given that they often do not have the massive exposure to input (in terms of daily contact hours) that L1 learners have over the course of 12–13 years, which would include, of course, literacy and massive amounts of written input.

Overall Summary and Discussion

In this chapter, we've seen the observations we started with emerge again and again. On the one hand, many L2 learners do not end up with an L2 representation that matches that of native speakers in their community. This differs from

L1 acquisition, in which convergence is taken for granted. On the other hand, we have also seen evidence for fairly high achievement on measures of L2 performance and competence. Researchers have proposed various explanations for apparent divergence from native-speaker competence. The FDH proposed that L2 learners lack access to UG and domain-specific acquisition mechanisms. The CPH proposed that L2 learners' age is the problem – after a certain age, L2 acquisition isn't possible. Representational deficit accounts propose that the problem is in the linguistic system, but that it's narrowly constrained. The SSH proposes that the problem is in the L2 parsing mechanisms. The Interface Hypothesis proposes that the problems lie not with the system or with the acquisition mechanisms, but rather with a general lack of ability to integrate information rapidly and efficiently across subsystems such as syntax and discourse. As we've considered each of these proposals, we've also seen that, in some cases, L2 learners do acquire aspects of the target language that look nativelike.

What do we make of all of this? First, it seems likely that Position 1 (L2 learners cannot become nativelike) is too strong. Evidence for poverty of the stimulus effects in L2 acquisition suggests that the L2 system is constrained in the same way that the L1 system is. Similarly, evidence from stages of development and orders of acquisition research (see Chapter 2) suggests that the process of L2 acquisition is similar to the process of L1 acquisition. In addition, it seems unlikely that the CPH is an accurate account of the data. This is because CPH work has a hard time separating age from other variables. It's also because there is some evidence for nativelikeness in adult L2 acquisition more generally. It's a bit harder to decide between Positions 2 (nativelikeness is possible in some domains but not others) and 3 (nativelikeness is possible), at least with the evidence we've presented here. In both cases, we've seen evidence for nativelikeness, and evidence against it. Essentially, researchers who take Position 2 have to explain why nativelikeness happens in some cases but not others. Similarly, researchers who take Position 3 have to explain why non-nativelikeness happens. Both sets of researchers agree that nativelikeness is not a given for all learners. Overall, we think the following statements are the most consistent with the evidence we have:

- It is possible for L2 learners to develop advanced proficiency in the L2.
- L2 learners acquire target-like mental representations for aspects of the L2 that are governed by UG, assuming they have been exposed to the relevant input.
- The aspects of the L2 that are not governed by UG (such as vocabulary, morphology, and discourse structure) will be acquired late, and may not be acquired at all.
- There are some documented cases of successful L2 acquisition, to the point that native speakers rate L2 speakers as nativelike. These cases are the exception, not the norm, but non-nativelikeness is probably not directly due to age of acquisition or lack of access to UG. Instead, the most likely source of non-nativelikeness is L2 learners' access to quality input in sufficient quantities.

In sum, 40 years of research has provided the following answer to the question "Can L2 learners become nativelike?" Some do; most don't. Given this, we think that it would be productive to start asking a different question: Given that some L2 learners achieve nativelike proficiency in their L2, why don't more L2 learners do so? We suspect that the answer

> Some L2 learners become nativelike; most don't.

to this will come down to the interaction of several factors, but one that has been relatively overlooked in the literature is the issue of input. Some researchers, such as Maria Pavesi, have compared groups of learners who have access to classroom input or naturalistic input (see Chapter 6). These researchers find group differences based on quantity or quality of input. Similarly, input has been lurking in the bushes in several of the proposals we've discussed in this chapter. For instance, it could be that the difference between early arrivals and late arrivals in much of the critical period work is due to the fact that children who arrive at the age of, say, 10, receive a significant portion of their schooling in English, have access to English-speaking peers, and overall, have access to more comprehensible English input than adults who arrive in their mid 20s. If this is the case, age and access to input are highly correlated. Given that input is a necessary condition for language acquisition, it seems that the type of input learners get will emerge as a major factor in L2 attainment. And as we saw in the case of L1 learners of null-subject languages, it may be literacy and massive exposure to written input that pushes some aspects of acquisition along (e.g., those involved in the Interface Hypothesis). Written input is much more complex and involves many more dependencies across clauses and sentences than everyday conversational input. This may be a much-understudied part of the picture of how learners develop nativelike representations and abilities.

What about Social Factors?

We know that one of the major factors that influences L2 acquisition is quantity and quality of input. Input doesn't exist in a vacuum, however, and the social environment someone is in may determine how much input they receive and how rich the input is. For example, Tokyo is home to a considerable number of expatriates from English-speaking countries. Many of them work in English-speaking offices, speak English at home with their families, and send their kids to English-medium instruction schools. These expatriates are in Japan temporarily, and the expectation is that they and their children will move back to their home country. For this to happen, their kids need to have the English skills and the academic background to fit back in to their home country. Kids and adults in this environment might not learn much Japanese because most of their social interactions – home, school, other activities – take place in English. On the other hand, other expatriates in Japan, such as English teachers or missionaries, are exposed to different networks. In many cases, these expatriates work to integrate as much as possible into Japanese communities. They study Japanese and develop networks with Japanese people. Some marry Japanese citizens, and many send their children to Japanese schools. This gives them access to different social networks, all of which increase their access to rich input in Japanese. This still doesn't guarantee convergence on native-speaker norms, especially with respect to the writing system. The Japanese writing system is particularly complicated, and many expatriates do not need to read and write fluently to go about their daily lives. Some do learn to read and write Japanese fluently, though. What this example points to is that, to the extent that social factors influence the amount of input learners have access to, ultimate attainment will also be influenced by these factors.

Recap

Here are some of the main ideas we discussed in this chapter.

- Native speakers of a particular language differ from each other in terms of their steady-state language skills. Because of this, nativelikeness is a difficult construct to define in L2 acquisition.
- The Fundamental Difference Hypothesis proposes that L2 acquisition differs from L1 acquisition in terms of both the process of acquisition and the nature of the system being acquired.
- The Critical Period Hypothesis was originally a proposal about L1 acquisition and proposed that if children are not exposed to L1 input within a critical period, they will not acquire their L1. Researchers have applied the CPH to L2 acquisition, but because age, access to input, instruction, and exposure are all confounded for adult learners, it is difficult to state definitively that the Critical Period Hypothesis applies to adult L2 acquisition.
- There is a substantial amount of evidence that suggests that L2 learners develop the same kinds of syntactic intuitions as native speakers of that language. This suggests that nativelikeness, at least in the domain of syntax, is possible.
- The Interface Hypothesis proposes that to the extent that optionality persists in L2 grammars, it is found at the interfaces between different linguistic modules, and at the interface between the linguistic system and other systems, such as discourse and pragmatic knowledge.

REFERENCES AND READINGS

- Abrahamsson, N. & Hyltenstam, K. (2009). Age of onset and nativelikeness in an L2: Listener perception versus linguistic scrutiny. *Language Learning*, 59, 249–306.
- Birdsong, D. & Molis, M. (2001). On the evidence for maturational effects in second language acquisition. *Journal of Memory and Language*, 44, 235–249.

- Bley-Vroman, R. (1989). What is the logical problem of foreign language learning? In S. Gass & J. Schacter (Eds.), *Linguistic perspectives on second language acquisition* (pp. 41–68). Cambridge: Cambridge University Press.
- Bley-Vroman, R. (2009). The evolving context of the fundamental difference hypothesis. *Studies in Second Language Acquisition*, 31, 175–198.
- Clahsen, H. & Felser, C. (2006). Grammatical processing in language learners. *Applied Psycholinguistics*, 27, 3–42.
- Ioup, G., Boustagui, M., El Tigi, M., & Mosel, M. (1994). Reexamining the Critical Period Hypothesis. *Studies in Second Language Acquisition*, 16, 73–98.
- Johnson, J. & Newport, E. (1989). Critical period effects in second language learning: The influence of maturational state on the acquisition of English as an L2. *Cognitive Psychology*, 21, 60–99.
- Johnson, J. & Newport, E. (1991). Critical period effects on universal properties of language: The status of subjacency in the acquisition of an L2. *Cognition*, 39, 215–258.
- Kanno, K. (1997). The acquisition of null/overt pronominals in Japanese. *Second Language Research*, 13, 265–287.
- Lardiere, D. (1998). Dissociating syntax from morphology in a divergent second language end-state grammar. *Second Language Research*, 14, 359–375.
- Lenneberg, E. (1967). *The biological foundations of language*. New York: John Wiley & Sons.
- Marinis, T., Roberts, L., Felser, C., & Clahsen, H. (2005). Gaps in second language processing. *Studies in Second Language Acquisition*, 27, 53–78.
- Pavesi, M. (1986). Markedness, discoursal modes and relative clause formation in a formal and informal context. *Studies in Second Language Acquisition*, 8, 38–53.
- Pliatiskas, C. & Marinis, T. (2013). Processing empty categories in an L2: When naturalistic input fills the (intermediate) gap. *Bilingualism: Language and Cognition*, 16, 167–182.
- Schwartz, B. (1998). The second language instinct. *Lingua*, 108, 133–160.
- Schwartz, B. & Sprouse, R. (1996). Second language cognitive states and the Full Transfer/Full Access model. *Second Language Research*, 12, 40–72.
- Sorace, A. (2011). Pinning down the concept of "interface" in bilingualism. *Linguistic Approaches to Bilingualism*, 1, 1–33.
- Sorace, A. & Filiaci, F. (2006). Anaphora resolution in near-native speakers of Italian. *Second Language Research*, 22, 339–369.
- White, L. (2003). *Second language acquisition and universal grammar*. Cambridge: Cambridge University Press.

FOLLOWING UP

1. In some circles of L2 research, the idea of whether someone can become native-like or not is questioned because of the definition of native. That is, some researchers question whether there is such a thing as a native speaker and, if there is, whether they all have the same competence in language. Clearly, native speakers diverge on some aspects of language but not on others. Which

of the following do you think are the places where native speakers are more or less likely to diverge? (Consider what it means for natives to be from the "same community.")

- underlying syntax (e.g., constraints on *wh*-movement such as those reviewed in this chapter)
- words and their meanings (e.g., whether the word *politics* means the same thing to all native speakers)
- social appropriateness (e.g., what to say when someone says that a parent has just died)
- forms of verbs (e.g., infrequent verbs in the past such as *strive*)
- inflections on nouns (e.g., adding plural markers such as the 'z' sound on *dog* when saying "dogs" as opposed to the 's' sound added to *cat* when saying "cats")

2. Review your responses from question 1 and now ask "So when we talk about L2 learners becoming nativelike, how should we phrase the question to make it more precise?"

3. In what ways are the Fundamental Difference Hypothesis and the Critical Period Hypothesis related? How do they overlap? Do you think that scholars who believe in one have objections to the points raised in the other or do you think they would more or less agree?

4. Try to articulate on your own three of the basic ideas behind the arguments that nativelikeness is possible in some domains but not others. Can you give examples?

5. Review the Exemplary Study in this chapter and then read the original article in its entirety. How would you revise the summary in this chapter to add additional information? What information would you add, and why that particular information? Hint: Consider creating a table comparing results from the two participants to demonstrate their knowledge and ability.

6. Find ten non-native speakers of English in your community who speak English fairly well in your opinion. Ask them to judge the following sentences. Is each sentence a possible English sentence (sounds OK) or not a possible sentence (doesn't sound OK)? Note: The contraction of *want to* to *wanna* is typical in English and perfectly fine in spoken language, so don't let people get confused that *wanna* is "bad English." The question is does the person accept *wanna* in each sentence as used?

    a. Who do you wanna ask to the party?
    b. What do you wanna make for the picnic?

   c. Who do you wanna call Mary on the phone?
   d. What do you wanna call Mary if she asks for a nickname?
   e. Who do you wanna fire the employee?
   f. What do you wanna fire from this list?

Do your participants' reactions jive with your intuitions about good and bad uses of *wanna*? How about other native speakers? If there is general agreement, would you say these non-natives are nativelike in what they "know" about how *wanna* works in English?

6 | Does Instruction Make a Difference?

Although SLA as a field of research was inspired by early research on child L1 acquisition (see Chapter 1), almost from the beginning research on L2 acquisition began to concern itself with instruction. In other words, researchers asked whether explicit instruction on how language works coupled with practice impacts acquisition in some way. For many readers, the answer may seem intuitively obvious: Of course instruction impacts acquisition! After all, haven't most of us learned a language through some kind of instruction plus practice? As we will see in this chapter, the answer isn't so obvious. In fact, for most people what they did consciously as learners and what actually happened to them unconsciously during acquisition may be unrelated. To understand what instruction does or doesn't do in acquisition, we will begin by looking at instruction and ordered development. But before we do, we need to touch on the issue of **explicit knowledge** versus **implicit knowledge** of language.

Explicit knowledge of language is conscious knowledge. It is often verbalizable, such as "to talk about someone else, add an -s sound to the end of the verb, for example *I/you/we see* versus *he/she sees*." Learners of English might have this explicit knowledge. In a language like Spanish, learners might have a conscious, explicit rule such as "adjectives must agree with nouns so that *un libro es blanco* but *una casa es blanca* ('a book is white-MASC' but 'a house is white-FEM')". Learners might pick up such rules from textbooks, teacher explanations, the Internet, or other places.

Implicit knowledge, on the other hand, is unconscious knowledge. Generally, it is not verbalizable and it bears little resemblance to explicit knowledge. For example, in the case of Spanish noun and adjective agreement, the underlying implicit knowledge might be described by linguists as something like this: "learners' systems know that nouns must 'move up' in the phrase in which they are found in order to get their abstract feature related to gender checked." This probably sounds esoteric and may not make much sense to you (i.e., What's a phrase? What does "move up" mean? What is feature checking?), but see Chapters 4 and 5. The point is that implicit knowledge is qualitatively different from explicit knowledge, which is why most people – native speakers and language learners – cannot verbalize it. As an example of your own implicit knowledge, try to explain the following: You know that re- can be added to verbs to mean to do something again (e.g., *paint/*

repaint, record/rerecord). Why are the following impossible in English? *bake* → **rebake, pet the dog* → **repet the dog, stare at him* → **restare at him*? In short, what's "the rule" for adding *re-* to verbs to mean 'do again'?

Within research on the effects of instruction, an important question is this: To what extent does instruction affect the underlying implicit knowledge that learners have regarding language? We know that instruction can affect explicit knowledge. We see this every time an instructor teaches something, learners practice it, and then the teacher gives a paper-and-pencil test. But acquisition is not about the development of explicit knowledge; acquisition involves the development of implicit knowledge – what we have referred to off and on in this book as underlying mental representation. We also know that implicit knowledge develops as a by-product of input processing in which there is a focus on meaning. We also know that implicit knowledge is qualitatively different from explicit knowledge; that is, it is not explicit knowledge that somehow is now "automatic" and "unconscious." So a fundamental question in the sections that follow is this: Does instruction influence the development of underlying implicit knowledge? (In Chapter 7, we will look at whether there is any relationship between explicit and implicit knowledge.)

Instruction and Ordered Development

You may recall from Chapter 2 that **ordered development** is well documented in L2 acquisition, just as it is in L1 acquisition. Learners acquire morphemes (e.g., verb inflections, noun inflections, articles, linking verbs, auxiliaries) in a certain order over time. In addition, learners have demonstrated clear staged development in the acquisition of particular aspects of language, such as negation, question formation, and other parts of sentence structure.

Our first foray into the question of whether or not instruction makes a difference is to note that the research on ordered development has happened in and out of classrooms. It seems that whether language is learned in classrooms or not makes no difference in ordered development: Order still shows up. As just one example, you may want to review the Exemplary Study by Rod Ellis published in 1989 that appears in Chapter 2. In that study, Ellis sought to determine whether the staged development in the acquisition of German word order that had been documented for non-classroom immigrant learners in Germany would also show up in exclusively classroom learners of German in the United Kingdom. What he found was that it did: The stages of acquisition of German word order were the same in and out of the classroom.

Other such studies have all revealed the same thing. For example, also in the latter part of the 1980s, Maria Pavesi published a study in which she compared what she called formal and informal learners of English as an L2. Their L1 was Italian. The formal learners were all English as foreign language students in Italy. The informal learners were immigrants living in the United Kingdom who had little to no formal training in English and largely "picked up" English from work and friends. The vast majority of these learners were waiters. As Pavesi notes, the major distinction between the formal and informal contexts for her was not just whether learners received explicit instruction but also the type of input learners are exposed to. In formal contexts, such as classrooms, learners are often exposed to more complicated and **planned discourse**. Planned discourse is speech that is not spontaneous and conversational, but rather prepared before it is produced, such as the discourse found in a formal speech (that is read out loud), readings, literature, and so on. Such discourse may contain many more instances of linguistic features not found in everyday spoken language. The informal learners were not exposed to such discourse, at least not on a regular basis like the formal learners.

Pavesi tested her groups on relative clause formation. (You may wish to review the more detailed discussion in Chapter 2 on markedness and relative clauses.) What Pavesi found was that both formal and informal learners obeyed the acquisition orders found for relative clauses. For example, they were able to produce relative clauses on subjects (*Bill is the man who wrote this chapter*) before relative clauses on objects (*Bill is the man who Megan met in 2010*). In turn, they produced subject relative clauses before indirect relative clauses (*Bill is the man Alessandro sent an email to in 1996*), and so on. So learning context (formal versus informal) did not alter the sequence in which these Italian learners of English acquired relative clause formation. (We will return to this study in a later section of this chapter on ultimate attainment.)

Pavesi did find one difference between her formal and informal learners unrelated to ordered development. Her formal learners, when producing non-nativelike relative clauses, tended to use resumptive pronouns in a clause such as *Bill is the man who Alessandro sent an email to him in 1996* more than nouns, as in *Bill is the man who Alessandro sent an email to the man in 1996*. In these two examples you will see that the difference is whether *to him* or *to the man* was inserted into the relative clause. The informal learners showed the reverse, preferring full nouns when producing non-nativelike relative clauses. It is important to note, however, that this difference in "strategy" when producing relative clauses did not alter the sequence; again, subject clauses before direct object clauses before indirect object clauses, and so on. More germane to the present discussion is this: Why would the instructed learners insert anything at all? Clearly, inserting a pronoun copy or a noun copy into the relative clause is not English and certainly was not something they were taught. In a sense, then, the classroom learners were doing the same thing as the non-classroom learners: They just preferred pronouns instead of nouns. While interesting, this does not demonstrate any significant effect of instruction.

If we reviewed all of the studies on ordered development and instruction, we would not find one that actually shows instruction (for formal contexts) altering ordered development in any real way. Interestingly, there are some studies that show negative effects of instruction on ordered development. What we mean by negative effects will become clear in a moment. One study was reported by Patsy Lightbown and appears in this chapter as the Exemplary Study, so you can review that study there. The other study is by Manfred Pienemann and was published in the 1980s.

> If we reviewed all of the studies on ordered development and instruction, we would not find one that actually shows instruction altering ordered development in any real way.

Manfred Pienemann looked at children acquiring German word order (again, see Chapter 2 for details on the acquisition of German word order in the Exemplary Study in that chapter). Pienemann had children who were at different stages of the acquisition of word order. He found two things. One was that no matter what he tried to teach the children, they could not skip stages in the developmental sequence. Instruction did not alter the ordered development. The second finding in his study had to do with readiness. He found that his participants benefitted from instruction only if the instruction was on something related to the next stage of development. If the instruction was "too advanced," it either had no effect or, in the case of one participant, had a detrimental effect. Pienemann found that for that particular participant, she reverted to an earlier stage of development. In short, the advanced instruction actually caused her to regress. Hence, a negative effect for instruction.

Based on his research, Pienemann coined the term "teachability" and launched what he called **the teachability hypothesis**, namely, that instruction was only beneficial if it targeted the next stage in a developmental sequence. Anything other than teaching the next thing the learner was developmentally ready for would result in either no effect or possibly negative effects. Research since the 1980s on this hypothesis has yielded mixed results. In their 2017 book, Bronwen Patricia Dyson and Gisela Håkansson summarize the research on the teachability hypothesis. They point out that the evidence for beneficial or detrimental effects of instruction are mixed. However, the research is consistent in that stages cannot be skipped or changed. Once again, instruction does not seem to alter ordered development.

Consider this ...

The research has shown that instruction does not alter ordered development. The data used in most of the research is spontaneous or semi-spontaneous oral data, not paper-and-pencil tests. Does the fact that ordered development is unaffected by instruction mean that the underlying implicit knowledge is not affected by instruction? Most researchers would argue that yes, it does mean that implicit knowledge is not affected. How would you make the argument?

To conclude this section, we will point out several things. First, research on instruction and ordered development has been conducted from different frameworks, using various kinds of assessment tasks to see what learners know and can do, and has been conducted in various contexts (e.g., with children, with adolescents, with adults, with different languages in different countries). Ordered development always seems to assert itself, so it is probably not the case that we haven't tried the right instructional technique or we have found that instruction has no impact on this kind of learner but may have an impact on a different kind of learner. Second, although it is now accepted that instruction does not seem to alter ordered development in any significant way, if at all, it does not necessarily follow that instruction has absolutely no effect. The next sections of this chapter discuss the effects of instruction unrelated to ordered development.

Exemplary Study

Lightbown, P. M. (1983). Exploring relationships between developmental and instructional sequences in second language acquisition. In H. W. Seliger & M. H. Long (Eds.), *Classroom oriented research* (pp. 217–245). Rowley, MA: Newbury House.

Participants

- 36 students in grade 6
- L1 = French; L2 = English
- location: Quebec
- students rarely used English outside of class including with friends, business, TV and so on

Major Target Item

- various morphemes in English, but we will focus here on -*ing* (*He's eating*) and 3rd person -*s* (*He eats*)
- recall that -*ing* is acquired relatively early and 3rd person–*s* is acquired relatively late

Materials and Procedure

- Participants were recorded three times during the sixth grade, spaced at roughly equal intervals.
- Each participant was engaged in "picture games" consisting of the participant describing a picture and the interviewer trying to determine which picture (from an array) the participant was describing.
- The pictures were designed to create "obligatory contexts" for the use of -*ing* and -*s* on verbs.

Results

- At the first recording, learners were producing correct -*ing* verbs about 56 percent of the time; by the third recording, their correct use of -*ing* dropped to about 30 percent.
- Use of 3rd person -*s* started at about 5 percent and increased to about 20 percent.
- Interestingly, bare verbs (uninflected verbs as in *He take the cake* for "He's taking the cake") were used about 42 percent of the time at the first recording, increased to about 60 percent, then dropped to about 52 percent.
- In short, learners got worse overall at using verbs in English to talk about actions in progress and iterative (repeated) activities over the course of the year.
- When the researchers looked at textbook materials and what teachers emphasized in class (i.e., explicitly worked on), they could see no relationship between that and what the learners were doing with verbs.

Conclusion

- Although there was a strong focus on grammatical accuracy in the learners' ESL classrooms, this did not affect their acquisition of English verbal morphemes.
- What is more, the increase in bare verbs shows natural acquisition processes asserting themselves, given that this is where learners normally start when producing verbs in English; in short, these classroom learners' internal systems were "overriding" what was happening in class. That is, they were overriding the emphasis on -*ing* and -*s* to "start at the beginning."

Instruction and Rate of Development

Another area of focus for research on the effects of instruction has been **rate of development**. Rate of development refers to the relative speed with which learners progress through ordered development. One claim has been that classroom learners progress through ordered development more quickly than non-classroom learners; that is, their rate of development is faster. This idea was first launched by Michael Long in a well-known essay he published in 1983, "Does second language instruction make a difference?" He reviewed almost a dozen studies comparing classroom and non-classroom learners. None of the studies showed that ordered development could be altered, but he did find that six of the studies concluded that acquisition seemed to proceed faster under instruction. The rest of the studies showed no effect or at best a marginal effect.

In a 1988 essay, Bill VanPatten argued that the findings of the research reviewed by Long must be taken with caution for several reasons. One major reason is that it is problematic to conclude that it is actual instruction on formal properties of language that distinguish classroom and non-classroom environments. As Maria Pavesi pointed out in her research (see the previous section on instruction and ordered development), there is a qualitative difference in input and discourse when we compare classrooms and non-classrooms. The spoken everyday language of non-classrooms that immigrant learners tend to encounter is not as rich, elaborate, and complicated as classroom language. This is especially true when we consider the push to make classroom learners read written texts as soon as possible. Written texts contain longer sentences compared to everyday spoken language and they also contain many more subordinate clauses of varying types. This kind of language pushes learners to process formal features of language and hold them in working memory as they make their way through sentences. In a sense, the language of written texts is "more challenging" and may push learners in a classroom to do more internal mental work than learners in non-classrooms who aren't working at being literate. Classroom input and written texts also contain more examples of marked aspects of language and a broader range of vocabulary. All of these differences most likely work to give classroom learners richer input compared to non-classroom learners, especially when the latter are not working toward any degree of literacy.

VanPatten also argued that it might not be appropriate to compare classroom and non-classroom learners, especially if the latter consist of economically and politically motivated immigrants. Their reasons for learning a language may be quite different from those of classroom learners and their support for acquisition may be less. What is more, they may not have as much access to input and speakers of the language as researchers think they do. Consider for a moment the

Italian immigrants in Pavesi's study. Why were they in the UK? And what were their occupations? Clearly, they were there for economic reasons and not to learn English. They worked largely in service, with most of them being waiters. How much English does a waiter need to learn to be a waiter in the UK? And who are the friends and networks of people with whom these waiters interact? Many must have families and live in neighborhoods with other immigrants. Who do they identify with? Thus, their interactions with native speakers of British English may be limited. Compare this scenario to one of the authors of this book. He emigrated to the UK from Italy to pursue graduate work, eventually earning a Ph.D. in Applied Linguistics. He married an English-speaking Irish woman and raised his children in the London area. His network and support group consists not of other Italian speakers but instead of native speakers of English, including his immediate family. This is another instance in which social factors influence acquisition, a point we will return to later in this chapter.

The point of these comparisons is that motivation and the consequences of that motivation for learning a language may profoundly

> No strong case can be made for instruction speeding up acquisition. Classroom learners may be faster than non-classroom learners for a variety of reasons unrelated to instruction.

affect how fast and how far one goes in the acquisition process. The research comparing classroom and non-classroom learners has tended not to take such factors into consideration. For this reason, we must take with a grain of salt that it is the focus on formal elements of the classroom that causes the differences that Long observed in his review of studies back in 1983. With that said, we can't rule out completely that instruction isn't an important variable in such studies either. Instead, we are simply saying no strong case can be made for instruction speeding up acquisition. Classroom learners may be faster than non-classroom learners for a variety of reasons: the quality of input, motivation, access to interaction with speakers of the language, among others, as well as instruction itself (if at all).

Since the 1980s, there has been little direct work comparing classroom and non-classroom learners. As we will see in a later section, most research on the effects of instruction has focused on short-term comparative studies of classroom learners only. So for now, it seems that the jury is out on whether instruction on formal features of language is the causative variable to explain why, in some cases, classroom learners seem to acquire language faster than non-classroom learners. What is more, if there is an effect on rate, it is not clear if the rate is on explicit knowledge or implicit knowledge. Classrooms may help learners build up explicit knowledge quickly; but they may or may not accelerate the development of implicit knowledge. Much depends on what is measured in the research (i.e., what kind of "tests" are given to learners). We will discuss this issue in a later section in this chapter.

Instruction and Ultimate Attainment

Somewhat related to rate of acquisition is ultimate attainment. **Ultimate attainment** refers to how far learners progress and to what degree they approach anything that looks nativelike. You may recall from Chapter 5, which asked whether learners can become nativelike, that although nativelikeness seems to be possible, it is not the norm for most L2 learners. In this section, we will discuss the extent to which instruction affects how far learners get in acquisition.

Very little research has been conducted in this area and little research can be used to address the question in an indirect way. For the present discussion, we will focus on two studies that are suggestive. The first is the Maria Pavesi study reviewed in the first section of this chapter. Pavesi compared formal (classroom) and informal (non-classroom) learners of English with Italian as an L1. She looked at their acquisition of relative clauses. You may recall that she found that instruction did not alter ordered development: Both groups acquired relative clauses in the same order. She did find that there was a strategy difference when producing non-native relative clauses. The classroom group tended to use resumptive pronouns (e.g., *Bill is the man who Megan met him seven years ago*) while non-classroom learners tended to use nouns (e.g., *Bill is the man who Megan met the man seven years ago*).

Pavesi also found one other difference between the two groups. While the order of acquisition was the same for both groups of learners, significantly more classroom learners acquired more types of relative clauses than non-classroom learners. You may remember that the order of acquisition is this: subject clause → direct object clause → indirect object clause → oblique clause → genitive clause → object of comparison clause. Pavesi found that many more classroom learners showed knowledge of and ability with object of comparison clauses compared with non-classroom learners, for example. This did not mean that non-classroom learners did not acquire object of comparison clauses. Some did. The point is that significantly more classroom learners than non-classroom learners did.

One interpretation of this particular finding is that somehow classrooms help learners get further down the acquisition path. That is, classroom learners may reach higher levels of ultimate attainment for some things in language when they are compared to non-classroom learners. Pavesi herself did not conclude that these results were necessarily a reflection of instruction on relative clauses. Instead, her conclusion was that classroom learners, because of the focus on high degrees of literacy, tend to get more elaborate input (see the discussion in the previous section on rate of acquisition). More elaborate input contains more relative clauses and more types of relative clauses. Non-classroom learners, if exposed largely to spoken speech, would encounter many fewer relative clauses and fewer types of relative clause. For Pavesi, then, the differences she found in ultimate attainment for her two groups of learners comes down to quality (and possibly quantity) of input.

To be sure, as we said earlier, we cannot completely rule out an effect for instruction itself for higher levels of ability with relative clauses in Pavesi's study. Another study that compares advanced classroom and advanced non-classroom learners might shed some light on this issue. Jason Rothman published a study in 2008 in which he looked at classroom and non-classroom learners of Spanish as L2 with English as L1. He was interested in their acquisition and use of the preterit and imperfect verb forms in Spanish. The preterit and imperfect are past-tense verb forms used to encode information about how a speaker views a particular event relative to a point in time in the past. The distinction between the two and how they are used involves complex and abstract information that we cannot describe in this chapter. What is critical here are two things: (1) much of the difference in use between the two verb forms is difficult to teach and is not readily clear from the input that learners hear or see; (2) English has no such contrasting verb forms so learners cannot transfer any knowledge or ability with the past tense into learning Spanish as an L2.

Rothman tested his learners of Spanish using a cloze-selection task based on Goldilocks and the Three Bears as well as a sentence-level completion task. The cloze-selection task required the participants to read the story and select from the verb choices available. The sentence-level completion task was basically a fill-in-the-blank test in which participants had to write in a verb form based on what they understood from the sentence. He also tested a group of native speakers of Spanish for comparative purposes.

Rothman's results are somewhat surprising. On the Goldilocks cloze-selection test, there was no significant difference in how the native speakers and the non-classroom learners performed. However, there was a significant difference in how the native speakers performed and how the classroom learners performed, as well as a significant difference between how the non-classroom and the classroom learners performed. In all comparisons, the natives and the non-classroom learners performed at higher levels compared to the classroom group. On the sentence-level completion task, Rothman obtained the same results: The native and non-classroom learners performed similarly, with both groups better than the classroom learners.

What Rothman's results suggest is that the classroom learners did not fare as well as the non-classroom learners; that is, they weren't getting as far in acquisition. So perhaps classroom instruction (and the classroom learners did receive regular instruction on the past-tense verb forms throughout their studies of Spanish) was actually detrimental. Before accepting this conclusion, we need to examine one other possibility: namely, that the non-classroom group was already at a higher level of proficiency compared to the classroom group. If this were the case, then we would expect them to perform better. Rothman did not include a general test of proficiency so there could have been a real difference between the groups from the outset. However, an interesting aspect of his study might lead us to lean more toward the detrimental effect of instruction in this particular case. When Rothman analyzed the actual non-nativelike responses, he found that the classroom learners were non-nativelike precisely on those items on which they could apply pedagogical rules they had learned. These rules are simplified and somewhat erroneous in what they describe. For example, one such rule is that stative verbs such as 'be' and 'have' typically occur in the imperfect. This led the classroom learners in Rothman's study to overuse the imperfect with these verbs when the preterit was required. The non-classroom learners had no access to such a rule. Another example is with the verb *querer*, for which learners are taught lexical translations; in the imperfect the verb means 'want' but in the preterit it means 'tried to.' This is not necessarily the case (certainly they don't mean two different things to native speakers), and in the tests that Rothman used he noticed the classroom learners not using the preterit with *querer* when it indeed meant 'want.' Again, the non-classroom learners did not exhibit this kind of error, as they had no recourse to such pedagogical rules.

If classroom learners are filtering the input through pedagogical rules by attaching the wrong function or meaning to items they encounter in the input, this may slow down acquisition and affect ultimate attainment

In short, Rothman's research is suggestive: If classroom learners are learning and applying pedagogical rules and/or if they filter the input through these pedagogical rules by attaching the wrong function or meaning to items they encounter in the language surrounding them, this may slow down acquisition and/or negatively affect ultimate attainment.

Missing from the research on ultimate attainment are **long-term studies**. That is, there is no real research that looks at how instruction at one time affects learners many years down the road. Such research would be extremely difficult to conduct for all kinds of reasons. But the main reason is that such a study cannot control for the most important **intervening variable**: input. An intervening variable is a factor that influences the outcomes of a study that a researcher cannot account for or control. In the case of ultimate attainment, a researcher cannot control the variation of quantity and quality of input, and interaction with that input, that learners receive over the years. Most recent research on the effects of instruction (over the last several decades) has focused on short-term studies of the effects of instruction. We will turn our attention to this kind of research in the next section.

What about Social Factors?

As mentioned in Chapter 5, identity is a powerful factor that shapes and guides how we feel about language acquisition as well as our behaviors in acquiring another language. Scholars working in the area of social context and identity offer clear examples of how a learner's feelings toward the environment or how that learner feels about being part of another culture may work against acquisition. Bonnie Norton, for example, wrote about Mai in 1997. Mai was a Vietnamese immigrant who'd made tremendous effort and sacrifice to attend an evening ESL course to improve her English. However, the teacher's method and the focus on students bothered Mai so much she eventually stopped attending. This clearly affected how the classroom might have helped Mai in any way. Socially, she just couldn't connect with that particular classroom community. And way back in the late 1970s John Schumann described what he called the pidginization process. In a longitudinal case study, Schumann examined Alberto's development of English. Alberto was an economically motivated immigrant from Central America who had a low-paying job in the Boston area. Schumann found that Alberto's English hardly developed during the time Schumann studied him and attributed this in part to Alberto's non-identification with the new culture he was in. Alberto seemed to be fine with "good enough to get the job done." He had no real intention of integrating into a new culture.

In short, both context and identity can affect learner motivation, which in turn affects the efforts they make to engage with the second language. This is true both in and out of the classroom. As such, these factors affect rate and ultimate attainment.

The Effects of Instruction and Short-Term Studies

It is fair to say that dozens of studies – well over a hundred – have been conducted on the effects of instruction on L2 acquisition using what is called **short-term** research design. By this, we mean that measurement of what learners can do or what they know is conducted immediately after instruction or soon after (usually within a month). Only a handful of studies have examined the effects of instruction over a longer period (i.e., six months to a year), which we will discuss a bit later. These short-term studies may take place in a classroom with whole groups of students as participants or they may take place in laboratories where participants undergo a treatment individually via computer-mediated instruction. In most such research, the standard design is: (1) pre-test the learners to see what they know or can do with linguistic feature X, (2) provide some kind of treatment (instruction) on X, (3) post-test the learners and compare results to the pre-test. If for (2) there are different kinds of treatments being compared, then in step (3) the research also compares the groups' performance relative to each other.

Analyses of this line of research (called **meta-analyses**), in which all eligible studies are submitted to statistical analysis to determine the strength of any effects of instruction, have concluded that instruction makes a difference. (Eligibility includes such things as appropriate and full reporting of statistical information, inclusion of such things as means, standard deviations, sample sizes, and so on, for all groups in a study.) For example, John Norris and Lourdes Ortega published one such meta-analysis in 2000. After combing through the many studies that had been conducted prior to 2000, they found that 49 met the criteria to be included in a meta-analysis. Their conclusion was that there did seem to be some benefit to instruction. That is, overall, the studies showed that learners were better on post-test measures than on pre-test measures. However, Norris and Ortega offered several very important caveats regarding this finding – caveats that we will review in a minute.

In 2010, Nina Spada and Yasuyo Tomita published another meta-analysis. They located 41 eligible studies investigating whether explicit instruction (that is, explaining things to learners / giving them "rules" as part of the instructional treatment) yielded different outcomes from implicit instruction (instructional treatment in which explanation about what was being learned was not included). What they determined was that, overall, there was an effect for instruction and the effect was greater for learners engaged in explicit instruction. Again, "effect" was determined by comparing post-test scores to pre-test scores. A similar study was conducted by Jaemyung Goo and his colleagues, published in 2015 with similar results.

At first blush, it seems that instruction does make a difference. These meta-analyses, which summarize all the eligible research, point to positive effects for instruction on grammatical properties of language. At the same time, a number of questions arise that cause us to take such conclusions with caution. These questions include the following:

- What is it that the researcher is measuring? What does it mean to "know" something? In particular, does the research on the effects of instruction measure explicit knowledge or implicit knowledge (and what does the researcher think is in the implicit knowledge)?
- What kind of task can be used to measure what learners know and how do we know it is a valid measurement?
- If we are looking at what learners can do after treatment, the same questions apply about what is measured and how it is measured.
- What is the nature of the treatment? What is it trying to affect? Does the treatment attempt to affect explicit knowledge or implicit knowledge (or something else)?

- How does the treatment reflect what we know about acquisition more generally and what does the researcher believe he or she is "altering" in the learner? That is, what underlying "processes" does the instruction attempt to affect?

Norris and Ortega, for example, provide a significant caveat in their discussion that it is not clear that most of the studies they included in their meta-analysis measured implicit knowledge. In fact, the opposite seemed to be true: 90 percent of the studies in the meta-analysis used tests that probably measured explicit knowledge. They suggest that had different kinds of tests been used, then the outcome for the effects of instruction they observed might have been different. Catherine Doughty, in a 2003 critique of such research, argued that there is a bias toward explicit knowledge and the testing of explicit knowledge in research on the effects of instruction.

> According to a number of scholars, there is a bias toward the testing of explicit knowledge in research on the effects of instruction.

To see what all of this means, let's imagine a researcher is interested in whether instruction makes a difference in the acquisition of passive structures such as *The cow was kicked by the horse*. Let's suppose that the researcher uses Chinese and Turkish learners of English as an L2, largely because these languages form passives differently from each other and quite differently from how passives are formed in English. The researcher gives a pre-test and finds the learners are terrible with passives. Then some kind of treatment or instruction is provided to learners on passives followed by a post-test similar to the one given as a pre-test. The learners all perform significantly better. The researcher concludes that instruction made a difference. In this fictitious but stereotypical study, we have to ask ourselves how learners were tested on their knowledge of passives and how that test avoided learners using the explicit knowledge they gained during the treatment as opposed to any fundamental change in underlying implicit knowledge. What if the researcher asked the learners to "judge" sentences by indicating whether the sentence was grammatical or ungrammatical or "good" or "bad," as in these three examples (the first is good; the second two are not):

> The cow was kicked by the horse.
> The cat was bitten the dog.
> The mouse trapped by the cat.

Asking learners to judge sentences about something they have just learned about most likely invites them to use their new explicit knowledge. "Now let's see. I just learned about passives. So is this sentence trying to be a passive? Is it correctly formed? No it's not. Oh, there's a *by* missing in this sentence ..." Alternatively, as in some published research, our participants might be given a prompt and asked to write out a sentence. In our fictitious passive study, participants might get a picture of a cat being bitten by a dog. On a piece of paper or on a computer screen, the participant is told to complete this sentence based on what is in the picture: "The cat _____." Again, this type of measurement invites the use of explicit knowledge. "Let's see now. We just learned about passives so I'm assuming they want me to use a passive here. How was that formed again? Oh yeah, I need a form of 'be' and also I have to use 'by.' I think it's 'the cat is bited by the dog." Note that the learner doesn't have to get the past participle correct in order to engage explicit knowledge. The learner is consciously applying what he or she remembers about the overall rule.

As we said above, research on the effects of instruction cannot mimic what happens in classrooms; we know that instruction "makes a difference" for test-taking in classrooms. Research has to have measurements that probe underlying implicit knowledge that is qualitatively different from explicit knowledge. This has proven to be elusive for researchers. Let's look at a different example to see the opposite: how instruction is questionable if we attempt to measure implicit knowledge.

In 2012, Bill VanPatten and his colleagues, Gregory Keating and Michael Leeser, published a paper in which they used what is called **self-paced reading** to determine learners' sensitivity to violations of various structures in Spanish (the learners' L1 was English). In self-paced reading, a participant sits in front of a computer screen and reads a sentence in bits and pieces. After reading the sentences, the participant answers a comprehension question about the content of what was just read, not about its well-formedness as a sentence (i.e., they are not asked to judge whether a sentence was good or bad). So what a participant initially sees on the screen is a series of blanks, such as this:

_____ _____ _____ _____ _____ _____

As the participant presses a button, a blank disappears to reveal part of the sentence, as in:

Now _____ _____ _____ _____ _____

When the participant presses the button again, the part that was just revealed disappears and the next part appears, as in:

_____ I lay _____ _____ _____ _____

And this continues with each button press, as in

_____ _____ me _____ _____ _____ [press button]
_____ _____ _____ down _____ _____ [press button]
_____ _____ _____ _____ to _____ [press button]
_____ _____ _____ _____ _____ sleep [press button]

In short, the participant reads at his or her own pace, with each piece of the sentence appearing one at time, hence the name "self-paced reading." As buttons are pressed, this procedure pushes the reader to keep in mind what he or she just read to "build the sentence" and its meaning. Researchers manipulate parts of sentences to include wrong or odd things and the software records the reading time for each segment (we will see examples in a minute). The researcher then compares these reading times with the segments from other sentences in which nothing was wrong or odd. After the participant reads a sentence, a button press reveals a question about the content of the sentence, thus encouraging the reader to focus on meaning and not on how the sentence is formed. What this kind of research demonstrates is that even if learners are focused on meaning, there are generally slightly longer reading times on sentence segments that contain wrong or odd things compared to those that don't.

Here are two examples from VanPatten, Keating, and Leeser's study. Both sentences mean 'Right now I'm drinking a soda in the cafeteria.' However, the second sentence is ungrammatical in that verb form means 'he's drinking' not 'I'm drinking.' That is, the verb and subject do not match. (Note: The slash '/' indicates the segments that appeared one at a time during self-paced reading.)

Ahora /yo /tomo /un refresco/ en/ la cafetería. [match]
Ahora/ yo /toma/ un refresco/ en/ la cafetería. [do not match]

The sentence was followed by a comprehension question "In the sentence you just read, the person is drinking something cold. True or False?" VanPatten, Keating, and Leeser measured the reading times on the verb forms and the phrase immediately after the verb (called the "spillover region" – sometimes there is a lag in reading and the longer reading time happens in the spillover region).

They also looked at sentences such as the following. Again, the first sentence is grammatical and the second is ungrammatical and both mean 'Robert no longer travels to France because he has no money.' (The ungrammaticality has to do with word order in that Spanish puts the verb between the 'no' and the 'longer' whereas English puts the verb after 'longer.')

Roberto/ no viaja más/ a Francia/ porque/ no tiene/ dinero. [word order like Spanish]
Roberto/ no más viaja/ a Francia/ porque/ no tiene/ dinero. [word order like English]

The sentence was followed by a comprehension question "In the sentence you just read, the person has extra money for travel. True or false?" What the researchers compared were the reading times on *no viaja más* and *no más viaja* as well as the spillover region *a Francia*. Their participants were native speakers of Spanish and intermediate-level learners of Spanish who were taking their first courses in Spanish literature and culture. Note that this was not a study on effects of instruction: that is, there was no pre-test, treatment, and post-test. The researchers were simply testing learners on their underlying knowledge of particular features of

Spanish to answer a question unrelated to instruction. But the study and results are actually relevant to the discussion at hand.

What VanPatten, Keating, and Leeser found was that on the sentences where the verb did not match the subject, native speakers slowed down on the expected areas of the sentence when there was a mismatch. The L2 learners did not. However, on the sentences where word order was an issue, both native speakers and the L2 learners slowed down. What is significant about these findings is that learners are taught subject–verb agreement and practice it almost from the first day of learning. It is also something they receive feedback on and are tested on. However, the word order with *no VERB más* is not taught and is a very infrequent structure in the language these learners were exposed to. In short, on the thing for which they did not receive instruction, these intermediate learners performed in a manner similar to native speakers. On the thing for which they did receive instruction and feedback over the years, they showed no sensitivity to grammatical violations. The question is this: What happened to all that instruction, practice, feedback, and testing on verb forms? And how could these learners perform like native speakers on something else for which they did not receive instruction, practice, and so on? For the second question, we know this to be a poverty of the stimulus situation (see Chapters 2 and 5). Learners have come to know more about the language than what they were exposed to. However, for the first question, it is not clear what happened to all the instruction, practice, and so on regarding subject–verb agreement in Spanish. All we can suggest here is that, as in the case of the Lightbown study and others like it, instruction does not seem to override how such things as verb forms get into learners' mental representation. Something internal to the learner is in charge of that.

Before continuing, it might be beneficial to make an observation about research methodology. In this regard, two interesting things emerge from the VanPatten, Keating, and Leeser study. First, the study shows how something like self-paced reading can be used to measure underlying implicit knowledge – or lack of it. Because participants' attention is on reading for meaning and reading times are measures of unconsciously "detecting something funny," this kind of measurement may be more appropriate for use in research on the effects of instruction. A second interesting thing is that the researchers included completely unrelated structures, which increases the internal validity of the study. Thus, the results of the *no VERB más* reading times have to be an indication of implicit knowledge because such structures are not taught or practiced. Thus, the results of subject–verb reading times – in which no sensitivity was demonstrated – suggest that in the implicit knowledge of the learners, subject–verb agreement just wasn't there yet. We can only make this conclusion because the researchers had other structures for comparison – structures on which the learners had no instruction or practice. (For the record, the researchers also had a third structure – also not taught or practiced in Spanish language classrooms and for which the learners showed sensitivity to ungrammaticality just like native speakers – but we want to keep the presentation simple here.)

Consider this …

We said early on in this chapter that there is a qualitative difference between explicit knowledge and implicit knowledge. One way to look at this is that explicit knowledge tests "rules": the kinds of rules we find in textbooks, teacher explanations, online sites, and so on. Implicit knowledge, on the other hand, does not look like rules as teachers and students think of rules. As Bill VanPatten and Jason Rothman have argued in a 2014 publication, mental representation cannot be rules in the classic sense. Language is too abstract and complex to be captured by textbook rules. Even a rule as seemingly simple as "subjects have nominative case and objects have accusative case" is violated in English whenever *and* is used as in "Me and Bob are going" as opposed to "Bob and I are going." This is because what actually underlies how subject pronouns and object pronouns are used is much more abstract than the textbook rule. (By the way, try saying this to yourself: "I and Bob are going." Doesn't it sound awful?) So we may not make headway in research on the effects of instruction until researchers grapple with the nature of implicit knowledge as opposed to explicit "rules."

The point we are making, as we did in earlier sections of this chapter, is not that instruction makes no difference. Instead, the point is that we cannot rely on the research to tell us instruction does make a difference – at least not on the underlying implicit knowledge we are interested in. As stated earlier, there is a clear and overwhelming bias toward testing explicit knowledge in the research on the effects of instruction.

Absent so far in this discussion are issues related to several of the questions we listed earlier. They are repeated here:

- What is the nature of the treatment? What is it trying to affect?
- How does the treatment reflect what we know about acquisition more generally and what does the researcher believe he or she is "altering" in the learner?

To date, no systematic analysis of treatments has been conducted on the research regarding the effects of instruction. Two of the meta-analyses referred to earlier (Spada & Tomita, Goo et al.) did separate what they call explicit instruction from implicit instruction. The basic difference between explicit and implicit instruction in the meta-analyses centers on whether teachers (or computers) teach participants rules and whether participants know what they are learning and/or "practicing." Under explicit instruction, learners get rules and know what they are learning; under implicit instruction, learners don't get rules and presumably don't know what they're learning. Unfortunately, such a division of treatments is too broad to be meaningful because within each group there is such variation in what is actually taught and how it is taught as to render the two categories meaningless. Some of these matters will be addressed in the next chapter on the roles of explicit and implicit learning, but for now we can examine one example to see the problem. In these meta-analyses, explicit instruction may contain a treatment in which learners read a rule, write out sentences and practice, and perform other kinds of activities. Implicit instruction may contain a treatment in which learners hear sentences, one after the other and then select from several pictures to indicate what they understood the sentence to mean. Clearly, we are comparing apples and oranges when we lump studies under one category or another. That is, we cannot tease out if the results are due to explicit versus implicit instruction or the actual treatment used in particular studies.

What is more, this broad definition of explicit versus implicit learning ignores the fundamental problem we have identified above: the inherent bias in the research on testing explicit knowledge and not understanding that implicit knowledge is qualitatively different.

Before concluding, we should touch on the issue of longer-term effects of instruction. As mentioned in the section on ultimate attainment earlier, the problems of doing actual long-term research (i.e., over years) to see if the effects of instruction exist are insurmountable. Still, there have been a handful of studies that have looked at **the long(er)-term effects** of instruction, meaning after several months to a year. In 2004, Bill VanPatten and Claudia Fernández published a study in which they reviewed the four studies that could be considered longer-term. In none of those studies did the effects of instruction show up at a later date. That is, when the researchers went back to test learners' performance on the things they were taught, the short-term effects had disappeared. In VanPatten and Fernández's own study using processing instruction, they tested learners eight months after instruction. They found that although learners performed significantly better on the delayed post-test compared to the pre-test, their scores had still declined significantly after the short-term post-test. One could speculate that if VanPatten and Fernández had returned several months later and tested again, they might find the effects of their treatment to have disappeared altogether – in line with the studies they reviewed as part of the background to their own research.

> In none of the longer-term studies (in which researchers have tested learners up to a year later) did the effects of instruction show up. Short-term effects seem to disappear over time.

We conclude this section with the same caveat we have stated in previous sections. Even though the research to date does not suggest that instruction has short-term effects on implicit knowledge, this does not necessarily mean that it couldn't.

As we pointed out, we need more sophisticated research designs that use measurements (tests) that attempt to test implicit knowledge and not explicit knowledge. For now, the best conclusion about research on the effects of instruction is this: Instruction clearly helps explicit knowledge, at least in the short run. It is not clear what it does, if anything, for the implicit mental representation we call "language."

Recap

Here are some major ideas and topics covered in this chapter.

- There is a qualitative difference between explicit and implicit knowledge of language. Researchers are interested in the development of implicit knowledge.
- Instruction on formal features of language does not affect ordered development such as morpheme orders and staged development. Instruction does not change the order in which things are acquired.
- It is not clear that instruction on formal features of language speeds up acquisition. There are important intervening variables (e.g., quality of input) that need to be considered when comparing those who get instruction and those who do not.
- It is not clear that instruction on formal features of language affects ultimate attainment. It is almost impossible to do this kind of research.
- It is not clear that instruction on formal features of language affects short-term gains in acquisition. Too much of the research is biased toward the testing of explicit knowledge.
- For the research on the effects of instruction to make advances, it needs to consider ways in which to assess implicit knowledge along with a consideration of what implicit knowledge actually is.

REFERENCES AND READINGS

- Doughty, C. J. (2003). Instructed SLA: Constraints, compensation, and enhancement. In C. J. Doughty & M. H. Long (Eds.), *The handbook of second language acquisition* (pp. 206–257). New York: Blackwell.
- Dyson, B. P. & Håkansson, G. (2017). *Understanding second language processing: A focus on processability theory.* Amsterdam: John Benjamins.
- Ellis, R. (1989). Are classroom and naturalistic acquisition the same? A study of the classroom acquisition of the German word order rules. *Studies in Second Language Acquisition*, 11, 303–328.
- Goo, J., Granena, G., Yilmaz, Y., & Novella, M. (2015). Implicit and explicit instruction in second language learning: Norris and Ortega (2000) revisited and updated. In P. Rebuschat (Ed.), *Implicit and explicit learning of languages* (pp. 443–482). Amsterdam: John Benjamins.

- Long, M. H. (1983). Does second language instruction make a difference? A review of research. *TESOL Quarterly*, 17, 359–382.
- Norris, J. & Ortega, L. (2000). Effectiveness of second language instruction: A research synthesis and quantitative meta-analysis. *Language Learning*, 50, 417–528.
- Norton, B. (1997). Language, identity, and the ownership of English. *TESOL Quarterly*, 31, 409–429.
- Pavesi, M. (1986). Markedness, discoursal modes, and relative clause formation in a formal and an informal context. *Studies in Second Language Acquisition*, 8, 38–55.
- Pienemann, M. (1984). Psychological constraints on the teachability of languages. *Studies in Second Language Acquisition*, 6, 186–214.
- Rothman, J. (2008). Aspect selection in adult second language Spanish and the Competing Systems hypothesis: When pedagogical and linguistic rules conflict. *Languages in Contrast*, 8, 74–106.
- Schumann, J. (1978). *The pidginization hypothesis.* Rowley, MA: Newbury House.
- Spada, N. & Tomita, Y. (2010). Interactions between type of instruction and type of language feature: A meta-analysis. *Language Learning*, 60, 263–308.
- VanPatten, B. (1988). How juries get hung: Problems with the evidence for the effects of a focus on form. *Language Learning*, 38, 243–260.
- VanPatten, B. (2016). Why explicit knowledge cannot turn into implicit knowledge. *Foreign Language Annals*, 49, 650–657.
- VanPatten, B. & Fernández, C. (2004). The long-term effects of processing instruction. In B. VanPatten (Ed.), *Processing instruction: Theory, research, and commentary* (pp. 273–289). Mahwah, NJ: Erlbaum.
- VanPatten, B. & Rothman, J. (2014). Against "rules." In A. Benati, C. Laval, & M. J. Arche (Eds.), *The grammar dimension in instructed second language acquisition: Theory, research, and practice* (pp. 15–35). London: Bloomsbury.
- VanPatten, B., Keating, G. D., & Leeser, M. J. (2012). Missing verbal inflections as a representational issue: Evidence from on-line methodology. *Linguistic Approaches to Bilingualism*, 2, 109–140.

FOLLOWING UP

1. Explicit and implicit knowledge do not just differ in terms of whether the knowledge is verbalizable or not. The two knowledge types also differ in terms of substance (what that knowledge actually is). Read either VanPatten and Rothman, "Against 'rules'" or VanPatten, "Why explicit information cannot become implicit knowledge" (see References and Readings) and prepare a 100-word summary (or less) on implicit knowledge. Then conduct your own research to see if you can find different definitions of the nature of (implicit) linguistic knowledge.

2. Explain why you agree or do not agree with the following statement: Because instruction in grammar does not affect ordered development, there is no need to worry about grammar in language teaching.

3. A recurring theme in L2 research concerns the types of assessments we use to measure L2 knowledge and ability. Conduct a search on the following types of tasks in order to define each and offer examples, explaining what the task attempts to measure.

   • grammaticality judgments
   • truth-value tests
   • sentence-combination tasks
   • information-gap tasks
   • self-paced reading.

4. One of the findings of long(er)-term research is that the effects of instruction seem to fade after time. In the handful of studies we have that actually measure development or knowledge many months later or up to a year later, we see marked declines in performance on tests. In most cases, learners are back where they were before instruction. Make an argument for why this would be the case. (Hint: What are the data for language acquisition? How does language get in your head?)

5. Pavesi's research suggests there is a difference in the type of language learners are exposed to in and out of the classroom, especially if classrooms are dealing with literacy. Select a reading from a second-year or intermediate-level text in the language you teach or will teach. At the same time, record an hour of conversation between two people in the same language (or use dialogue from TV or a movie if you don't have access to speakers; reality TV would be best). For both data sets, analyze them for the following.

   • length of sentence (i.e., mean number of words per sentence)
   • ratio of sentences with embedded clauses to single-clause sentences
   • percentage of person–number marking on verbs (i.e., 1st singular, 2nd singular, 3rd singular, and so on)
   • something else you would like to look at.

   Present your findings and decide whether indeed the language in the two environments is different.

6. Imagine a teacher or someone else saying, "Of course instruction makes a difference. I see it all the time in my students." What would you say to this person?

7. Conduct some bibliographic research on the teaching of pronunciation or the teaching of vocabulary. Try to find at least five studies. How do they measure the effects of instruction? Are the issues raised in this chapter valid for those areas of instructed SLA as well?

What Role Does Explicit Learning Play in L2 Acquisition?

In Chapter 6, we concluded that instruction on the formal properties of language does little to alter acquisition. In this chapter, we look at a somewhat related issue, namely, the role of explicit learning. As we will see, the issues are different in that in Chapter 6 we looked at what effect, if any, outside interventions by teachers and textbooks have on acquisition. In this chapter, we focus on what the learner does during comprehension.

But before we get into the topic, let's begin with something that is generally accepted by researchers regardless of their theoretical orientations: that the result of L2 acquisition is an implicit system. By implicit we mean that learners cannot articulate what is the content of the mental representation we call language. In this book we tend toward a generative perspective on language but what we claim is equally true if you take, say, a usage-based perspective: Whatever language is, it exists as an implicit system in the learner's mind/brain. You may recall from Chapter 6 that explicit knowledge is what a person can articulate about language such as "To make a verb in the past in English add an -ed." Generally, such knowledge comes from textbooks, teachers, internet sites, and perhaps the learner's own conscious observations about how he or she *thinks* the language works (e.g., "Oh. I have to put the adverb here and not there!" "Oh. Looks like I have to insert a *do* to make a question."). Implicit knowledge, on the other hand, is knowledge that cannot be articulated, such as why *re-* can combine with *paint* and *write* to make the verbs *repaint* and *rewrite* but can't combine with *sleep* and *pet* to make **resleep* and **repet*. Another example would be knowledge that you can make a progressive out of verbs like *eat* and *die* (e.g., "The man is eating." "The man is dying.") but not *seem* and *know* (e.g., "*The man is seeming sad." "*The man is knowing me.")

What is more, if a learner can articulate a rule in some way, this does not mean that what the learner says is how language is represented in the mind/brain. Typically, rules found in textbooks and given by teachers are not psychologically real – meaning that what the rule says is not what winds up in people's heads. So when we talk about what gets learned in L2 acquisition, we are not talking about rules in the classic sense but something quite different. Here's an example given by Bill VanPatten in several of his publications. In Spanish, objects of verbs are sometimes marked by the tiny word *a*. Textbooks and teachers refer to this as "personal *a*" because it generally marks some kind of person as an object of a verb. Here is a typical rule that learners may read.

In Spanish, when the direct object is a person, it is preceded by the preposition *a*. The personal *a* is not used when the direct object is not a person or is an animal for which no personal feelings are felt.

Now let's look at some samples of language.

(1) a. María conoce a Juan.
'Maria knows John.'

b. María conoce la materia.
'Maria knows the subject.'

This rule seems to work in (1a) and (1b): *Juan* is a person and the name is marked with an *a*, but *subject* is not a person so there is no *a*. But what happens with the following examples?

(2) a. ¿Conoces un buen médico?
'Do you know a good doctor?'

b. Tengo una hermana.
'I have a sister.'

(3) a. El camion sigue al carro.
'The truck is following the car.'

b. El chico asustó al coyote.
'The boy scared the coyote.'

In (2a) and (2b), both doctor and sister are people but no *a* is used to mark them as objects of the verb. And in (3a) and (3b) neither a car nor a coyote is a person and yet the *a* is used. In short, the pedagogical textbook rule that students learn does not reflect what winds up in the mental representation of both L1 and L2 learners.

It is worth reminding ourselves of additional facts about acquisition that contribute to the understanding that learners are building an implicit system over time. As we have seen in this book, acquisition is ordered and piecemeal. There are stages of development for syntactic and morphological properties of language. Ordered development cannot be traced to teaching and instructional environments. In addition, learners come to know more about language than what they are exposed to, what we have called poverty of the stimulus (POS) situations in previous chapters. With POS situations, learners show evidence of knowing things that are possible about language, as well as things that are not possible, that they haven't been exposed to. And as we saw in Chapter 6, the effects of trying to teach the formal properties of language are severely limited in that they do not affect ordered development in any substantial way. In short, learners are doing things to and with language that they are not aware of. So if learners wind up with an implicit mental representation of language, and that representation bears no resemblance to textbook rules or rules the learner gets from external sources, how does that system get in the learner's mind/brain? Does explicit learning have anything to do with the development of that system? And just what is explicit learning? These are the questions that underlie the discussion in this chapter.

A Brief Discussion of "Learning"

It may seem odd to the reader of this book, but learning is an ill-defined concept in L2 research. That is, researchers often assume a definition of learning but don't lay out their idea of just what learning is. In other words, researchers know that learning happens, but they often aren't specific about what processes the learner is undergoing to learn something. The issue of explicit learning is also muddled because we find that researchers use the terms explicit teaching and explicit learning interchangeably. Explicit teaching involves instructors or online delivery systems overtly teaching learners such things as "Verbs must agree with their subjects. This is how it happens in Spanish" and then providing learners with practice to "internalize" what has been explicitly taught. Explicit learning is presumed to happen during the phase of practice in which learners' overt attention is on learning the rule in question. In a 2015 essay, for example, Nick Ellis, defines explicit learning as form-focused instruction. In that same essay, he describes implicit learning as something that happens to the learner internally by way of mechanisms involved in general learning (e.g., frequency tabulations of occurrences in the input, blocking). So, for Ellis, implicit learning is internal to the learner and controlled by that learner, but explicit learning is external to the learner and controlled by something else. However, relating explicit learning to explicit teaching environments means that researchers often leave what is actually learned and how it is learned undefined. Although we can define explicit teaching – and researchers regularly do when they describe an experiment – explicit learning is often simply assumed. In other words, researchers assume a clear correspondence between what is taught and what is learned. The underlying processes and mechanisms for explicit learning are generally left unspecified.

If we turn to psychology, learning involves the development of new cognitive structures. For example, a child learns over time what a "bird" is, developing a cognitive structure that has information in it such as "has feathers," "has wings," "can fly," and so on. Later, that cognitive structure is altered when the child encounters penguins, emus, and ostriches, for example. But exactly how does the cognitive structure develop in the first place? Clearly, from processing stimuli in the environment. The child hears that the robin on the tree branch is a bird, that the canary inside the cage at Aunt Tracy's house is a bird, and that the bald eagle on a sign is a bird. From these encounters, learning mechanisms (unspecified for now) begin to tally relevant characteristics and from these tallies the more abstract concept of "bird" emerges. Thus, when a child sees a blue jay for the first time, that child says "Bird!" The child forms some kind of abstract concept of "bird" based on various interactions with birds. So learning happens as a result of processing data from the environment. Exactly what that processing is we will leave for books on psychology.

Is language acquisition any different? Yes and no. To create a mental representation of language, learners have to process data from the environment. But in the case of language acquisition, those data aren't rules but actual streams of speech (either spoken or signed). The learner somehow processes the data, and then internal mechanisms cull from those data to build an implicit system. We will see a bit later what, exactly, we mean by processing, but for now the question is this: To what extent do learners process linguistic data in the input explicitly? Theoretically, there are three positions on the matter: Explicit processing of the data is necessary, explicit processing is not necessary but beneficial, explicit processing is neither necessary nor beneficial. (Note that from here on in we will use **explicit processing** and **explicit learning** interchangeably.) The issue with these positions is that it is not always clear what a researcher means by "explicit learning." Even though we have defined it here as the explicit processing of input data (given the fundamental role of input) it's not clear that all researchers do so. As we said above, explicit learning is often inferred by researchers when (1) explicit teaching is involved (see above) and/or (2) learners can state a rule or articulate what they have learned (i.e., demonstrate explicit knowledge). What is more, researchers often don't make reference to *how* learners process input data or to *what* they process in the data. This makes the task of discussing the role of explicit learning a bit challenging.

> To create a mental representation of language, learners have to process data from the environment. But in the case of language acquisition, those data aren't rules but actual streams of speech (either spoken or signed).

Consider this ...

Think of abstract concepts that you have in your head; for example, *liberty, justice, comprehension, mathematics*, and *the universe*. If pushed, you could probably eke out some kind of definition as you reflect on what these concepts are. But how did they get in your head? Did you memorize a definition? Did you focus on the word *liberty* and then go about learning it purposefully? If you are like most people, concepts such as these "sneak" into your head through exposure. Try to think of concepts you deliberately learned (i.e., concepts such as "hate" not activities such as "baking a cake"). How much non-explicit processing do you think happens on a daily basis?

To date, the field of SLA has focused on two broad questions related to explicit learning. The first is whether explicit knowledge can somehow turn into implicit knowledge. The second is whether explicit knowledge or explicit learning can influence the development of implicit knowledge. As we get into these issues, we will see how sometimes they get a bit confused.

Can Explicit Knowledge Turn into Implicit Knowledge?

We begin by noting that the first contemporary distinction between the roles of explicit and implicit knowledge in L2 acquisition was articulated by Stephen Krashen in the late 1970s and early 1980s. Krashen distinguished between learning and acquisition. In Krashen's terms, **learning** involves intentional focus on the learning of rules through some kind of explanation and practice. The learner is consciously aware of what he or she is doing and the purpose of the effort is to learn the grammar (rules, sounds, and so on). The result is some kind of explicit knowledge. At the time of Krashen's writing, he was envisioning learning as part of traditional language classes (and classes we still see today): Teachers and textbooks present, learners practice, and performance is assessed via tests to see if the learners have "internalized" what was presented and practiced. **Acquisition**, on the other hand, happens as a by-product of input processing in communicative contexts. To state this another way, acquisition happens through sustained interaction with comprehensible input. The learner is not actively focused on learning rules, sounds, and so on but instead is actively attempting to understand what someone is saying (or signing). No conscious awareness of the formal properties of language is involved. Krashen argued that there is no relationship between explicit knowledge and implicit knowledge and, most importantly, that explicit knowledge cannot become implicit knowledge. If we return to our example from Spanish with the so-called "personal *a*," Krashen would argue that the rule that learners are given cannot turn into the implicit knowledge that underlies the examples we saw in (1a) through (3b). Krashen's position is what's called a **no interface position**. That is, he argued that the two knowledge systems are distinct from each other and do not interact.

> In the 1970s and early 1980s, Stephen Krashen argued for a "no interface" position; namely that explicit and implicit knowledge systems are distinct from each other and do not interact.

Early on, Krashen's distinction between learning and acquisition was met with criticism, as was his no interface position. But since the 1970s, a good deal of research supports the claim that explicit knowledge cannot turn into implicit knowledge. Bonnie Schwartz, for example, provided a solid updating of the distinction between explicit and implicit knowledge in her 1993 essay. Instead of talking about learning and acquisition, she made the distinction between competence on the one hand and learned linguistic knowledge on the other, as well as between performance and learned linguistic behavior. She used competence in the Chomskyan sense and in the way we use mental representation in this book, whereas learned linguistic knowledge is the kind we typically find that learners have based on textbook rules. Performance is what learners do with their competence whereas learned linguistic behavior is what they do with their learned linguistic knowledge. She argued, from a generative perspective, that competence and learned linguistic knowledge are qualitatively different and one cannot turn into the other. She also argued that performance and learned linguistic behavior are different, and one does not lead to the other. Important here is that competence (and the performance based on it) is not learned in any explicit way but can only be learned through the processing of input coupled with language-specific internal mechanisms such as Universal Grammar. For this reason, learned linguistic knowledge cannot turn into competence because competence can only develop as a result of processing input. (If you want to read about a concrete example of what Schwartz meant, see Bill VanPatten's 2016 essay cited in Chapter 6. It also appears in the references for this chapter.)

Although we say that most scholars within and without the generative tradition adopt the position that explicit and implicit knowledge do not interact, there is one exception: the position adopted in **skill acquisition theory** – although as we will see in a moment, there is some misunderstanding of what skill theory actually claims.

Robert DeKeyser is the name most associated with skill acquisition theory (2014). Under this theory, skills develop out of some kind of practice. To begin, adults typically have skills in a wide range of areas, such as driving, cooking, or playing a sport, and most of these are skills acquired in adolescence or adulthood. DeKeyser and his colleagues argue that L2 acquisition should be seen as another instance of skill learning. This means that the general stages of acquiring any skill are also relevant for L2 learning. These stages involve three kinds of knowledge: **declarative knowledge**, **procedural knowledge**, and **automatized knowledge**.

The most common way that people explain each of these types of knowledge is with respect to driving. When someone first learns to drive, the person teaching them shows them where the important parts of the car are and explains the basic process of driving. A first-time driver might be told which pedal is the gas pedal, which pedal is the brake, how the gearshift works, where the turn signals are, how to execute smooth turns, how to keep alert to other drivers, how to stop correctly, among many other things. All of this information helps learners develop some kind of declarative knowledge. Declarative knowledge is not the most important type of knowledge for executing skills, but this isn't because the knowledge is inherently complicated. For example, it's easy enough to understand that if you want to signal a left-hand turn, you press the lever on the left side of the steering wheel down. What matters, though, is the ability to do this when you approach a left turn. This type of knowledge is called procedural knowledge. Procedural knowledge is *knowledge how*, and it encompasses the ability to execute a task in some way. Procedural knowledge emerges from actually doing the task that you are supposed to do. So while you might have declarative knowledge about the necessity of putting your turn indicator on when making a left turn, procedural knowledge develops only when you actually do this when making a left turn.

Procedural knowledge lies on a continuum from partly automatized to fully automatized. Skills that are automatized can be performed quickly and accurately with little to no attention, and with few errors. So as novice drivers improve, reaching for the lever that activates the turn signal becomes second nature, and instances of moving it in the opposite direction from the turn they want to signal also decrease. Skills that are fully automatized aren't necessarily always performed perfectly – even skilled drivers sometimes forget to signal, or indicate a right-hand turn when they intend a left-hand one. Skill acquisition theory has a long history and a wide research base within the field of cognitive psychology, and there is evidence that many skills – driving, swimming, cooking, and so on – involve the interaction between declarative, procedural, and automatized knowledge.

Now let's consider how skill acquisition theory applies to L2 acquisition. Skill acquisition theorists assume that linguistic skills are like any other kind of skill. In other words, DeKeyser and his colleagues do not assume that linguistic knowledge or skill is any different from any other kind of knowledge or skill. Because of this assumption, it makes sense that learners would benefit from explicit rules and practice for the development of L2 skills. Explicit rules are the equivalent of declarative knowledge (even though they don't have to be), and practice is what is necessary for declarative knowledge to become procedural knowledge. More practice over time leads to the automatization of knowledge. The naïve reader might assume that under skill acquisition theory, explicit or declarative knowledge turns into procedural and automatized knowledge – and that the latter are equivalent to implicit knowledge. It is not clear that skill theorists would accept this. While there is a relationship between automatized and procedural knowledge, skill theorists don't really claim that declarative knowledge turns into procedural knowledge. The reader may notice that we used the term "emerge" as in "procedural knowledge emerges." It is not clear in skill theory what exactly procedural knowledge is but it is qualitatively different from declarative knowledge and is not "derived" from it. What is more, it would be wrong to conclude that under skill theory, explicit knowledge turns into implicit knowledge. These terms aren't even used in skill theory. Instead, learners somehow develop procedural knowledge that

> It would be wrong to conclude that under skill theory, explicit knowledge becomes implicit knowledge. These terms aren't even used in skill theory.

subsequently gets automatized. As should be clear from the discussion above, skill acquisition theory is a theory that explains how humans learn to perform behaviors. Because of that, the terms declarative and procedural *knowledge* are a bit of a red herring – skill acquisition theory isn't really a theory of knowledge. It's a theory of behavior.

DeKeyser and other researchers who subscribe to skill acquisition theory do not claim that skill acquisition theory accounts for all of SLA, or that it is the only process by which L2 acquisition takes place. Instead, DeKeyser limits skill acquisition theory to adult instructed L2 learners who are relative beginners learning relatively simple structures and who have a relatively high level of linguistic aptitude. DeKeyser doesn't think that all of these factors have to be in place. Similarly, he suggests that low-aptitude adults will have a harder time forming the kinds of declarative representations that would enable them to automatize this knowledge. And he doesn't think skill acquisition theory accounts for language learning at levels beyond beginning-level learners. Advanced learners are exposed to more input, which makes it more likely that they will be able to engage the input and, thus, that implicit learning can (will) happen. DeKeyser probably takes the strongest position in favor of declarative knowledge of researchers working in SLA today, yet even he doesn't argue that explicit knowledge is the only – or the most important – factor in SLA. Rather, he argues that in specific contexts, declarative knowledge is important because it can facilitate the development of procedural and automatized knowledge.

Consider this ...

We have limited our focus on what is acquired in L2 acquisition to the mental representations for language. We have not talked much at all about linguistic *skill*. In your mind, what is skill? Is it the ability to communicate? If so, what does this mean? And what is the relationship between skill and mental representation as we have talked about it in this book?

We conclude this section by saying that few scholars, if any, believe that explicit knowledge turns into implicit knowledge. The question for most scholars is whether explicit knowledge can somehow influence the development of implicit knowledge. This would suggest that somehow explicit knowledge is used during the processing of input and thus explicit learning is implicated in the development of implicit knowledge. We turn our attention to this position in the next section.

Can Explicit Knowledge/Learning Influence the Development of Implicit Knowledge?

Probably most researchers agree with the premise that the development of implicit knowledge can be influenced by explicit knowledge or explicit learning. But researchers are not in agreement about what this means. Some researchers, like Rod Ellis, believe in what is called a **weak interface** between explicit and implicit knowledge. According to these scholars, explicit knowledge can influence the development of the implicit system in some way. However, the mechanisms for how this happens are not clear, and the evidence is the same as the evidence we reviewed in Chapter 6 on the effects of instruction. That evidence is problematic at best. Because the research on instruction – and thus the research on explicit knowledge and learning affecting the implicit system – is biased toward testing explicit knowledge, we have no good evidence for the basic claim that explicit learning somehow affects the development of implicit knowledge. The best reasonable conclusion is that explicit learning affects the development of explicit knowledge. Even if the research clearly suggested that explicit learning affects implicit knowledge, there remains the problem of the learning mechanisms themselves. If, as Rod Ellis and others claim, there is an interface between explicit knowledge and implicit knowledge, just what is that interface? How does it work? What learning mechanism "connects" the two knowledge systems? What does it mean for one system to "influence" the other when we know they are qualitatively different? Researchers who argue for such an interface really haven't addressed these questions; instead, they assume that because there are two knowledge systems, they influence each other. In a sense, the assumption that this interface exists may reflect the socio-cultural context in which much L2 instruction takes place: classrooms. The assumptions work like this: We know learners are taught a lot of explicit knowledge about the second language, so it must be useful to them in some way. If it weren't, we wouldn't spend so much time focusing on it. This reasoning is circular, and, as we've seen, there isn't much evidence that instruction influences the development of the underlying mental representation for language.

> Some researchers believe in a "weak interface" model; that somehow explicit knowledge can influence the development of implicit knowledge. However, the mechanisms for how this happens are not clear.

One of the most significant hypotheses to emerge regarding explicit learning is **the Noticing Hypothesis**. The Noticing Hypothesis was formulated by Richard Schmidt in a 1990 publication. The hypothesis states that learners have to notice (i.e., be aware of) formal features in the input in order for these forms to become intake and subsequently be acquired. The Noticing Hypothesis does not state that this (conscious) awareness becomes intake. Rather, the claim is that the language acquisition mechanisms are more likely to make use of data in the input if the learner is somehow aware of those data. If we go back to our example of the personal *a* in Spanish, the claim under the Noticing Hypothesis is that somehow learners must consciously register the *a* when they encounter it. In other words, if they are to acquire personal *a*, they can't "skip over it" in the input; it has to somehow enter their focal attention during the processing of input.

What is important to understand about the Noticing Hypothesis is that what gets noticed can only be detectable surface features of languages such as verb endings and what they mean or noun endings and what they mean or, in our example, something like the personal *a*. In its original form, the Noticing Hypothesis was not meant to apply to complex syntax or even some superficially simple syntac-

> In its original form, the Noticing Hypothesis was not meant to apply to complex syntax or even to some superficially simple syntactic operations – only to detectable surface features of language such as verb and noun endings and what they mean.

tic operations. Thus, researchers often talk about "noticing" past-tense endings, case endings, and plural markers, for example, but never about "the conjugated verb in German is always in second place" or "object pronouns in Spanish never appear between an inflected verb and an infinitive." What is more, the Noticing Hypothesis is limited to what is observable in sentences and not what is hidden or impossible in a language. In our example of the personal *a*, is it possible to notice when *a* is not used? How do you notice things that aren't there? This observation makes the Noticing Hypothesis at best limited in its application to L2 acquisition. Let's go back to an example from the introduction to this chapter to better illustrate the limited scope of the Noticing Hypothesis. Learners can easily "notice" in the input that *re-* can combine with verbs to mean something like "do again." They hear *repaint, redo, rewrite, redesign*, and so on. And yet, at some point they wind up with a linguistic system that tells them that **resleep, *repet, *rebake, *resneeze*, and **redrink* are not possible. How does this happen? How did the noticing of *re-* with some verbs lead to the ungrammaticality of *re-* with other verbs? It can't be because learners just haven't encountered them yet. After all, there are grammatical things we haven't encountered, yet we know they are grammatical. In the *re-* example, you may not have encountered *reinvite* but when you hear it, you know it sounds OK (even though it's not in the dictionary!). Language is full of things that we know are possible and impossible that we can't have acquired because we "noticed" them in the input.

What is more, noticing is at best a fuzzy concept. Over the years, Richard Schmidt attempted to clarify just what noticing was, but in the end, the concept continued to elude an easy definition, which in turn led to difficulty conducting empirical research. Just how does the researcher operationalize a construct that is not well defined? What has happened is that a number of researchers have used the Noticing Hypothesis to motivate research on instructed L2 acquisition (Chapter

6). In such research, they might compare one group who has prior explicit knowledge of a formal feature of language with one that does not. The learners are then exposed to the same input, and if the group with prior knowledge performs better on a post-test on that formal feature, the researcher concludes that noticing helped. That is, learners are able to somehow deploy explicit knowledge during the processing of input, resulting in greater gains than the group that did not get explicit knowledge. If the shortcomings of this kind of research are not clear, we invite the reader to review the criticisms of instructed L2 research in Chapter 6. But again, the major obstacles in this research are (1) demonstrating that "noticing" happened (that is, that something explicit happened during input processing) and (2) relying too much on tests on which learners can use explicit knowledge in some way or another. (See also some of the problems in using noticing to discuss interaction, Chapter 3.)

Some recent research is beginning to use online methods such as eye-tracking to see where learner attention is directed during processing. However, this research has not yet focused on the intersection of noticing and acquisition – that is, how learners have to notice something in order to acquire it. Instead, it has largely focused on whether learners can detect things they have already been exposed to in the input or might have learned from a book, from a teacher, or from the Internet. For example, in a study called "Coming Eye-to-Eye With Noticing," published in 2013, Patti Spinner, Susan Gass, and Jennifer Behney examined second-semester university learners of Italian and whether their eye movements indicated noticing cues on articles and nouns in order to determine what gender a noun is. Participants read sentences such as *Poi la carne è troppo* ... on a computer screen and off to the side was a box with four adjective choices: *grassa, grasso, grasse,* and *grassi* (i.e., 'So the meat was too ... fatty'). They tracked their unconscious eye movements to see where they went in order to determine which version of the adjective to select. They found that learners' eye movements went to both articles and nouns to determine gender, not just to the nouns, for example. However, this is not a study of how learners acquire adjective agreement or the gender of nouns to begin with. This use of eye-tracking is more like a test of whether they have gender agreement and what cues they use to make that agreement in a very conscious way – as they might do when taking a paper-and-pencil test with multiple-choice answers. Thus, it is too soon to tell whether this line of research will shed any light on the fundamental question of whether learners have to notice (explicitly process) formal features in order to acquire them. We will see later why there are additional problems with any strong version of noticing when we review just what is involved in processing a sentence.

> **Consider this …**
>
> We will see in a bit what some possible criticisms of the Noticing Hypothesis are. But for now, ask yourself this question: Is it possible to notice something that's not in the input? In other words, if you can only notice what you see or hear, how do you come to know what is impossible in a given language?

There are some scholars who have been critical of the Noticing Hypothesis, among them John Truscott and John Williams. In a 1998 essay, Truscott argues that it makes little sense to say that learners have to notice formal features in the input. His argument rests on two ideas. The first is along the lines we've laid out here: The nature of the mental representations learners acquire is too complex and abstract to be clearly related to the surface features of the input. The second is along the lines we laid out in Chapter 6: There is no convincing evidence that information about language influences the development of mental representations for that language. We'll return to Truscott's first argument at the end of this chapter with a detailed example. Williams, in a series of essays and empirical studies, has argued that noticing involving some kind of awareness is not necessary for acquisition. Coming from a psychological perspective and not a linguistic perspective (such as Truscott's), Williams suggests that we first need to understand how implicit learning works and what exactly is learned implicitly. Only after doing that can we determine to what extent any kind of explicit learning contributes to acquisition.

> We may first need to understand how implicit learning works and what exactly is learned implicitly. Only after doing that can we determine to what extent any kind of explicit learning contributes to acquisition.

Although it was not intended to address the relationship between explicit learning and processing, there is some research that provides some evidence that helps us answer this question. In a series of studies, Bill VanPatten and his colleagues have shown that explicit knowledge does not necessarily get deployed during the processing of input and that the question of whether or not it does is much more complicated than we might think. In a 2013 study, VanPatten and his colleagues were interested in the intersection of the first-noun strategy and the processing of different structures in Spanish, French, German, and Russian. The first-noun strategy claims there is a universal tendency in learners to begin the process of acquisition by assuming the first noun or pronoun they encounter when comprehending a sentence is the subject/agent (see Chapter 4 for some discussion). VanPatten and his colleagues identified four learning problems in the languages they were interested in:

- Spanish: object-verb-subject (OVS) sequences are problematic as in *Lo ve la chica* (lit: him sees the girl, 'The girl sees him'). The tendency would be for learners to think the *lo* is the subject/agent and misinterpret the sentence as 'He sees the girl.'
- German: OVS sequences are problematic as in *Den Mann hört die Frau* (lit: the man-ACC hears the woman-NOM 'The woman hears the man'). The tendency would be for the learners to think *Den Mann* is the subject/agent and misinterpret the sentence as 'The man hears the woman.'
- Russian: OVS sequences are problematic as in *Собаку слышит кошка* (lit: the dog-ACC hears the cat-NOM 'The cat hears the dog'). The tendency would be for the learners to think *Собаку* is the subject/agent and misinterpret the sentence as 'The dog hears the cat.'
- French: causative structures with *faire* as in *Le père fait lire la lettre à la mère* (lit : the man makes to read a letter to the mother 'The man makes the mother read a letter'). The tendency would be for the learners to think the father is reading the letter and to misinterpret the sentence as something like 'The father is reading a letter to the mother.'

In their experiment, half of the learners in each language got information on the problem (e.g., *lo* is not a subject pronoun so don't interpret it as one) and half did not. During the treatment, learners were exposed to mixtures of sentences (e.g., in German some were OVS and some were SVO) and were asked to match what they heard to one of two pictures (e.g., a man listening to a woman and a woman listening to a man). All conditions and languages were matched for vocabulary as well as problematic versus non-problematic sentences to process. The researchers measured how long it took learners to begin processing sentences correctly. They found that for the Spanish and Russian groups, information about processing strategies did nothing to influence the rate at which these participants began to process sentences accurately, whereas the participants in the German and French groups who got the information on the processing problem prior to hearing sentences began to correctly process the problematic sentences sooner than those who did not get such explanation. So it appears that explicit processing helped in two of the four cases. The question of course is what was different about those cases. The most interesting cases are the German and Russian groups. Both German and Russian mark case on nouns but do it differently: German marks the article whereas Russian (which doesn't have articles) marks the noun. Why would this make a difference? It's not clear why it would. The point is that the question of whether explicit processing (deploying explicit information during real-time comprehension) makes a difference or not is much more complicated than some claims would lead us to believe. What is also important about this particular kind of research is that VanPatten and his colleagues do not rely on tests of knowledge but on tests of processing (i.e., sentence interpretation). Although this is a step in the right direction, we cannot claim here that such research is definitive. It is, at this point, suggestive and warrants continued investigation.

Other researchers have begun to use online measures to explicitly test the relationship between explicit information and input processing. In a 2015 study (see the Exemplary Study summarized in this chapter), Sible Andringa and Maja Curcic used eye-tracking to investigate whether participants who were provided with explicit information interacted with input differently than participants who did not receive explicit information (similar to the VanPatten et al. study just reviewed). They investigated whether novice learners who were told that animate nouns were marked with *al* in Esperanto were able to use this information to attend to the relevant cues in the input. They hypothesized that these participants might have been more likely to attend to the relevant cue (the presence or absence of *al*) and use this knowledge to help them process sentences. Andringa and Curcic provided their participants with input in a semi-artificial version of Esperanto (semi-artificial because Esperanto doesn't actually mark animate direct objects with *al*). In the input their participants were exposed to, animate direct objects were marked with the preposition *al*, and inanimate direct objects were not marked with a preposition. The authors hypothesized that if learners were sensitive to this distribution in the preposition *al*, they would use the presence of the preposition to predict that the upcoming noun would be animate. They measured this by having learners hear a sentence while pictures were displayed on a screen. The authors hypothesized that if participants were aware of the grammatical function of *al*, when they heard the preposition, their eyes would unconsciously move toward the picture of an animate noun on the computer screen in front of them. In short, if explicit information makes a difference in whether participants relied on *al* to anticipate the direct object, the results should show that participants who received explicit information had a higher proportion of looks to the correct picture when they heard *al*. These results, however, were in the opposite direction to what the authors predicted. Although the group who received explicit information processed the input differently than the group that did not receive explicit information, this difference didn't make them more likely to look at the right picture sooner than the implicit group. Instead, it just made them more indecisive in their processing of the differential object marking sentences. In other words, it doesn't seem like explicit information helped these participants use object marking as a disambiguating cue during real-time processing of input.

Exemplary Study

Andringa, S. & Curcic, M. (2015). How explicit knowledge affects online second language processing: Evidence from differential object marking acquisition. *Studies in Second Language Acquisition, 37,* 237–268.

Participants

- 51 L1 Dutch speakers with no prior knowledge of either Spanish or Esperanto
- 2 groups: the explicit group ($n = 26$) got explicit information and an input treatment task, and the implicit group ($n = 25$) got only the input treatment task

Materials

- Input treatment based on a semi-artificial version of Esperanto:

  - vocabulary: 10 animate nouns, 10 inanimate nouns, 19 transitive verbs, 6 intransitive verbs, 5 adjectives
  - syntax: SVO word order
  - included differential object marking by marking animate direct objects with the preposition *al*
  - 104 black-and-white pictures that represented everyday objects and activities
  - 104 sentences that described the pictures and were presented auditorily
  - 52 sentences were contexts for differential object marking; 26 had animate direct objects and 26 had inanimate direct objects
  - explicit group: a differential object marking rule explanation in Dutch using two example sentences

- Visual word eye-tracking task as a measure of implicit processing:

  - participants picked the image that matched the last word in a recorded sentence
  - pictures were presented in pairs; one quarter of them had two animate nouns; one quarter had two inanimate nouns; one half had an animate and an inanimate noun
  - 36 experimental sentences; 18 with animate nouns and 18 with inanimate nouns
  - sentences with animate nouns and a choice between an animate and inanimate picture should have evidence of looks to the animate picture when encountering the preposition *al*
  - no anticipatory looks when the pictures match in animacy

- Auditory grammaticality judgment task as a measure of syntactic knowledge:

- o　participants heard a sentence describing a picture with a transitive activity
- o　rated the sentence as grammatical or ungrammatical
- o　stated whether the decision was based on feel or rule
- o　8 grammatical sentences (four with *al* and an animate object; four with no preposition and an inanimate object)
- o　8 ungrammatical sentences (*al* and an inanimate object; no preposition and an animate object)

Results

- The group that got explicit information did significantly better on the grammaticality judgment task than the group that got only input.
- Both groups performed equally well in choosing the correct picture in the eye-tracking task, indicating that both groups had understood the treatment equally well.
- Anticipatory looks

  - o　Implicit learners showed a gradual increase in looks toward the correct picture.
  - o　Explicit learners showed a decrease in looks toward the correct picture before they show an increase in looks toward the correct picture.
  - o　Neither group used the preposition *al* to predict the animate noun.

Putting Explicit Learning into Perspective

In this section we lay out what the underlying problem is in talking about the role of explicit learning/processing (or even noticing) during acquisition. Let's remind ourselves of several things before continuing.

1. In the case of L2 acquisition we know that the result is the development of an implicit, abstract, and complex system. The result is not the development of an explicit system – even if learners get one along the way.
2. Learning is defined as processing external stimuli in some way that is subsequently used by internal mechanisms to build a linguistic system. That is, something "encodes" the data as the learner hears or reads it so that it can be eligible as data for linguistic development. This is called input processing.

When we begin to scrutinize just what must be going on during acquisition, we see just how complicated learning is. For example, let's imagine a learner hears a simple sentence such as 'Megan is reading a book.' At the same time, the learner encounters this sentence as descriptive of an event in which Megan is, indeed, reading a book. So the learner's "job" is to map what he or she hears onto the meaning conveyed by the event. This sounds easy enough, but let's peel back the layers on this example. Here's what must happen for language to develop.

- The learner tags 'Megan' as referring to the person in question. As a result, the word 'Megan' is tagged with particular properties: it is a noun ([+N, –V]), it represents a proper name, and so on. At the same time, the processing mechanism begins to project sentence structure. Given that 'Megan' is a noun, it is probably the subject so the learner's processor creates something like this upon hearing the word: [TP [SPEC Megan] [T ...]. This abstract information is how the system must encode that something is a subject.
- The learner then hears 'is.' The learner must determine what this little word is. Is it part of 'Megan'? Maybe a case marker to indicate nominative case (e.g., Megan-is-NOM). Is it a verb? If so, a main verb or an auxiliary? Maybe the learner can't make sense of it at all and it is simply dumped from processing for the time being as the learner moves on to the word 'reading.' But for the sake of argument, let's assume the learner does tag it as a verb and successfully as an auxiliary (which is doubtful in the early stages of acquisition, but again, we're assuming here for the sake of presentation). Let's also assume the learner knows that the situation is about what is going on now and not in the past or the future. The learner encodes all of this information along with 'is': [–N, +V], [+aux], [+T], [+pres, –past], [–plural]. Note: We're not saying the learner does encode all of this information nor all of it at once, we're just indicating that if the learner could encode all of the information, that is what the learner would wind up with. Now the learner has projected something like this for the sentence: [TP [SPEC Megan] [T is ...].
- The learner then hears 'reading.' The learner links this to the actual act of reading, so the meaning of 'reading' is encoded. At the same time, the learner knows this is the main verb, and given that 'is' has wound up in the TP (tense phrase), this verb must be in the VP. Also given that 'is' is marked with tense, the verb 'reading' must be non-finite. So in addition to the meaning of 'reading,' the processor encodes the verb with this information: [N, +V], [–T], [+progressive, –perfective]. At this point, the processor has built this sentence structure in real time: [TP [SPEC Megan] [T is [VP [SPEC –] [V reading ...].
- Then the learner encounters 'a book.' Here the processor must determine whether there is one word 'abook' or two words 'a book' given the prosody of how this phrase is pronounced. (Depending on how fast the sentence is spoken, there are some conditions under which the learner might think he or she is hearing 'readinga' and 'book.') If the learner successfully determines that these are two words, then the processor must decide what 'a' is and what 'book' is. Given the

strong stress on 'book' the processor probably decides that it is a content word and refers to the book in the event under question. So the processor ascribes it the meaning of 'book' as well as these features: [+N, −V], [+count], and possibly others. If the learner's processor figures out that 'a' is a determiner, the processor has to figure out from the situation whether it is definite or indefinite. For the sake of argument, let's just say the processor correctly marks 'a' as an indefinite determiner. This would mean it ascribes to this function word the following properties: [+D], [−spec, −def]. At this point, the processor builds the sentence structure this way: [TP [SPEC Megan] [T is] [VP [SPEC −] [V reading] [DP [SPEC] [D a] [NP book]]]].

- Sentence computation is complete, the processor is happy, properties have been ascribed in a way that makes sense, and meaning and form are mapped onto each other.

The question now for the role of explicit and implicit learning is what parts of this process happen explicitly and what parts happen implicitly? The reader might now see the problem with attributing any strong or beneficial role to explicit learning (as processing) once we delineate what must be learned. There is no scenario we can think of where a learner engages conscious processes to attribute properties such as [−N, +V], [−T], [+progressive, −perfective] to the word 'reading' in our example. There is also no scenario where in real time a learner projects syntactic constituents such as TP, VP, DP, and so on, as well as the dependencies among them, consciously or with some kind of awareness. In this example, we have left out other elements of the formal properties of language that are present alongside the morphosyntactic properties we have highlighted here, such as phonology (sound classes, syllable structure and syllable segments, prosody or pitch, stress, and intonational contour of the sentence). So while processing the syntactic units of the sentence to build structure, and tagging meaning onto morphological units as well, the learner is also processing things such as which parts of words and the sentence get strong stress and which get weak stress, that English syllables can end in consonants, and so on. Clearly, the assignment of properties to words and the building of sentence structure must happen outside of awareness. If not, could the learner ever make it past the first word? Conscious explicit processing of formal features would be exceedingly slow and acquisition might not happen at all.

> Clearly, the assignment of properties to words and the building of sentence structure must happen outside of awareness. If this were not the case, conscious explicit processing of formal elements would be exceedingly slow and acquisition might not happen at all.

To be sure, our example is one in which the learner is successful with all parts of the sentence – and our example is a relatively simple one. Imagine if the sentence were more complicated (e.g., 'I'm pretty sure Megan is reading a book right now at a coffee shop somewhere.'). It is clear from research (see, for example, Chapter 2) that learners get bits and pieces of language over time. They are not successful at processing all parts of a sentence in the beginning and even intermediate stages. This is because the learner is most likely struggling to get basic meaning of content words from the input and mapping those onto the event talked about. The learner might miss or not process function words and possibly not map certain inflections onto their meaning and vice versa. Nonetheless, for whatever the learner actually processes in the input at any given point in time, the formal features of language and sentence structure must be processed outside of awareness.

We have limited our example to a simple sentence in English. Let's imagine that the next sentence the learner hears is 'She likes it very much.' Now the learner must not only process all the words and compute sentence structure as before, but there is the added layer of antecedence-pronoun indexing. The learner must somehow link in real time that 'she' is a pronoun and is indexed to 'Megan' while 'it' is a pronoun and is indexed to 'book.' What conscious or explicit processing could be involved in this scenario? In the case of 'she' the learner has to somehow encode the formal properties of the word (e.g., [+N,−V] [pro] [+fem] and so on) as well as its index to Megan. The learner must do the same for 'it' (e.g., Megan$_i$ is reading a book$_j$. She$_i$ likes it$_j$ very much.').

What all of this means, then, is that when we break down how learning happens in a moment-by-moment analysis of comprehending a sentence – that is, when we get into the weeds of processing the formal elements in language – we get a clearer picture of the learning problem. Against a definition of learning that includes processing and against the learning problem outlined here, we are better able to judge whether or not language acquisition happens with explicit learning. Our conclusion is that explicit learning is largely excluded from learning the formal elements of language. Instead, its role might be to figure out "what something means" and by "means" we actually mean what dictionary definition can be given to that word or phrase. For example, "Oh. That word must mean 'book'!" or "Oh. He must be referring to what happened yesterday!" and even "Oh. 'She' refers to Megan!" So explicit processes and learning are used to uncover meaning, but implicit processes and learning are used to map formal properties onto that meaning. These are some of the issues that John Truscott raised in his 1998 essay and we hope to have illustrated them here in an accessible way.

Consider this …

We have excluded from our discussion any role of the L1 in processing (see Chapter 4). Is there L1 influence during the processing of input or does the learner rely on universal properties of language processing? Although an important question, does the presence of the L1 impact the implicit processing of formal features of the L1 during real-time comprehension?

With the above scenario laid out, we are also better able to sit back and assess the various positions on explicit and implicit learning. The debate is, in a sense, a result of three issues: (1) whether or not the researcher considers the fundamental role of input as data for acquisition; (2) how the researcher views the nature of language; (3) how the researcher defines learning and its relationship to processing input data. It seems to us that the field has not reached consensus on the role of explicit/implicit learning largely because researchers have not come to consensus on these three basic issues. As long as the researcher believes that language is something like what we see in textbooks, then explicit learning can play a role in L2 acquisition. But if the researcher believes language to be something much more abstract and complex, then that researcher might conclude that explicit learning plays little to no role in acquisition.

What about Social Factors?

Throughout this book we have touched upon ways in which social factors (context, relationships between speakers, and so on) impact acquisition from an external perspective – largely the quantity and quality of input and interaction a learner receives (or seeks out). We have also touched on how social factors can relate to internal issues such as identity and its impact on learner willingness to engage, for example. Regarding the role of explicit learning as explicit processing, there is not much to say about how social factors might bear upon the questions at hand. Processing as an unconscious phenomenon that exists outside of awareness is largely linguistic in nature and it is difficult to conceive of ways in which social context or social factors would affect that processing. Once a learner is engaged in actively trying to comprehend a sentence, the mechanisms for processing kick in.

Recap

In this chapter, we have touched on these major points.

- What learning is in its general sense (the creation of new cognitive structures).
- Language acquisition must be linked to input in some way, such that a major part of language learning is processing data in communicatively embedded input.
- Scholars have debated to what extent explicit learning is involved in language acquisition, with two major positions taken: no interface and weak interface.
- The Noticing Hypothesis is one of the most widely discussed positions that some kind of conscious registration of the formal properties of language is necessary for acquisition.

- A continued problem in the debate on the role of explicit learning is a lack of what it means to learn language (i.e., what the processes are) and a vagueness about what is acquired (i.e., what the formal properties of language are).
- How complicated and abstract the processing is of even a simple sentence such as "Megan is reading a book," suggesting a very limited role, if any, for explicit learning during the acquisition of the formal properties of language.

REFERENCES AND READINGS

- Andringa, S. & Curcic, M. (2015). How explicit knowledge affects online second language processing. *Studies in Second Language Acquisition, 37,* 237–268.
- DeKeyser, R. (2014). Skill acquisition theory. In B. VanPatten & J. Williams (Eds.), *Theories in second language acquisition.* New York: Routledge.
- Ellis, N. (2015). Implicit AND explicit learning of languages. In P. Rebuschat (Ed.), *Implicit and explicit learning of languages* (pp. 1–23). Amsterdam: John Benjamins.
- Ellis, R. (2005). Measuring implicit and explicit knowledge of an L2: A psychometric study. *Studies in Second Language Acquisition, 27,* 141–172.
- Hulstijn, J. (2005). Theoretical and empirical issues in the study of implicit and explicit second-language learning. *Studies in Second Language Acquisition, 27,* 129–140.
- Krashen, S. (1982). *Principles and practice in second language acquisition.* Oxford: Pergamon Press.
- Krashen, S. (1985). *The input hypothesis: Issues and implications.* London: Pearson-Longman.
- Rebuschat, P. (Ed.) (2015). *Implicit and explicit learning of languages.* Amsterdam: John Benjamins.
- Schmidt, R. (1990). The role of consciousness in second language learning. *Applied Linguistics* 112, 17–46.
- Schwartz, B. (1993). On explicit and negative evidence affecting and effecting competence and linguistic behavior. *Studies in Second Language Acquisition, 15,* 147–163.
- Spinner, P., Gass, S., & Behney, J. (2013). Coming eye-to-eye with noticing. In J. M. Bergsleithner, S. N. Frota, & J. K. Yoshioka (Eds.), *Noticing and second language acquisition: Studies in honor of Richard Schmidt* (pp. 227–246). Honolulu, HI: University of Hawai'i National Foreign Language Resource Center.
- Truscott, J. (1998). Noticing in second language acquisition: A critical review. *Second Language Research, 14,* 103–135.
- VanPatten, B. (2016). Why explicit knowledge cannot turn into implicit knowledge. *Foreign Language Annals, 49,* 650–657.
- VanPatten, B., Borst, S., Collopy, E., Qualin, A., & Price, J. (2013). Explicit information, grammatical sensitivity, and the first-noun principle: A cross-linguistic study in processing instruction. *The Modern Language Journal, 92,* 506–527.
- VanPatten, B. & Rothman, J. (2015). What does current generative theory have to say about the explicit-implicit debate? In P. Rebuschat (Ed.), *Implicit and explicit learning of languages* (pp. 89–116). Amsterdam: John Benjamins.

- VanPatten, B. & Williams, J. (Eds.) (2015). *Theories in second language acquisition.* 2nd edition. New York: Routledge.
- Williams, J. (2013). Attention, awareness, and noticing in language processing and learning. In J. M. Bergsleithner, S. N. Frota, & J. K. Yoshioka (Eds.), *Noticing and second language acquisition: Studies in honor of Richard Schmidt* (pp. 39–57). Honolulu, HI: University of Hawai'i National Foreign Language Resource Center.

FOLLOWING UP

1. Conduct a review of L2 research where the terms explicit learning and implicit learning are used. Try to find instances in which the researcher actually defines the terms and also instances in which the researcher assumes the reader knows what is meant by the terms. What does your research demonstrate?

2. In B. VanPatten and J. Williams second and third editions of *Theories in second language acquisition*, various theoretical approaches are presented by experts in those approaches. One of their tasks is to review the "explicit/implicit" debate. First, review what VanPatten and Williams say about the debate in their first chapter and then review what the individual contributors say about this topic. What do you find?

3. Review the section of the chapter called "Putting Explicit Learning into Perspective." Can you summarize in your own words what the principal argument is in this section?

4. In language-teaching circles, people heatedly debate whether teaching and practicing grammar is necessary or beneficial. After reading Chapter 6 and the present chapter, why do you think this debate exists among teachers?

5. In both Chapter 6 and in this chapter, we have stated that explicit and implicit knowledge are qualitatively different. What does it mean for something to be qualitatively different from something else? Can you explain what this means for explicit and implicit knowledge of language?

6. Read one of the following from the References and Further Readings section. Prepare a 1,000 word (maximum) summary of the main ideas.

   - Hulstijn, "Theoretical and empirical issues in the study of implicit and explicit second-language learning"
   - VanPatten & Rothman, "What does current generative theory have to say about the explicit-implicit debate?"
   - Williams, "Attention, awareness, and noticing in language processing and learning."

8   What Are Individual Differences and How Do They Affect L2 Acquisition?

Individual differences are a fact of life. One person differs from the next on a range of factors, such as intelligence, height, shoe size, athleticism, and memory. Even people with the same eye color don't have exactly the same eye color. The question of whether such differences come from innate characteristics (nature) or from their environment (nurture) is an old one in philosophy. At least in the case of L1 acquisition, the answer seems to be "both." Children are biologically predisposed to acquire a language (nature) and they acquire the language they are exposed to along with the social norms that govern its use (nurture). Child language acquisition is considered part of normal human development because all children acquire the language of the speech community in which they are raised. One of the obvious ways in which L2 acquisition differs from L1 acquisition is that adults seem to vary a good deal more in rate and ultimate attainment (how far they get) in L2 acquisition than children acquiring their L1 do. That said, as we will see shortly, there are individual differences in L1 acquisition as well. For some time, L2 researchers have looked to individual differences as a way to explain the apparently wider range of outcomes for L2 learners. In this chapter, we examine whether individual differences play a role in L2 acquisition, which factors play a role, and how individual differences interact with the role of input. First, though, we review the work on individual differences in L1 acquisition. We'll do this so that we have some context for individual differences in L2 acquisition. In this latter section, we will review the three main factors researchers have looked at: aptitude, working memory, and motivation. We'll then end the chapter with a discussion of what aspects of L2 acquisition individual differences explain.

Individual Differences in L1 Acquisition

One common assumption about child language acquisition is that it is rapid and relatively uniform. This assumption is based on two observations. The first is that children seem to "pick up" their native language without much effort. The second is that all normally developing children acquire language in a predictable order. While the second observation is accurate – children do pass through predictable stages in the acquisition of the L1 – it's less true that language acquisition is quick and easy. The fact that, in the absence of major cognitive deficits, human children acquire their L1 means that it is easy to assume that child language acquisition is effortless. This assumption masks individual variation in both child language development and L1 ultimate attainment as well as the

There is variation in both child language development and L1 ultimate attainment.

thousands of hours it takes children to acquire the basics of language. One of the major ways in which individual children differ is rate of acquisition. For example, most children begin to understand individual words between 8 and 10 months of age. In other words, it takes some children 25 percent more time to understand individual words. Another major individual difference in early child language acquisition is vocabulary size. For all children, vocabulary size increases as they get older. However, at any given age, there is a wide range in the number of words that children know. For example, research suggests that at 10 months of age, children understand an average number of 67 words, with a median of 41 words. In other words, half of the children have a vocabulary size of less than 41 words, and the other half have a vocabulary size of more than 41 words. In order to bring the average number of words to 67, many of the children who know more than 67 words know many more than 67 words. This is quite a bit of individual variation, and, indeed, the range of the number of common words that those children understood went from zero to 144. Vocabulary size matters because it predicts both language comprehension and syntactic development, which means that differences in vocabulary size predict other differences that persist throughout the course of child language acquisition.

One way that differences in vocabulary size persist is in the relationship between comprehension and production. Production normally follows comprehension. So children who are slower to comprehend language are also slower to produce language. There is also a relationship between vocabulary size and grammatical development. Children start putting two words together when they have a vocabulary size between 50 and 100 words. Children who are slower to acquire vocabulary are thus also slower to enter the two-word stage of grammatical development. Utterance length and complexity start increasing exponentially when children have a vocabulary somewhere between 300 and 600 words. Again, when this happens depends on the size of the child's vocabulary.

In addition to the above, children have been observed to fall into two broad groups regarding how they use language to communicate. One group is called the referential group. This type of child begins the one-word stage of acquisition by naming things largely using nouns (e.g., *horsie, mommy*). The other group of children is called holistic. This group tends to use more chunks of language to express emotions, treating the chunks like one-word items. A classic example is *silli-in-it*, which is an unanalyzed reproduction of "silly, isn't it?" Verbs tend to predominate in the speech of these children. Even with these differences, however, we still see the predictable ordered acquisition referred to in Chapters 1 and 2. In short, although all typically developing children pass through predictable developmental stages, there are individual differences among children in terms of how fast they pass through these stages.

Although it seems like all native speakers of a language have the same mental representation for that language, adult native speakers can and do diverge from each other. One of the most obvious ways is in vocabulary knowledge. In addition, there is evidence that there are differences between syntactic and semantic knowledge in adult native English speakers. For example, some adults find it difficult to interpret passive sentences correctly, especially when the syntactic and semantic cues conflict. These speakers find sentences like *the dog was bitten by the man* (which means *the man bit the dog*) more confusing than sentences like *the man was bitten by the dog* (which means *the dog bit the man*). In the former case, the word order (dog-bite-man) lines up with the real-world knowledge that dogs are far more likely to bite men than men are to bite dogs, even though the passive voice gives the alternate interpretation. When passive sentences have a meaning that conflicts with real-world knowledge, some speakers misinterpret them. In addition, some adult native English speakers interpret the sentences *every basket has a dog in it* and *every dog is in a basket* as meaning the same thing while others don't. Let's picture, for instance, a dog kennel that has three dogs and three baskets. Both sentences are true if each basket has a dog in it. However, what happens when there are three baskets but four dogs? There could be two baskets each with one dog and the third with two dogs. This would make both sentences still true. Then there could be three baskets each with one dog and the fourth dog is lying on the ground. Now only one of the sentences is true. In other words, the first sentence is a statement about whether all *baskets* are filled, and the second sentence is a statement about where the *dogs* are. In short, adults can differ from each other in the extent to which certain syntactic and semantic structures are acquired. These differences are usually not evident to other native speakers of a language. Thus, it is easy to assume that L1 acquisition is easy, unproblematic, and uniform. However, research from linguistics suggests that this assumption isn't accurate. There are individual differences in L1 acquisition, both in the course of development and in outcomes.

> Ultimate attainment in L1 acquisition seems to depend more on exposure than on learner-internal factors.

Researchers have suggested that these differences are due to an interaction between learner-internal factors (e.g., communication styles) and learner-external factors (e.g., exposure to the target language). However, ultimate attainment seems to depend more on exposure to the language than on learner-internal factors.

The factor that seems to predict L1 syntactic knowledge the best is education. Ewa Dabrowska has conducted a series of studies investigating whether a college education makes a difference in how native English speakers perform on tests of grammatical knowledge. These structures include passive voice and sentences like those with *every* mentioned above. Dabrowska has found that participants with a college education get all of the questions right on these tests but that there is much more variation among the participants with only a high school education. Some of these participants perform like the college students and get all of the questions right, but others perform much worse. Dabrowska argues that education is the causal factor in these differences in syntactic knowledge and performance. It's likely that what education does is give people access to a wider range of input. Once people get to college, they are exposed to a wider range of texts and probably read more than people who do not go to college – or they have read much more prior to going to college. Both the passive voice and the sentences with *every basket* discussed above (the target structures in Dabrowska's work) are much more frequent in written language than they are in spoken language. Thus, people who read frequently and widely are more likely to be exposed to the relevant input. Thus, it's possible that the differences among native speakers in Dabrowska's work have as much to do with quantity and quality of input as with education, and that education is the vehicle for relevant input. Either way, it's clear that (1) there are individual differences in L1 acquisition that extend beyond vocabulary size, and (2) the usual account of these differences is that they are due to a combination of exposure, education, and literacy. Individual differences are also influenced by the interaction between learner-internal factors and the environment. For instance, children growing up in the same household show variation in rate of acquisition. These differences can't be attributed solely to the environment because children who grow up in the same household share their linguistic environment. In short, individual differences in child language acquisition are probably due to a mix of learner-internal factors and environmental factors, such as education and access to input.

Individual Differences in L2 Acquisition

Superficially, L1 and L2 acquisition seem to have major differences in outcomes. While L1 learners will acquire their L1, L2 learners are not guaranteed to acquire the L2 and fall within a wide range of non-nativelikeness. Such differences need an explanation, and research on individual differences in SLA has attempted to explain why some people progress farther in L2 acquisition than others do. What is more, individual differences should be able to explain outcomes independently from the central roles of input, interaction, and general exposure. In this chapter, we will focus on three main subsets of individual differences in L2 research: language aptitude, working memory, and motivation. All three of these are learner-internal factors, but aptitude and working memory can be thought of as cognitive factors, while motivation is closer to a personality factor that is sometimes also related to social factors. Although working memory is a factor in L1 acquisition, neither language aptitude nor motivation is thought to influence L1 acquisition. Thus, a major role for either aptitude or motivation in adult L2 acquisition would point to a substantial difference between L1 and L2 acquisition. Before we discuss individual difference factors in more detail, it's important to reiterate that when we talk about L2 acquisition we are talking about the underlying processes that create the abstract, complex, and implicit system we have consistently called "mental representation" in this book. Let's begin with those individual differences that are internal to the learner.

Language Aptitude

Language aptitude is defined as an individual's ability to acquire an L2. Like most cognitive attributes, it is hypothesized to be innate and relatively fixed. In the United States, concern for aptitude for L2 learning can be traced to World War II and the army's desire to identify military personnel who would make good L2 learners. The US military was – and still is – interested in identifying individuals who have a "special" ability to learn an L2 on the premise that investing in language instruction for these persons is a more efficient use of resources than investing in language instruction for people with a low or average ability to acquire an L2. Thus, from the beginning, work on L2 aptitude assumed that some adults were more suited to L2 learning than others, and researchers set out to identify which factors or abilities predicted success in language learning.

An underlying premise of linguistic aptitude was that it varied among the population in the same way that eye color and height do.

The foundation of aptitude research dates to the work of John Carroll and Stanley Sapon in the 1950s. They set out to identify the abilities that make an individual a good language learner and then developed the first aptitude test, which is called the Modern Language Aptitude Test (MLAT). Carroll and Sapon hypothesized that linguistic aptitude is a relatively fixed set of abilities. In other words, linguistic aptitude varies among the population in the same way that eye color and height do. Carroll and Sapon identified four abilities that they hypothesized underlay a general language-learning ability:

- **Phonetic coding ability** refers to an individual's ability to identify individual sounds, particularly those that are not contrastive in English, and to form associations between sounds and symbols.
- **Grammatical sensitivity** refers to an individual's ability to identify the syntactic function of words or phrases in sentences.

- **Inductive learning ability** has to do with how well an individual can generalize to a rule based on a set of language materials.
- **Rote learning ability** has to do with how well an individual can learn arbitrary associations between sounds and meanings.

Carroll and Sapon then developed a test – the MLAT – that tested each of these subcomponents and refined the test based on how classroom language learners scored on the test. In other words, they assumed that learners who perform well on classroom assessments have high language aptitude and refined the test so that it identifies those learners. Not surprisingly, scores on the MLAT correlate strongly with classroom language learners' performance, and thus the MLAT has good predictive validity in instructional settings. Although other aptitude tests, such as the Pimsleur language battery, the Hi-LAB, the LLAMA aptitude test and the Canal-F Test, have been developed in the years since the MLAT was developed, the MLAT remains the foundational aptitude test. Some of the more recent tests, such as the LLAMA aptitude test, are closely modeled on the MLAT, and others test similar abilities. To this day, the MLAT and its close cousin, the LLAMA, remain the most frequently used aptitude tests in L2 research.

Consider this ...

John Carroll and Stanley Sapon initially developed their definition of linguistic aptitude in the 1950s. At this time, linguistics was just beginning to undergo the evolution from structural to generative linguistics described in Chapter 1. To a large extent, linguistics and language teaching were still governed by the assumptions of structural linguistics and behaviorism. How might these assumptions have informed Carroll and Sapon's definition of aptitude? Do you think if they saw language differently (i.e., as a complex, abstract, and implicit representation not resembling textbook rules or patterns) they might have gone about their research a different way?

Over the years, researchers have investigated whether aptitude scores correlate with outcomes in L2 acquisition. If aptitude plays a role in L2 ultimate attainment, we would expect to see a strong correlation between performance on a measure of linguistic knowledge and scores on the aptitude test. Robert DeKeyser conducted a study with Hungarian learners of English living in the United States to see whether such a relationship exists. DeKeyser administered a grammaticality judgment test and a Hungarian version of the grammatical sensitivity subsection of the MLAT to L1 Hungarian speakers who were L2 learners of English and had lived in the United States for at least ten years. DeKeyser found that there was a strong correlation between aptitude scores and scores on the test for participants who had arrived in the United States after the age of 16, but not for those who had arrived before then. Similarly, Niclas Abrahamsson and Kenneth Hyltenstam investigated the relationship between aptitude scores, age of arrival, and ultimate attainment in L1 Spanish speakers who were L2 Swedish speakers. They found that all of their near-native participants who had an age of arrival in Sweden after the age of 12 had aptitude scores that were higher than the average aptitude score for the participants who had arrived before the age of 12. The results of these two studies aren't that unusual in the literature – successful L2 learners have been found to have above-average aptitude scores in a variety of studies. Based on results like these, researchers such as Peter Skehan have argued that aptitude should be seen as central to explaining individual variation in L2 acquisition.

Recently, however, some researchers have challenged the centrality of aptitude as a major explanatory variable in L2 acquisition. These challenges have been both conceptual and empirical. The first conceptual challenge is that the construct of aptitude, and therefore the design of the aptitude test, rests on assumptions about language that may or may not be warranted. Bill VanPatten and some of his colleagues have argued that the MLAT assumes that language acquisition consists mostly of explicit rule learning. This is also how most L2 classrooms treat language – students memorize vocabulary and learn rules – so it's not surprising that outcomes on the MLAT should correlate closely with outcomes in formal language classrooms. It's also not surprising that scores on the MLAT should correlate with a lot of the outcome measures used in ultimate attainment research. For instance, as mentioned above, Robert DeKeyser found a strong correlation between MLAT scores and scores on a grammaticality judgment test. DeKeyser's grammaticality judgment test contained a number of items that reflected explicit rule learning (as opposed to intuitions when such tests are used with native speakers), so it is, again, not surprising that two tests of rule knowledge should correlate with each other. VanPatten and his colleagues have argued that language acquisition should be conceptualized as fundamentally involving input processing, and that any regularities in learners' grammars are a by-product of processing the input. When acquisition is thought of as being primarily about input processing and comprehending linguistic input, and not about learning rules, it makes less sense that learners' analytic ability should predict outcomes in language acquisition. In other words, the question changes. It's not about whether some learners are better at learning rules than other learners; it's about how learners process input in real time.

A premise underlying aptitude is that it involves explicit rule learning. When acquisition is thought of as being primarily about processing and comprehending linguistic input, and not about learning rules, it makes less sense that learners' analytic ability should predict outcomes in language acquisition.

VanPatten and his colleagues have published two studies that investigated the relationship between learners' processing behaviors and aptitude. The first of these investigated whether aptitude predicted the speed at which L1 English speakers shifted to a new processing strategy in Spanish, French, German, or Russian, and is summarized in the Exemplary Study. The second one, conducted by Bill VanPatten and Megan Smith, investigated whether aptitude scores were related to naïve learners' (absolute beginners) processing and acquisition of complement + head word order in Japanese L2 when their L1 was English (see Chapter 4 for a discussion of heads and complements). In both of these studies, individuals differed from each other in terms of how quickly they moved toward L2-like processing or how much they were able to project beyond the input. In both of these studies, however, aptitude scores did not predict or correlate with which learners did what or how fast they came to do it. It's not that these studies show no evidence of individual differences. Instead, they suggest that aptitude is not the source of individual differences in the observed results when the focus is taken off rule learning.

Exemplary Study

VanPatten, B., Collopy, E., Borst, S., Price, J., & Qualin, A. (2013). Explicit information, grammatical sensitivity, and the first-noun principle: A cross-linguistic study in processing instruction. *The Modern Language Journal*, 97, 506–527.

Background

- Language learners tend to interpret the first noun in a sentence as the subject or agent.
- This presents a problem with interpreting non-canonical word orders, such as object-verb-subject structures in Spanish or scrambled sentences in Russian.
- Processing instruction (PI) is an intervention designed to push learners away from relying on the first-noun principle (FNP).
- In PI, input is manipulated so that both the subject and the object are capable of performing the action, and learners hear a mix of SVO, OVS, and OV sentences.
- PI includes information about the target structure and feedback so that learners know when they misinterpret sentences.

- The words-in-sentences section of the MLAT, which tests for grammatical sensitivity, has been found to have strong correlations with scores on measures of grammatical knowledge in previous research.

Research Questions

- Does explicit information (EI) influence how quickly learners of Spanish, German, French, or Russian move away from the FNP and correctly interpret sentences in which the first noun is not the agent?
- Does grammatical sensitivity correlate with outcomes on the PI task, regardless of the presence of explicit information?

Participants

- 42 third-semester Spanish learners, split between a group that got explicit information (+EI) and a group that did not get explicit information (−EI)
- 46 third-semester German learners, split between a +EI and a −EI group
- 44 third-semester Russian learners, split between a +EI and a −EI group
- 48 third-semester French learners, split between a +EI and a −EI group

Materials

- PI materials with and without explicit information
- PI materials had pictures and audio files that provided input on OVS structures in Spanish, German, and Russian, and the causative *faire* construction in French
- the words-in-sentences section of the MLAT

Results

- Spanish: no effect for explicit information or grammatical sensitivity
- German: an effect for explicit information; grammatical sensitivity correlated with how fast the +EI group progressed but not with the −EI group's progress
- Russian: no effect for explicit information or grammatical sensitivity
- French: an effect for explicit information, but not for grammatical sensitivity

Conclusion

- The results run counter to findings of previous research. The authors conclude that aptitude as grammatical sensitivity does not relate to how learners process input, which is assumed to be an integral part of how acquisition happens.

Other challenges have come from researchers who question the conceptualization of aptitude. Aptitude, like most other cognitive variables, was originally hypothesized to be relatively fixed. This means that, regardless of the context or the type of learning a situation called for, an individual's aptitude would be the same. This means that aptitude should be independent of other cognitive variables, such as intelligence. It also means that linguistic aptitude and education should not be related to each other. Researchers have begun to challenge these assumptions. The biggest initial challenges have come from outside of L2 research. Individual differences are an area of research in cognitive psychology more generally and many psychologists have argued that individual differences are more related to specific situations and are less fixed than earlier generations of researchers had thought. Based on this work, some researchers have argued that L2 researchers need to pay more attention to how individual learners are situated in their own contexts, as well as to how they respond to those contexts. In other words, some learners might have a better analytic ability than others, but that only matters if learners are in a context that calls for analytic abilities. In addition, some evidence suggests that linguistic aptitude is modulated by other factors, such as education. The challenges to the basic construct of aptitude don't necessarily challenge traditional conceptions of language or of aptitude as such; instead, they raise the possibility that what looks like an effect for aptitude actually has other, more diverse, sources. In line with the above, Peter Robinson has offered a more complex and nuanced view of aptitude in a number of publications. However, his work is focused almost exclusively on the relationship between instruction and aptitude (or aptitude complexes) and thus does not extend beyond what we might consider largely explicit learning (Chapters 6 and 7). In other words, following in the more general work on aptitude, the concern is for how instructed learners perform in focused environments where much of their attention is directed (explicitly or implicitly) to how language works as well as working with language itself.

In short, much of the research on the role of language aptitude in L2 acquisition has found that learners with higher scores on aptitude tests tend to do better on tests of L2 knowledge. This is especially true when the tests of L2 knowledge tap learners' knowledge of explicit rules. On the other hand, other research has found that when the measures of linguistic knowledge reflect learners' input processing, comprehension, or abstract implicit knowledge, the relationship between aptitude scores and task performance disappears. Like most things, results tend to reflect researchers' working assumptions about the nature of language, the nature of language acquisition, and the tasks they use in their research. Because of this, the role of linguistic aptitude in L2 acquisition more generally is not clear. What is clear, however, is that it does not play the central predictive role that Carroll and Sapon initially hypothesized.

> ## Consider this ...
>
> Concern for linguistic aptitude originated in the military and is still a concern today. However, in educational contexts and in language acquisition outside of the military, aptitude has largely been of interest only to researchers. That is, the "practical" applications of aptitude research have not been of concern as they have been in the military. Why do you think this is so? Do you think, for example, that in schools and universities there should be tests of aptitude to put students into different groups or to promote language learning among some students and not others?

Working Memory

Working memory is another individual difference that has received a significant amount of attention in L2 acquisition literature. Working memory (WM) is a construct that was originally developed in cognitive psychology. Working memory is the part of human cognition that allows us to temporarily store and manipulate information during comprehension. For example, effective note-taking involves working memory. To take notes, you have to listen to the speaker, pay attention to what the speaker is saying, and remember enough of it to write it down. Because the lecturer often speaks faster than you can write, you have to have enough processing resources to take in new information while recording older information. The WM storage component is what allows you to keep things active in your mind while focusing on something else, and processing capacity is what allows you to pay attention to the other task. Working memory is thought to be related to individuals' ability to process information, and thus may influence how efficiently learners process an unfamiliar language.

Working memory is a complex phenomenon consisting of various components that we won't describe in detail here. However, tests of WM are important to understand and will describe the most used test: the reading span test. In the reading span test, a person is asked to read a series of unconnected sentences aloud. The unconnected sentences are presented in blocks of increasing size: 3 sentences, then 4 sentences, then 5 sentences, then 6 sentences. To keep people from simply memorizing the end of a sentence, it is typical to include a reaction to each sentence's meaning (e.g., whether it makes sense or not). At the end of each block, a person is cued to recall the last word of each sentence. At some point, the person fails to recall all of the items in a block and is assigned a score to indicate where he or she fell on the reading span test. There are some variations on the reading span test but all involve the basic components of blocks of sentences of increasing numbers of sentences per block plus a cued recall at the end of the block. The idea is that this kind of recall test taps the processing capacity that learners have during comprehension and that this processing capacity is reflective of working memory. In L1 research, such tests have shown to correlate highly with reading comprehension.

Reading span tests are not used in child L1 acquisition for obvious reasons, and so no research has been done to correlate reading span scores in, say, 2- and 3-year olds and their syntactic or grammatical development or their comprehension of language. Instead, child L1 researchers have looked at one component of working memory called **phonological short-term memory.** Phonological short-term memory governs how much verbal information someone can remember at any given time. In children learning their L1, phonological short-term memory is measured by their ability to repeat non-words. Children with a high phonological short-term memory capacity learn real vocabulary faster, have a larger vocabulary, and thus usually acquire syntax faster than children with a lower phonological short-term memory. Overall, children who have a high working memory capacity also tend to have strong reading skills and are better able to comprehend complex sentences than children with a low working memory capacity. This suggests that working memory is related in some way to linguistic ability in children; the more you can comprehend, the more language you get.

In the L2 literature, researchers have hypothesized that WM is related to the acquisition of L2 vocabulary and syntax. Researchers have also hypothesized that WM is related to L2 fluency and reading comprehension skills. With respect to L2 vocabulary, phonological short-term memory has been found to predict learners' ability to acquire new vocabulary in an L2. In addition, learners with a high phonological short-term memory capacity tend to do better on tests of morphosyntactic knowledge. The results of this research suggest that phonological short-term memory contributes to L2 learning. This may be because language is primarily a verbal system, and it is processed in phonological short-term memory first. Better phonological short-term memory capacity then leads to more linguistic processing (i.e., comprehension), which leads to faster and/or better L2 development.

In addition to work that looks at the role of phonological short-term memory in L2 acquisition, researchers have also investigated whether working memory capacity as a whole predicts syntactic knowledge. For example, Alan Juffs investigated whether working memory capacity as measured by a reading span task influenced how non-native English speakers processed complex sentences. Juffs was interested in whether reading span scores were related to how L2 English speakers from different L1 backgrounds processed different kinds of sentences with *wh*-gaps. You might remember from Chapter 5 that *wh*-gaps in English involve moving a word from its original position in the sentence to a position earlier in the sentence. *Wh*-gaps occur in *wh*-questions and in relative clauses (e.g., *Which teacher did John say was going to be late?* is related to *John said which teacher was going to be late?*). In addition to a reading span task, Juffs gave L1 Chinese,

L1 Japanese, and L1 Spanish speakers who spoke English as an L2 a reading task that asked them to indicate whether sentences containing *wh*-gaps, like those in (1), were grammatical.

(1) a.   *Who$_i$ did Ann meet the teacher after she saw e$_i$ on Tuesday?
     b.   Who$_i$ does the nurse know e$_i$ saw the patient last week?

A computer recorded participants' reading times. Slower reading times on the word immediately following the gap would indicate that participants are reintegrating the *wh*-word into the gap position. Overall, Juffs found that L1 background was a factor in the results, with L1 Spanish speakers performing the closest to native English speakers and the L1 Japanese group demonstrating the most difficulty processing these kinds of sentences. However, working memory capacity did not seem to influence performance for any of the L2 learners.

Like the results of aptitude research, the results of research on the effects of working memory in L2 acquisition are mixed.

Like the results of aptitude research, the results of research on the effects of working memory in L2 acquisition are mixed. There is some evidence, for instance, that phonological short-term memory capacity predicts vocabulary learning. One limitation of this research is that most of it has been done in explicit or semi-explicit learning conditions. For example, one common design for vocabulary research is to present participants with L1/L2 vocabulary pairs, ask them to memorize the vocabulary, and then give them a vocabulary post-test. This kind of task asks participants to memorize words and it gives them a test of memory capacity. It could be that the results of these two tasks are correlated because they are both memory tasks. Memorized vocabulary isn't necessarily vocabulary that has become intake and then incorporated into the linguistic system. Vocabulary is like anything else in language; it is ultimately acquired through learners' interaction with aural and written input in communicative contexts. With respect to working memory capacity more generally, there is some evidence that working memory is related to L1 sentence processing. However, the effects of working memory in L2 sentence processing do not seem to be independent of the influence of the L1.

Consider this ...

At the conceptual level, the possible role of working memory makes sense in language acquisition. If working memory is related to comprehension, and comprehension (processing input) is a necessary part of acquisition, then working memory should be related to acquisition. Can you think of any flaws in this argument? Is there a piece of acquisition that research in working memory might not be considering?

Motivation

Researchers have been discussing the possible role of motivation in L2 acquisition since the early days of L2 acquisition research. Unlike aptitude and working memory, both of which are cognitive factors, motivation is an affective factor. Although motivation is usually expressed in thoughts and opinions (e.g., "Spanish class is *so* boring!"), these reflect an individual's emotions, experiences in the world, and short- and long-term goals. In addition, although aptitude and working memory are usually thought of as relatively fixed factors, motivation is more variable. It changes as a function of a learner's feelings about something and their experience of the world. Thus, motivation can be affected by external social factors. Motivation researchers recognize the fundamental ebb and flow of motivation and define it as involving a process by which learners direct their attention toward goals. So motivation has to do with the process that helps learners reach their goals for acquiring an L2.

Second language motivation research has its roots in Robert Gardner and Wallace Lambert's work in the late 1960s. These researchers were interested in the dynamics of living in a bilingual and bicultural society in Canada. Gardner and Lambert hypothesized that learners' social contexts and goals for language learning would influence individual outcomes. They distinguished between integrative and instrumental motivation. The term **integrative motivation** refers to an individual's perspective on the target language and culture. In particular, people with a strong integrative motivation have a positive orientation to the target culture. This is usually accompanied by relatively higher degrees of openness to new experiences. It can also be reflected in positive impressions of speakers of the target language and a desire or willingness to communicate with speakers of the target language. The other main type of motivation is instrumental motivation. The term **instrumental motivation** refers to more of a practical need the learner has for the language, usually in order to do a job. Instrumental motivation may not be limited to a job – it can also include things like passing an entrance exam or other high-stakes test or completing some education in the target language. Both instrumental and integrative motivation are primarily about social contexts: affinity for culture, relationship building and maintenance, and success at work and school. Over the years, this distinction became less pronounced. Gardner, for instance, argued that, at some level, instrumental motivations are also integrative because they indicate some willingness to interact with other communities. Instrumental and integrative motivation are important because they influence what language(s) learners study and whether they seek out opportunities to interact in the target language and develop their skills. Learners without some basic level of motivation won't engage the learning process.

Consider this ...

Gardner and Lambert were working in Canada where there were two relatively homogeneous communities – French-speaking and English-speaking. They were also working in a context in which bilingualism was a legal requirement, if not a social norm. At the same time, due to historical and social factors, the two communities were largely independent of each other in that people went to different churches and sent their children to different schools. In this context, the idea of integrative motivation makes a lot of sense: There are political and social factors that make the idea of "crossing cultures" seem possible or desirable. Can you think of cases in which learning an L2 might be important but in which integrative motivation would not be a major factor? What about cases in which learning an L2 might depend primarily on instrumental motivation? How might different types of motivation influence how much of the L2 learners acquire?

By the early 1990s, research on motivation had shifted from focusing primarily on the social context for language learning to focusing on classroom contexts. There was also an effort to bring the constructs of motivation more in line with the research in psychology on motivation. This body of research focused on the interaction between social context, learner-internal factors (such as self-efficacy), and classroom and course contexts (e.g., what the classroom incentives are). One of the insights from this period of research is that motivation ebbs and flows over time. On any given day, and in any given class period, a learner's motivation may be low or it may be high. One question is how to measure the relationship between motivation at any given point in time and learning of one particular aspect of the language. At the same time, however, because motivation ebbs and flows, and because language acquisition is a long-term process, what matters most is not the moment-by-moment motivation but the long-term commitment to language acquisition goals.

As more researchers with different backgrounds became interested in motivation, the focus shifted again. This shift is the result of a number of factors. One of these is that the world changed significantly between the 1960s, when Gardner and Lambert started their research, and the early decades of the twenty-first century. As the pace of globalization increased and English became a global lingua franca, the construct of integrative motivation made less sense. For instance, English is the language of scientific publication, and it's the language of many science departments in universities across the world. This means that Japanese scientists might never leave Japan, and they might speak Japanese at home and in some aspects of their professional lives, but they would also need fairly technical English skills to conduct other aspects of their professional careers. It's not clear what the integrative motivation would be here – the Japanese scientist doesn't need to have a particular affinity for England or the United States, for example, to need English skills. Consequently, Zoltan Dörnyei and other L2 motivation researchers have argued that the construct of integrative motivation should be expanded and reconceptualized so that it better fits with constructs of self-conception in psychology research. They have done so by introducing the idea of the learner's **self-concept**.

Self-concept has to do with how learners see themselves, including who they are today (both positive and negative attributes), and who they might become. Dörnyei calls this the **L2 motivational self-system**, and it includes three aspects: the **Ideal L2 Self**, the **Ought-to L2 Self**, and the learning environment. The Ideal L2 Self draws on ideas from psychology about how people grow and change. The basic idea is that who individuals imagine themselves to be in the future is important for directing their attention to those goals. So the Ideal L2 Self is essentially who learners consider themselves to be with respect to the L2. It's a way to incorporate L2 skills into learners' conceptions of themselves. If they don't currently have the skills they want, the Ideal L2 Self helps orient learners to different aspects of the language-learning task. The Ought-to L2 Self includes the beliefs or expectations that learners have about who they should be or how they should behave. Ideally, the Ideal L2 Self and the Ought-to L2 Self should work together, but this may not always be the case. Both of these self-concepts are influenced by learners' experiences, learning environments, and social contexts. Overall, motivation research today considers motivation on a number of different levels:

> L2 motivation research finds that learners' self-concept is a key factor in a larger constellation of factors that influence how far learners get in L2 acquisition.

learners' goals, learners' self-concept, the social context for learning, and the interaction between learner-internal factors and their educational and social contexts. The key insight from L2 motivational research is that learners' self-concept is a key factor in a larger constellation of factors that influences how far learners get in L2 acquisition.

What Do Individual Differences Explain?

Many L2 researchers assume that individual differences, such as working memory, aptitude, and motivation, play an important role in determining outcomes for L2 learners. It seems to us that individual differences may help explain the rate of acquisition and why some learners acquire more of an L2 than other learners, but they do not really explain *how* language gets into the learner's head, and they don't really explain *what* language gets into the learner's head.

Throughout this book, we have focused on four central observations about L2 acquisition. These observations are: (1) L2 development is ordered and relatively impervious to outside intervention; (2) input is central to language acquisition; (3) instruction has a limited role to play in influencing the L2 acquisition process or how far learners get; and (4) explicit knowledge and learning play little to no role in L2 acquisition. None of the research on individual differences changes any of these observations. For instance, stages of development and acquisition orders show up in different populations of L2 learners and are not affected by a learner's L1 or by instruction. There is no evidence that aptitude or working memory changes acquisition orders. Aptitude, it is true, has been found to predict learners' outcomes in two areas: classroom performance and scores on certain kinds of grammaticality judgment tasks. This sounds like aptitude might influence the development of the internal linguistic system. However, one of the problems with the research that supports the role of aptitude in L2 acquisition is that it tends to rely on tests of explicit knowledge or material learned explicitly. And, as we discussed in Chapter 7, explicit knowledge and learning play little to no role in the development of the linguistic system. When aptitude is studied in conjunction with tasks that require learners to process input, the relationship between task performance and aptitude scores disappears. Similarly, there is no evidence that these individual difference factors influence whether learners show poverty of the stimulus effects in the L2. Remember that poverty of the stimulus effects (discussed in Chapters 3 and 5) show up when people show that they know something about the language that they could not have acquired based only on the information in the input. They are also usually subtle enough that they are not explicitly taught in language classrooms. Poverty of the stimulus effects show up when learners project beyond the input to which they were exposed in order to create a mental representation for the target language. Most studies that have investigated poverty of the stimulus effects in L2 acquisition find that L2 learners have the same judgments as native speakers. This suggests that poverty of the stimulus effects are not subject to individual differences. So while individual differences do not influence the type of system learners acquire, they do play a secondary role.

Individual Differences and Rate of Acquisition

Motivation matters for language learners not because it changes how they acquire language but because it keeps them oriented to long-term goals and influences whether they choose to seek out opportunities to learn and use the language beyond the classroom.

Individual differences such as aptitude, working memory, and motivation are usually invoked, alongside the apparent influence of the L1 on L2 acquisition, to explain the apparent failure of L2 learners to converge on target-like L2 knowledge. We have seen that individual differences do not actually have much explanatory power when it comes to explaining the process of language acquisition and the nature of the system that learners acquire. That said, individual differences do have some explanatory power in terms of outcomes. This is because learners' individual circumstances and choices influence how they interact with the input and what input they have access to. In other words, motivation matters for language learners not because it changes how they acquire language but because it keeps them oriented to long-term goals and influences whether they choose to seek out opportunities to learn and use the language beyond the classroom. In short, motivation keeps learners engaged in the (largely unconscious) language acquisition process. For example, one of the authors of this book was motivated to learn Japanese. She sought out short- and longer-term study-abroad opportunities, spending about a year in Japan as a high school student. She also worked there for a while as an adult. She acquired more Japanese than her classmates in her high school Japanese classes did. Without the motivation to learn Japanese, she probably would not have sought out those opportunities. That said, this motivation did not change the fact that she acquired her Japanese through interaction with the target-language input. In other words, the exposure to Japanese language input in communicative contexts was essential for her acquisition of Japanese. Her motivation had nothing to do with the internal mechanisms that work on language – but it was vitally important in that it helped her create the opportunities to have better access to input and then take advantage of them (and it kept her from giving up when the process was hard). This stands in contrast to another author of this book whose approach to the acquisition of French was the "good enough" approach. That author knows and speaks some French but readily admits he has no desire to learn more and has no desire to be part of the French-teaching profession. He does not identify with French speakers and does not want to be like them and his interaction with the French language-teaching profession has been negative in many ways, which in turn has impacted his motivation to seek out input and interaction with speakers. He does not read in French and seldom watches French movies any more. Interestingly, his motivation to learn French at the beginning was high. But as he interacted more and more with the French language-teaching profession, his attitude toward learning French changed. In essence, he has stopped learning French and is far short of any nativelike ability.

Similarly, working memory may influence how much of the input a learner can process at any given time, and thus may influence the rate at which learners acquire vocabulary. It's likely that vocabulary acquisition also influences syntactic development. This is because learners process input for meaning first, so the more they understand from the input, the more resources they have available for syntactic processing. Thus, learners with a higher working memory capacity may have more cognitive resources available to allocate to language processing and may acquire language somewhat faster than learners with less working memory capacity. Still, though, working memory capacity doesn't change the basic processes that underlie language acquisition. Learners need access to input, they have to process that input, and then their internal mechanisms have to "organize" the data.

Given that individual differences influence rate of acquisition and access to input but not the actual processes of acquisition, why have they received so much attention in L2 acquisition research? The answer to this question involves a couple of factors. First, two of the major individual difference factors – motivation and aptitude – emerged in specific social and historical contexts. In the case of motivation, this work came out of the Canadian context, where bilingualism is a social and political goal, but where the language communities themselves may have relatively little spontaneous interaction with each other. Aptitude research emerged in an era when linguistics and language teaching was dominated by behaviorism and structural linguistics, with its focus on rule learning and habit formation. Aptitude thus received a good deal of attention because the military was (and still is) looking for a way to identify good language learners.

The second, and probably more important, factor is that many SLA researchers assume that children and adults have access to the same kinds of input and spend the same amount of time on task. When we compare a child L1 learner after four years of input and interaction to an adult who has had four years of language classes, we find that the child has acquired much more of the target language. Because we assume that the acquisition contexts are the same, this seems to suggest that target-like L2 acquisition is the exception, not the rule, for L2 learners. Individual differences are thus proposed as an explanation for this fact. But let's examine this observation about time a little more closely. We know that children have acquired most of the target language by about the age of 5. By this point, children have been engaged in meaningful interaction with the target-language input at least eight hours a day for five years. This means that they have spent at least 14,600 hours acquiring their native language. Even then, children don't have adult-like knowledge of passive voice or of the semantic factors that are encoded in words like *each, every, all,* and *none.* In addition, children can't read and their vocabulary is limited to their immediate world. In contrast, an adult who takes four years of college-level Spanish has fewer hours of exposure to Spanish. Assuming that adult takes one Spanish class every semester for four years, that that class meets five days a week for an hour at a time, that the input is good, and that classes run for 15 weeks at a time, the adult has had about 600 hours interacting with target-language input. If we add some out-of-class exposure (not fill-in-the-blank-type homework), we could be generous and add another 100 hours. If the input isn't good, or if the class doesn't promote meaningful interaction with the input, the adult has even fewer hours of exposure to the target language. In other words, after four years of college-level Spanish, the adult has spent the same amount of time interacting with the target language as a child who is about 10 weeks old. Unlike the 10-week-old, however, the adult is expected to be a fluent speaker and reader of the target language. We wouldn't expect that of a 10-week-old, so it's likely not a fair expectation of the adult, either. In fact, given that input and time on task are necessary conditions for both L1 and L2 acquisition, it is not surprising that outcomes for L2 learners are more variable than they are for L1 learners. In fact, in many cases, it's surprising that L2 learners acquire as much as they do. And it is only the long-term learners, the ones who accumulate thousands of hours of good input and interaction with that input who approach nativelike abilities in some of the domains of language and language use. To be sure, it may not be just time on task that is the difference we see between child L1 outcomes and adult L2 outcomes. And to be sure, we noted that there are individual differences in L1 acquisition and outcomes. But the point here is that whatever individual differences are and whatever role they play in L2 acquisition, they have to be situated in a more complex picture of input and interaction over time – including time on task.

What about Social Factors?

Social factors, like community expectations of bilingualism, access to education, and access to language-learning opportunities, all influence outcomes for L2 learners. But they do so because they influence access to input and they influence how much time learners can spend interacting with the target language. For instance, in many parts of the United States, being a monolingual English speaker is the norm. Some communities may place a value on learning an L2, but it is not expected and opportunities for interaction with native speakers of other languages are rare. Thus, L2 learners have to seek out other opportunities for input and interaction and will be more highly motivated.

In contrast, in countries like Belgium where multilingualism is the norm, the social world is different. Signs may be in multiple languages, shopkeepers may speak multiple languages, and people have access to better input and more opportunities for meaningful interaction with the target-language input, and are therefore more likely to acquire the L2 with a greater degree of proficiency. One of the authors recalls a visit to Denmark where he discovered how important it was among teenagers to speak English. There was peer pressure to learn English. As he heard from one person, "If you can't speak English by high school, you're a nerd." When he probed, he found that kids in Denmark developed a lot of strategies outside of the classroom to get access to English. Music (largely from the US) seemed to be a number one source of input for this group. That author makes no claims about the reality of this situation at the time of writing this book, but this was his experience some 20 years ago when he visited. The anecdote reminds us, though, that it is good for us to ask, as we travel, about people's attitudes toward language acquisition to discern just what the social context is that fosters acquisition or doesn't foster it.

Recap

Here is a summary of the major ideas covered in this chapter.

- Individual differences are evident in L1 acquisition. They usually show up in vocabulary knowledge and in some types of syntactic knowledge. Researchers trace individual differences in L1 acquisition to education and socio-economic status.
- Individual differences, such as aptitude, working memory, and motivation, have been proposed to account for the variation in outcomes for L2 learners.
- Aptitude is hypothesized to be fixed and to vary among people in the same way physical traits vary.
- Working memory has to do with how much information people can keep active and process at any given time.
- Motivation has to do with learners' long-term goals and orientation to the target language. Early motivation researchers distinguished between integrative and instrumental motivation, and researchers today see motivation as more fluid. Either way, it is the factor that keeps learners oriented to long-term goals.
- Individual differences do not play a significant role in what gets into learners' heads or how it gets there.
- Individual differences do influence how much access to input learners have, how much time they spend interacting with the input, and the quality of the input learners receive. Thus, they can influence rate of acquisition and overall outcomes. But individual differences do not change the fundamental linguistic and cognitive processes involved in either L1 or L2 acquisition.

REFERENCES AND READINGS

- Abrahamsson, N. & Hyltenstam, K. (2008). The robustness of aptitude effects in near-native second language acquisition. *Studies in Second Language Acquisition*, 30, 481–509.
- Carroll, J. & Sapon, S. (1959). *Modern language aptitude test*. San Antonio, TX: Psychological Corporation.
- Dabrowska, E. (2012). Different speakers, different grammars: Individual differences in native language attainment. *Linguistic Approaches to Bilingualism*, 2, 219–253.
- Dabrowska, E. & Street, J. (2006). Individual differences in language attainment: Comprehension of passive sentences by native and non-native English speakers. *Language Sciences*, 28, 604–615.

- DeKeyser, R. (2000). The robustness of critical period effects in L2 acquisition. *Studies in Second Language Acquisition*, 22, 499–533.
- Dörnyei, Z. (2009). The L2 motivational self system. In Z. Dörnyei & E. Ushioda (Eds.), *Motivation, language identity and the L2 self* (pp. 9–42). Bristol: Multilingual Matters.
- Dörnyei, Z. & Ushioda, E. (2009). Motivation, language identities and the L2 Self: A theoretical overview. In Z. Dörnyei & E. Ushioda (Eds.), *Motivation, language identity and the L2 self* (pp. 1–8). Bristol: Multilingual Matters.
- Gardner, R. & Lambert, W. (1959). Motivational variables in second-language acquisition. *Canadian Journal of Psychology/Revue canadienne de psychologie*, 13, 266–272.
- Gardner, R. & Lambert, W. (1972). *Attitudes and motivation in second-language learning*. Rowley, MA: Newbury House.
- Juffs, A. (2005). The influence of L1 on the processing of *wh*-movement in English as an L2. *Second Language Research*, 21, 121–151.
- Robinson, P. (2007). Aptitudes, abilities, contexts and practice. In R. M. DeKeyser (Ed.), *Practice in a second language: Perspectives from applied linguistics and cognitive psychology* (pp. 256–286). Cambridge: Cambridge University Press.
- Skehan, P. (2012). Language aptitude. In S. M. Gass & A. Mackey (Eds.), *The Routledge handbook of second language acquisition* (pp. 381–395). New York: Routledge.
- VanPatten, B., Collopy, E., Price, J., Borst, S., & Qualin, A. (2013). Explicit information, grammatical sensitivity, and the First-noun Principle: A cross-linguistic study in processing instruction. *The Modern Language Journal*, 97, 506–527.
- VanPatten, B. & Smith, M. (2015). Aptitude as grammatical sensitivity and the initial stages of learning Japanese as a L2: Parametric variation and case marking. *Studies in Second Language Acquisition*, 37, 135–165.

FOLLOWING UP

1. One of the ideas that emerged from this chapter is that individual differences in L2 acquisition may help explain ultimate attainment but not affect underlying processes. See if you can explain in your own words what this means.

2. In the chapter we briefly discussed individual differences in L1 acquisition. Do you think that perhaps individual differences in L1 acquisition carry over to L2 acquisition? That is, faster learners in L1 acquisition are faster learners in L2 acquisition? How might you research this? Consider doing a literature search on this topic and prepare a short summary.

3. Read the VanPatten and Smith article from *Studies in Second Language Acquisition* listed in References and Readings. Prepare a summary similar to how exemplary studies are done in this book. Then discuss any implications for additional research and/or for teaching that you think emerge from this kind of research.

4. Review the nature of reading span tests for working memory briefly described in this chapter. Then do an internet search on these other WM tests: digit span and word span. How do the tests differ? Do you think one is more valid than

the other? Note that the reading span test or some version of it has predominated in L2 research. Why do you think that is so?

5. Conduct a survey among ten people who are not in the field of language acquisition or language teaching but who have studied another language. Ask them "how far" they got and then ask them to what extent "motivation" has played a role in their outcome. What ideas emerge from what they tell you? Do they mention any factors other than motivation? When they talk about motivation, how do they talk about it?

Epilogue

As promised at the outset of this book, in this epilogue we return to the fundamental question that launched the field of L2 research in the 1970s and lurks in the background of contemporary research: Is L2 acquisition like L1 acquisition? By now, the astute reader may have guessed that the way this question is phrased is deceptively simple. Language acquisition is a complex phenomenon and to answer such a question we need to tease apart some aspects of acquisition covered in this book.

We can begin by thinking about language acquisition as an internal process and set of internal mechanisms as well as an external process or set of external mechanisms. For the internal processes we can ask ourselves this: Do L1 and L2 share the same internal process and mechanisms for the development of language? Our conclusion is that, to a large degree, they do. What is the evidence for this? We list it here.

- Both contexts (if not all contexts of language acquisition) require the same kind of raw data: communicatively embedded input (CEI). That is, both children learning an L1 and children, adolescents, and adults learning an L2 need to engage in contexts in which they hear and see language in communicative contexts. They must actively engage in comprehension and interaction with that input. Researchers have recognized the fundamental role of CEI in language acquisition since the 1960s with L1 acquisition and the 1970s with L2 acquisition. Nothing has surfaced in the research to challenge the critical role of CEI as the data from which internal mechanisms draw in order to create language in the mind/brain. That the data for both L1 and L2 acquisition are the same suggests that something internal to all learners is the same. That is, CEI is required because the mechanisms in the mind/brain require it regardless of context. This suggests a substantial similarity in the raw data for both L1 and L2 acquisition.
- In both L1 and L2 acquisition, we see ordered development. Neither child L1 learners nor child, adolescent, or adult L2 learners create idiosyncratic languages in their heads. Allowing for individual differences in rate and attainment, learners in both contexts follow predictable paths in the acquisition of language. In many cases, the paths for both L1 and L2 acquisition overlap or are very similar. We see that in both L1 acquisition and L2 acquisition, the

same factors seem to impact development: markedness, universals of language, Universal Grammar, and frequency in the input, among others. Something in both contexts constrains linguistic development in similar ways. This suggests something is the same about L1 and L2 acquisition. However, there is the issue of L1 influence in the L2 context, which we take up in the next bullet point.

- L2 learners have something internal to them that L1 learners do not: another language (or other languages). We know that L1 influence happens in L2 acquisition. At the same time, we know that this L1 influence is constrained or quickly attenuated when universals of language and acquisition come into play. This aspect of language transfer or influence would seem to be a big internal difference between L1 and L2 acquisition. At the same time, the first two points above hold. The presence or absence of another language in the mind/brain does not obviate the role of input and does not compromise ordered development. It might affect ordered development, but again, as we've seen, the effect is constrained. So as we see it, the presence of an L1 inside the mind/brain of the L2 learner does not alter the processes or block what the internal mechanisms responsible for language development do or must do. The L1 can, however, "gum up" the works and slow down the process in some areas or some cases. In short, the presence of an L1 in L2 acquisition does not cause the underlying processes and mechanisms to be different for the L2 learner; it simply makes them (in some cases) not as efficient.

- Neither L1 nor L2 acquisition seems particularly responsive to outside manipulation. Attempts at overtly correcting child L1 grammar results in sometimes hilarious and unexpected outcomes, as the example from David McNeill in Chapter 1 shows. Chapter 6 on the effects of instruction in L2 acquisition suggests that such effects are limited. Some L2 scholars would claim the effects of external manipulation via explicit teaching and practice are non-existent. Thus, in both contexts, acquisition proceeds along its own path with the only external influence being the actual input itself. This suggests something is the same about L1 and L2 acquisition.

- In both L1 and L2 acquisition, output as part of communicative interaction is not the causal factor in how language unfolds over time. In either context, when learners engage in communication and express their own meaning, they draw from a linguistic system already in their heads. However, in both contexts, being part of communicative interactions gets the learner more appropriate-level input. This limited or indirect role of output suggests that something is the same about L1 and L2 acquisition.

- From the above and other observations made in this book, we know that both L1 and L2 acquisition involve largely implicit internal processes. Although it appears that L2 learners tend to deliberately and explicitly go about learning another language (except for L2 children whose parents migrate to a new language culture), their attempts to do so do not directly impact all of the other things we've noted above. Explicit learning may serve more of an affective factor, a point we'll touch on below. For now, we note that in most contemporary L2 research circles, language acquisition *happens to* learners as they get involved in communicative events. And because the product – mental representation – is far richer, more complex, and more abstract than any explicit learning or processing could achieve, implicit processing and organization of linguistic data must underlie acquisition. This would suggest that something is the same about L1 and L2 acquisition.

With the above said, we do not suggest at all that the *outcomes* of L1 and L2 acquisition are the same. We have touched on ultimate attainment and nativelikeness at various points in this book, and most directly in Chapter 5. We would also point out, though, that the fact that learners attain different proficiency levels does not mean that the *underlying internal processes* that get them there are different. Now we turn our attention to external aspects of acquisition.

The flip side of the internal is the external. More specifically, do L1 and L2 acquisition share the same external process and mechanisms? And by external, we mean things that are not language specific: the social environment, motivation, aptitude, and so on. In this book we have not focused on the social environment, save for the recurring boxes labeled "What about Social Factors?" We did touch on individual differences such as motivation and aptitude in Chapter 8. In this next set of bullet points, we list both what we believe the research tells us as well as our own speculations about external processes and mechanisms.

- Motivation does not seem to affect underlying processes in L2 acquisition. Ordered development, the limited effects of instruction, the role of the L1, the role of universals and Universal Grammar, and other language and learner-internal aspects of acquisition are not altered or impacted in any discernible way depending on a learner's motivation or orientation toward the language or the culture, for example. Motivation seems to affect two things: (1) how far learners get (i.e., ultimate attainment), and (2) the explicit and external strategies learners use to go about the task of acquisition (e.g., taking classes, seeking out native speakers, watching movies, taking notes, making flash cards). Clearly, L1 learners do not engage such strategies nor is motivation implicated in L1 ultimate attainment. So there is some external difference between L1 and L2 acquisition regarding motivation as part of an individual's profile, although this difference doesn't affect internal underlying processes and mechanisms.
- There is little in the research on language aptitude that leads us to conclude that it affects the underlying implicit processes in acquisition, although there is clear evidence that it impacts explicit learning. Because there is no theoretical reason and no empirical evidence to connect explicit learning to underlying

implicit processes in acquisition, it is safe to conclude that the role of aptitude in acquisition is, at best, minimal. But because aptitude is related to explicit learning and because for many learners this is standard fare for "getting into a language," aptitude is an important part of the external processes and mechanisms for learners. Again, this sets L1 and L2 acquisition apart from each other, as aptitude in L1 learning is not considered a critical component implicated in the acquisition process. At the same time, aptitude does not affect underlying L2 processes, which is why we do not see aptitude affecting the role of input, ordered development, the role of the L1, the role of universals and Universal Grammar, and so on, as we have stated previously.

- None of the three authors of this book is a researcher in social factors in L2 acquisition although we are familiar with the scholarship in this area. So here we offer some speculation based on our reading. Social factors such as identity, power relationships, contextual roles, and others do not affect the underlying processes of acquisition. That is, social factors do not show up as variables that alter or affect ordered development, the role of input, the role of the L1, the role of universals and Universal Grammar, and so on. Instead, social factors are implicated in learners' willingness and ability to interact with level-appropriate input, as well as their expectations about their own and others' behavior. Social factors are implicated in learners' willingness and ability to seek out contexts that aid rather than hinder their acquisition. These are powerful external factors, to be sure. As such, this makes L2 acquisition externally different from L1 acquisition in that social factors are not implicated in L1 acquisition, save for socio-economic factors that affect dialects acquired and by-products of language acquisition (e.g., literacy, discursive skills). L1 learners, regardless of the social contexts into which they are born and regardless of the social factors involved in these contexts, acquire their L1 (assuming non-extreme cases such as "wild children" or abused children who are isolated from normal human interaction). In short, social factors are more important in the L2 context than they are in the L1 context even though, again, they do not affect underlying and internal processes specific to language.

From this discussion, we suggest to the reader that at their core (i.e., when it comes to internal linguistic aspects of language acquisition) L1 and L2 acquisition are fundamentally similar. However, outside of this core, when it comes to external factors that are not linguistic in nature, L1 and L2 acquisition may be fundamentally different. These differences do not affect underlying processes, but they will affect such things as motivation, rate of acquisition, eventual outcome, and in general how the L2 learner "feels" about the whole process of acquisition. Such things, in turn, affect the quantity and quality of CEI that learners are exposed to and their interactions with that input. Given the fundamental role of input in language acquisition, the effect of external factors is not trivial when it comes to both rate and outcome. At the same time, given the fundamental role of learner-*internal* factors responsible for the processing of language, these external factors are in a certain sense unimportant for how language itself comes to be represented over time in the learner's mind.

The point here is that how one addresses similarities and differences between L1 and L2 acquisition depends on what one is looking at. And the relative importance of internal and external factors is also dependent on whether one is looking at internal linguistic development or something else, such as outcome and attitudes toward L2 acquisition itself. As we see it, there is no problem in saying something such as L1 and L2 acquisition are both fundamentally similar and fundamentally different.

To be sure, there are some scholars out there who disagree with our assessment – while others agree. Such disagreement hinges on definitions of similarity and difference. For example, some scholars might argue that because there is an L1 present in L2 acquisition and because we know that the L1 influences L2 acquisition, L1 and L2 acquisition must be different. As we said above, it depends on how you examine such things. The presence of the L1 as a factor in L2 development does not obviate the role of input, the role of universals and Universal Grammar, the role of markedness, and it does not change the fact that L2 acquisition is ordered and follows developmental stages. Our view is that the L1 may slow things down or make L2 acquisition less efficient in some aspects of acquisition, but it does not change the fundamental underlying processes. To use a metaphor used elsewhere (see, for example, Bill VanPatten's 2017 book, *While We're on the Topic*, published by the American Council on the Teaching of Foreign Languages), let's imagine a woman going up six steps to a landing. She puts one foot on one step, then the other foot on the next step, and so on until she reaches the top. As long as she is physically unimpaired, she (and anyone like her) will perform the same procedure to get to the landing. Now let's imagine that same woman carrying a 30-pound suitcase. She will probably struggle somewhat to go up the steps – and she most likely will take more time. However, she still has to put one foot on one step, then get to the next step, then the next as she would without the suitcase. In both cases, she is fighting gravity and there is no way around it. The suitcase-less scenario would be akin to L1 acquisition while the suitcase scenario would be like L2 acquisition. The woman does the same thing in each scenario; she merely has extra baggage to contend with in the second situation. Are the two scenarios fundamentally similar or fundamentally different? We see them as fundamentally the same at their core (e.g., going up steps, the basic body/leg movements, fighting gravity).

Scholars involved in instructed L2 acquisition may also disagree with us. Many scholars in this line of research place a high emphasis on explicit processes in learning, and because of these explicit processes, they would argue that L1 and L2 acquisition are fundamentally different. But as we have pointed out in this book and as summarized above, it is not at all the case that explicit processes (including explicit learning) affect L2 acquisition in any significant way. We know that any observed short-term effects of instruction disappear with time. We know that ordered and staged development is not altered in any observable or significant way. We have also argued that explicit processes can't be at the core of input processing. So looking at the short term, a scholar might argue that L1 and L2 acquisition are different. Looking at what we have examined in this volume (e.g., ordered and staged development, long-term effects, the limited to non-role of explicit learning/processing), other scholars might conclude that L1 and L2 acquisition are basically the same because they are resistant to external attempts to alter the processes. We fall into the latter group.

Although our position is that, at their core, L1 and L2 acquisition are fundamentally similar processes, we understand that such a position is not popular among certain sectors of L2 research (as briefly mentioned above) and is certainly concerning to many teachers who look to L2 research for insights. But we think it is important to underscore fundamental similarity because, in our experience, both the field of SLA and the field of language teaching have tended to focus on the differences. When we let the differences drive how we view the world, we lose sight of the similarities. In the case of research, scholars may spend a good deal of time (and publishing) on things that, in the end, don't really tell us much about how acquisition actually happens or what it means for an L2 learner to "know" a language. They may not be able to link a narrow research agenda into the bigger picture of what it means to acquire a language. In the case of teaching, by focusing on differences, the profession may develop pedagogies and strategies for the classroom that work against what the mind/brain wants to do naturally and, indeed, what the mind/brain *needs* to do. So we believe that focusing on the fundamental similarity between L1 and L2 acquisition is a good reminder about the special nature of the human ability to acquire language. What this means for teaching is that teachers (and learners!) can relax: Given access to input, interaction with that input, and time, learners will acquire an L2. There are important differences between the two, but these should not be the determining factor in what we do. Finally, focusing on the similarities between L1 and L2 acquisition helps us see the complexity – and wonder – of language and language acquisition more clearly and helps us to contextualize the differences better.

Glossary

Acquisition. Steven Krashen's term for implicit learning. He defines L2 acquisition as something similar if not identical to what happens in child L1 acquisition. Learners are not aware of the processes they are engaged in or what they are acquiring. The result is **implicit knowledge**.

Automatized knowledge. In skill theory, knowledge that can be used in relevant contexts accurately and efficiently without conscious awareness of doing so.

Backsliding. The phenomenon by which a learner regresses to a developmental stage prior to the one he or she is in.

Behaviorism. A theory of learning prevalent in the twentieth century up until the 1970s. Learning was seen as the acquisition of behaviors (observable phenomena) in any living being (see also **operant conditioning**).

Blocking. A term used in usage-based approaches to describe how previous knowledge (either from the L1 or the L2) can inhibit the learning of something new. Example: The strong association between subject (a grammatical notion) and agent (a semantic notion) as in *Bill carried John* (Bill = both subject and agent) is forged early on in acquisition. This can impede the learning of passives where the subject is not the agent but the theme of the verb, as in *John was carried by Bill* (John = subject but he is not the agent of the verb *carry*; he is the theme of the verb *carry*).

Communicative output (communicatively embedded output). Language that the learner produces that is part of the expression and interpretation of meaning in a given context with a given (communicative) purpose. Contrast with **communicatively embedded input**.

Communicatively embedded input. See **input**.

Complementizer. A word that introduces a clause (e.g., Bill said *that* Megan is smart, Alessandro is the guy *who* speaks Italian, I don't know *if* he will join us for dinner).

Comprehensible input. That part of **input** that learners can make sense of in terms of meaning (i.e., what they can actually comprehend).

Critical period. A specific window of time during biological development in which stimuli for a particular ability have to be provided. If critical stimuli are not provided during this window of time, the ability cannot be acquired.

The Critical Period Hypothesis. An idea in language acquisition stating that if linguistic **input** is not provided before a child is five, the child will not be able to learn the language. Applied to L2 acquisition, it states that adults will not be able to acquire an L2 if they have not been exposed to appropriate input before adolescence, if not earlier.

Declarative knowledge. In skill theory, "knowledge *that*." Knowledge that can be verbalized and explained and that usually involves facts and details.

Developmental sequences. Stages in which a particular structure or feature of language is acquired over time. Examples include the developmental sequence for negation in English, for linking verbs in Spanish, and for basic sentence word order in German. Same as staged development or developmental stages.

Domain-specific learning mechanisms. Learning mechanisms that are specifically designed to process (and organize) linguistic input independently of other kinds of stimuli. These mechanisms are central to generative linguistics.

Explicit knowledge. Knowledge of language that is conscious and can be articulated by a person. Example: A learner of English can say "Third-person verbs in English end in -s." A learner of French can say "With partitives, don't use the article if the sentence is negative."

Explicit learning. Processing linguistic input with conscious attention paid to the formal properties of language.

Form–meaning connections. How a meaning is expressed linguistically (e.g., the connection between "cat" and its meaning as a feline, or the connection between -ed on a verb and the concept of "pastness").

Fossilization. A term coined by Larry Selinker in 1972 to refer to the process by which L2 learners' internal linguistic systems stop evolving. Fossilization results in a non-native linguistic system or parts of the system.

Full Access. The position claiming that the initial state of acquisition for L2 is just UG. There is no L1 transfer at the outset of L2 acquisition (similar to the Initial Hypothesis of Syntax).

Full Transfer/Full Access. The position claiming that the initial state of L2 acquisition is the L1 mental representation, but that learners have complete access to the contents of Universal Grammar that subsequently guide and constrain acquisition.

Functional categories/features. Refers to the abstract features of language provided by Universal Grammar such as Case, Number, Aspect, Tense, Complementizers, and so on.

Garden-path effects. Those "Huh?" moments that happen when comprehending sentences when the intended sentence structure is not the structure that the parser originally assigns to the sentence. The person usually has to stop and "reanalyze" the sentence.

General learning mechanisms. Cognitive structures designed to process information in the world and learn something from it. Unlike domain-specific learning mechanisms, which apply to language only, general learning mechanisms are used in all learning contexts (see Usage-based approaches).

Generative linguistics (generative revolution). The scientific study of language founded by Noam Chomsky in the late 1950s / early 1960s. Two basic ideas lay at the heart of generative linguistics (and still do): (1) only humans have language, so there is probably something innate about language; (2) people can generate an infinite number of sentences using a finite system of "rules," including sentences they've never heard before and couldn't be imitating from their environment. For example, *I know the man. I know the tall man. I know the tall man over there. I know the tall man over there in the brown coat. I know the tall man over there in the brown coat who is smoking a cigarette. I know the tall man over there in the brown coat who is smoking a cigarette and probably shouldn't be.* Minimalism is the current version of generative linguistics. **Universal Grammar (UG)** is a major construct in generative linguistics.

Generative tradition. See **generative linguistics**.

Grammatical sensitivity. The component of linguistic aptitude that is hypothesized to govern someone's ability to identify grammatical constructions.

Ideal L2 Self. A component of the L2 motivational self-system that includes how learners see themselves as users of the L2.

Implicit knowledge. Knowledge of language that exists outside of one's awareness whose contents can't be articulated by a person. Example: Except for trained linguists, people can't say why they prefer "Me and Alex went" compared with "I and Alex went." They simply say, "It sounds better." (See also **poverty of the stimulus** for examples of implicit knowledge.)

Implicit learning. Processing linguistic input without paying conscious attention to the formal properties of language.

Indeterminate intuitions. Intuitions about whether something is grammatical in a language that are "fuzzy" or not especially strong. For example, we might have a strong intuition that *undrink* is not a possible word (*I undrank the soda*) but we might not be sure about something like *strived* (is it *strove* or *strived* as in *He strove/strived to do it*? Hmmm. I'm not sure).

Inductive learning ability. The component of linguistic aptitude hypothesized to relate to how well an individual can "formulate a rule" based on a set of language stimuli.

Inflectional morpheme. Morphemes that are added to nouns and verbs that don't change the fundamental meaning of the root word and don't change its function (i.e., the noun remains a noun and the verb remains a verb). Example: A form of -*s* is added to the end of nouns to indicate plurality (*dog/dogs, house/houses, snack/snacks*).

Initial Hypothesis of Syntax. A position claiming that the initial state of acquisition for L1 and L2 is the same; that is, that both L1 and L2 learners begin the process of acquisition with just **Universal Grammar**. There is no L1 transfer at the outset of L2 acquisition.

Initial state. Refers to what learners bring to the task of acquisition at the outset. The concern is largely with whether they transfer all the properties of the L1 at the outset or not (see **L1 transfer, the Initial Hypothesis of Syntax, Full Transfer/Full Access,** and **Minimal Trees**).

Input. Refers to the language (in spoken, written, or signed forms) the learner is exposed to in communicative contexts. Also called **communicatively embedded input**.

Input Processing. Refers to how learners make form–meaning connections during comprehension/acquisition and how they process sentence structure during real-time comprehension.

Instrumental motivation. A desire to learn a language because it will be useful, usually for a professional or educational reason.

Intake. That subset of the **input** that learners can actually process at a given time and make use of for acquisition.

Integrative motivation. A desire to learn a language based on an interest in or affinity for aspects of the target language culture(s).

Interlanguage. A term coined by Larry Selinker that refers to an L2 learner's mental competence at any point in time during development.

Intervening variable. Refers to a variable that researchers do not account for or

cannot account for during experimenta-
tion, which may affect results. Example:
In research on the outcomes of classroom learning, very often researchers
cannot account for what learners do
outside of classrooms, which may affect
the results.

L1 influence. See **L1 transfer.**

L1 transfer. Refers to the influence that
the L1 has on L2 acquisition. It is not
clear what the influence is (for example, whether it's on **mental representation or input processing** or on both) or
exactly where it happens, and different
theories define it in slightly different
ways. It is a concept especially relevant to the idea of the **initial state.**

L2 motivational self-system. The ways
that learners think about themselves in
the present and who they want to be in
the future as related to the L2. This term
has replaced **integrative motivation.**

Language-related episode. Refers to when
learners engage in explicit discussion
about language during an interaction.

Learning. Steven Krashen's term for the
explicit learning of rules and properties
of language typical in many classrooms.
The result is **explicit knowledge.**

Lexical categories/features. Refers to the
concrete features of language provided
by Universal Grammar such as nouns,
verbs, adjectives, prepositions, and so
on.

Linguistic aptitude. An innate ability to
learn an L2 that varies among the population.

**Long-term studies/short-term stud-
ies.** Refers to research on instructed L2
acquisition and how long after a treatment the research measures the effects
of instruction. Typically, short term
refers to tests following immediately
after treatment or up to a month or two
later. Long term refers to testing learn-

ers many months or even a year after
treatment.

Long(er)-term effects. Refers to whether or
not the effects of instruction are evident
in **long-term studies.**

**Marked and unmarked structures (lesser/
more marked).** See **markedness.**

Markedness. A concept in linguistics with
differing definitions. In general, it refers
to how typical/frequent/simple or not
typical/infrequent/complex a linguistic structure or form is. The most typical, most frequent, and/or simplest are
termed unmarked or the least marked
structures/forms in a language. Example: In most languages that mark plurality, the plural form is more marked
than the singular, which is considered
unmarked. Thus *dog* is unmarked and
dogs is more marked. The latter is more
complex and is less frequent than the
singular form.

Meta-analysis. A large-scale analysis of
many studies focused on the same question or problem. For an example, see
Spada, N. & Tomita, Y. (2010). Interactions between type of instruction and
type of language feature: A meta-analysis. *Language Learning*, 60, 263–308.

The Minimal Trees Hypothesis. The position claiming that learners transfer only
the **lexical categories** from the L1 at the
outset, but not the **functional categories.** In other words, **L1 transfer** is constrained in the initial state.

Modified input. Input that is adjusted by
another speaker to a language learner
based on a perceived communication
problem.

Monitored output occurs when a learner
has formally studied grammar and can
apply consciously learned rules and formal features to edit speech or writing as
he or she produces it.

Morpheme. The smallest unit of language
that carries meaning. The simple word

book is one morpheme. The word *books* consists of two morphemes: the morpheme *book* and the plural marker *-s* that indicates "more than one." Another example of a morpheme is the prefix *un-* which denotes negation, as in *invite* and *uninvite* (and of course, *invite* as a simple word is also a morpheme).

Morpheme orders. The sequence in which morphemes are acquired over time. Example: In English, verbal inflectional morphemes are acquired in this order: *-ing* before *-ed* (regular past tense) before irregular past tense before 3rd-person *-s*.

Movement (Syntactic movement). An operation that takes a word or phrase from one part of the sentence and moves it to another part of the sentence. Movement happens without us knowing (e.g., "What did you eat?" represents movement of the *wh*-word *what* from its position as object of the verb *eat* : *You eat what? → What did you eat?*).

Nativelikeness. A mental representation for the L2 that is largely indistinguishable from that of native speakers of that language.

Negative evidence. Information about what is not possible in the target language, usually provided through error correction but also through **recasts**, for example.

Negotiation of meaning. The act of resolving comprehension problems during a communicative interaction.

No interface position. This is the position that implicit and explicit knowledge are distinct from each other and do not influence each other.

Noticing Hypothesis. Richard Schmidt's proposal that L2 learners need to be aware of formal properties in the input for acquisition to happen.

Noticing the gap. The idea that learners can compare what they produce to what they hear/read to see if there are differences.

Operant conditioning. A major construct in behaviorism that attributed learning to a combination of various factors, including stimulus, response, and feedback/reward. B. F. Skinner was one of the major twentieth-century figures and scholars in the field of behaviorism.

Ordered development. Refers to **morpheme orders, developmental sequences** and other phenomena suggesting that language follows particular paths as it develops in the learner's mind/brain over time. Example: For learners of English, the verbal morpheme *-ing* is always acquired before past-tense verbal morphemes, which in turn are always acquired before 3rd-person *-s*.

Ought-to L2 Self. The component of the L2 motivational self-system that includes how learners see themselves using the L2 in the future.

Output. Language that the learner produces (compare with **input**).

Output as practice. Language that the learner produces for the sake of producing the language or to explicitly try to learn something.

Parameter resetting. Refers to the "switching" of L1 values to L2 values for **functional and lexical features** during the course of acquisition.

Parser. The part of the mind that constructs a moment-by-moment interpretation of spoken or written language as it encounters it. Example: The moment the parser "hears" the word *the* it projects a noun phrase and if it "hears" it at the beginning of a sentence in English will most likely posit it as the subject noun phrase (until told otherwise as in **garden-path** experiences).

Phonetic coding ability. A component of linguistic aptitude referring to an individual's ability to identify individual sounds and to form associations between sounds and symbols.

Phonological short-term memory. People's capacity for recalling verbal information for short periods of time. Phonological short-term memory is thought to be related to vocabulary acquisition.

Planned discourse. Refers to non-interactive language that is written out or thought of prior to production, such as literary works, formal speeches that are read, or essays on subject matter. Unplanned discourse would be the spontaneous use of language found in interactions between two or more speakers.

Poverty of the stimulus. The situation that arises when people come to know more about language than they could have learned from exposure. Example: Speakers of English know that you can add *re-* to verbs like *paint, record*, and *decorate* to make new verbs: *repaint, rerecord, redecorate*. They also know that you cannot add *re-* to verbs like *pet* (a dog), *bake*, and *sleep : *repet, *rebake, *resleep*. Restrictions on the use of *re-* with verbs are not evident in the **input** English speakers are exposed to and no one ever tells them what they can and cannot do with *re-*.

Procedural knowledge. In skill theory, "knowledge *how*." It refers to the ability to execute a task without explicitly thinking about it even if the person has not yet developed **automatized knowledge**.

Process. The act of linking meaning with its form in the **input** during comprehension.

Processability Theory. A theory concerned with universal constraints on how learners process **communicative output** over time; that is, how they put words in serial order during real-time spontaneous speech.

Rate of development. Refers to the relative speed with which learners acquire language. Some are faster than others, for example.

Recast. When a speaker reformulates what a learner has just said in a more appropriate or nativelike way.

Rote learning ability. A component of linguistic aptitude hypothesized to relate to how well an individual can learn/memorize arbitrary associations between sounds and meanings.

Rule-like knowledge. Linguistic knowledge that shows a pattern or a systematic nature whether that system is adult-like or nativelike. For example, the child who consistently says *ated* and *wented* is showing systematicity with regular past-tense endings. This would be rule-like knowledge where the "rule" of regular past-tense endings is used with irregular verbs.

Salience. Not always well defined, it tends to refer to how a linguistic form or word "stands out" in the **input**. Salience can involve stress or position in a sentence, among other features. Example: In the sentence *Where did you go?* the *wh-*word *where* is salient as it carries stress and is in sentence-initial position. The auxiliary *did* is less salient as it does not carry stress and can even be contracted as in *Where'd you go?*

Self-concept. How learners see themselves; includes both positive and negative attributes.

Self-paced reading. A research tool to examine people's unconscious processing of sentences as they read for meaning. The participant pushes buttons to reveal parts of a sentence as they read, thus controlling the speed at which they read. For an example, see VanPatten, B., Keating, G. D., Leeser, M. J. (2012). Missing verbal inflections as a representational issue: Evidence from on-line methodology. *Linguistic Approaches to Bilingualism*, 2, 109–140.

Staged development. See **developmental sequences.**

Strong interface position. This is the position that **explicit knowledge** can become **implicit knowledge** in some way.

Structural linguistics. The major school of linguistic analysis prior to the Chomskyan revolution. Structural linguistics focused on patterns in order to state observable rules of language.

Teachability hypothesis. Refers to the claim that learners cannot be taught that which they are not ready for in terms of developmental sequences. To say this another way, instruction can only make a difference if learners are at the stage where the focus of instruction would be acquired anyway. Example: If a learner cannot produce verb separation in German (stage 3 of word order acquisition), that learner cannot be taught subject–verb inversion (stage 4) (see Chapter 2 for details on the acquisition of German word order).

U-shaped development. The phenomenon by which a learner begins to do something correctly, then seems to do it incorrectly, and then over time does it correctly again.

Ultimate attainment. Refers to how far learners get along the acquisition continuum or how close they get to native-likeness.

Universal Grammar (UG). An innate system in humans that constrains the nature of all languages. It consists of an inventory of basic features (e.g., Tense/Finiteness, Aspect, Case, Number) and principles (e.g., the nature of phrase structure). Example: All languages consist of hidden phrases that exist in a hierarchical manner (they stack on each other to make sentences) and all phrases consist of a head and its complement. There is no human language that does not exhibit this universal trait.

Universals (of language). Refers to the approach called typology of language in which languages are surveyed to see what features consistently co-occur (absolute universals) or are a strong tendency (weak universals). Example: An absolute universal is that all languages that have VSO word order also have prepositions (and not inflections, for example, to carry the same meaning as prepositions). A weak universal would be that SOV languages tend to have case marking (about 70 percent of SVO languages do, while only 14 percent of SVO languages have case marking).

Uptake. Refers to that moment in an interaction when a learner repeats something he or she just heard.

Usage-based approaches (UBAs). Approaches from the field of psychology that tie all human learning to an interaction between external stimuli and internal general learning mechanisms. A major component of UBAs is frequency and how it affects what gets picked up by the learner and in what linguistic environments.

The Valueless Features Hypothesis. The position claiming that L1 **lexical and functional categories** are transferred to the L2 in the initial state. However, the strength of the features associated with L1 functional categories does not transfer (see also **L1 transfer**).

Variation in L2 development. Refers to learners' use of different versions of a structure at a particular stage of acquisition. Example: Learners of Spanish in Stage 2 of the acquisition of the verbs *ser* and *estar* (both mean 'to be') make *ser* the default verb. However, *estar* is required in progressive constructions (e.g., *Juan está corriendo* 'John is running'). So learners use *ser* instead of *estar* for progressives. Variation occurs because learners can vacillate between *Juan es corre, Juan es correr,* and *Juan es corriendo.* And variation occurs across learners because learner A might have a "preference" for one version while learner B has a preference for another. Yet both are in the same stage: *ser* is the default verb.

Weak interface position. This is the position that explicit knowledge can somehow influence the development of implicit knowledge.

Working memory. The amount of information people can store and manipulate at any given time. Working memory varies among the population. Working memory is usually discussed in research on language comprehension.

Index